Inviting Angels into Your Li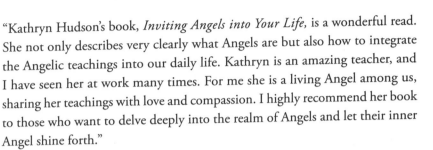

"Kathryn Hudson's book, *Inviting Angels into Your Life,* is a wonderful read. She not only describes very clearly what Angels are but also how to integrate the Angelic teachings into our daily life. Kathryn is an amazing teacher, and I have seen her at work many times. For me she is a living Angel among us, sharing her teachings with love and compassion. I highly recommend her book to those who want to delve deeply into the realm of Angels and let their inner Angel shine forth."

— **FRANS STIENE**, co-founder of the International House of Reiki
and author of *The Inner Heart of Reiki* and *Reiki Insights*

"At a time when we need Angels the most, *Inviting Angels into Your Life* is a bolstering and enjoyable resource and step-by-step manual for those of us who want to be more connected to—and, above all, aided by—Angels. Her fresh, intimate style brings us right into her connection with the Angelic world and invites us to feel at home there. The exercises are surprising in their power and simplicity—with an element of discovery and fun! As a veteran of Angelic connection, I am pleased to highly recommend working with Kathryn through this book and beyond."

— **KATHY TYLER**, co-creator of *The Original Angel Cards*
and *The Transformation Game*

"Like an able surfer gliding easily forward on a wave, I flowed through *Inviting Angels into Your Life* easily from exercise to exercise on a sort of Angelic wave, rendering my connection all the more tangible and fluid. Kathryn invites us to step into the driver's seat and recognize that our body is the vehicle that brings us into contact most directly with the Angelic realm and that the Angels (at our invitation) can assist and lift any barriers that crop up on our path. With this, the book facilitates more light and more joy in our life. What is unique is that this book recognizes and does not demean our human aspect. Yes, we are light, but we are also very human, with all of the emotions and experiences that entails. But what a relief, with the help of this book, to invite Angels in and to appreciate the immediate results of more ease and more peace on all levels. Often the most difficult step is opening that door to the Angels, inviting them in. Thanks to Kathryn, this movement is now simple."

— **THOMAS PHELIP**, Angel Therapist and author

INVITING ANGELS INTO YOUR LIFE

Assistance and Support from
the Angelic Realm

Kathryn Hudson

 FINDHORN PRESS

Findhorn Press
One Park Street
Rochester, Vermont 05767
www.findhornpress.com

Text stock is SFI certified

Findhorn Press is a division of Inner Traditions International

Originally published in French by Éditions Exergue/Éditions Trédaniel, under the title *Agir Avec les Anges*

Disclaimer

The information in this book is given in good faith and intended for information only. Neither author nor publisher can be held liable by any person for any loss or damage whatsoever which may arise from the use of this book or any of the information therein.

Cataloging-in-Publication data for this title is available from the Library of Congress

ISBN 978-1-64411-172-7 (print)
ISBN 978-1-64411-173-4 (ebook)

Printed and bound in the United States by Lake Book Manufacturing, Inc. The text stock is SFI certified. The Sustainable Forestry Initiative® program promotes sustainable forest management.

10 9 8 7 6 5 4 3 2 1

Edited by Nicky Leach
Text design and layout by Damian Keenan
This book was typeset in Adobe Garamond Pro, Calluna Sans and Museo with Fontin used as a display typeface.

To send correspondence to the author of this book, mail a first-class letter to the author c/o Inner Traditions • Bear & Company, One Park Street, Rochester, VT 05767, USA, and we will forward the communication, or contact the author directly at **http://kathrynhudson.net**

Contents

Living Large:
A Call to Action

I magine your favorite person in the whole world, the person with whom you feel incredibly comfortable, the one you most love being around. Go ahead. Close your eyes and visit the person for a few moments.

How easy it is to be with them. We can relax, breathe freely, laugh easily, never have to think twice before saying or doing what comes naturally to us—give them a hug, or our opinion, or simply sit in silence.

If you have such a person in your life, then you know that there is a kind of safety that you feel when you are with such a person, and that is a rare and beautiful gift. When we feel safe with someone and we are relaxed, our heart opens wide. Our light and our love shine through. That is the truth of our being, but unfortunately, rarely expressed as the world teaches us to remain so defended.

Now, close your eyes again and think of your least favorite person in the world. (Oh, go ahead. You know who I mean!)

Do you feel like hugging them? (Probably not.) How does it feel to be around them? Do you relax around them? Or do you have to weigh your words? Can you breathe? (Maybe not.) When we are in a situation that is disagreeable, often our very breath cuts off or diminishes in strength. But with breath comes life, so when we breathe less, we feel less; we live less. So in order to live, we really need to be able to breathe freely; we need the relaxation that comes from a heart that is open. An open heart is our large life force, our power!

Now go back to being with the two people, favorite and least favorite. Which situation makes you feel more powerful? Which less so?

Funny, isn't it? When we have our heart open we are more powerful, and when we have our heart closed we are less powerful. Funnier still, the world, which understands so little, teaches us the exact opposite: that to protect ourselves we must be defended and close our hearts, that open-heartedness is a weakness. When we are able to relax and be ourselves, we step naturally into our power, and we need that power for Large Life.

There are no accidents. If you are holding this book in your hands, the Angels are looking to help you step into your power, to relax and be yourself more, no matter the situation. As they are always around, their friendship and assistance can help us to know we are always safe so we can relax and allow in more health, more light and more joy, and enjoy a larger, more power-filled and powerful life.

Here, at the very beginning of our journey, consider yourself served!

. . . As in a game of tennis, imagine that this book is Life, and the Angels are lobbing the ball over the net to you, hoping you'll play. Service! (Angels love to play.)

. . . If the idea of duty calling suits you more (as with jury duty, for example), imagine that in this moment you are being served with a request to show up even more for your life purpose, in service to the wider community and supported by the Angels!

. . . Perhaps the most apt service metaphor is one of "being served," as in fine dining. Dinner is served. Take your place so that all manner of good things can be placed before you for your delight and nourishment.

Playing tennis, fulfilling civic duty, a delightful feast? Your choice. In all, consider yourself served—invited to play, asked to show up, and if you so desire, to accept the delights the Angels have in store for you.

With reference to popular religious dogma of our times, let's be clear: the pertinent phrase is, consider yourself "served" not "saved." This book is not about cowering as sinners, begging for scraps at a distant Father's table. How relaxed would we be in that situation? No, this is about accepting that we are already "saved." A seat is saved for us. We are already invited to the Table of Life, which is (very patiently) waiting for us to take our place.

Dinner—Life, that is . . . Large Life—is served. Will you come?

The invitation is all about relaxing and heart-wide-open fun. It is a reminder that we were never meant to be stiff. It is not natural to live defended, with our hearts closed to others; we are not destined to mourn our way through life but, rather, to remember that we've got "friends in high places" (Angels), so we can relax as we play this game called Life.

Once we understand that we are safe things become fun. We understand that we have never been alone and are not really separate from the Divine. We relax and enjoy this life when we get clear (because we have proof) that divine assistance (through the Presence of the Angels) is never far off, just waiting for us to remember that we are always held in Love. No matter how far the world may have caused us to stray, like the prodigal son in the Bible, we can feel secure in the knowledge that we are always welcome at the table. When we are ready, we are welcomed in with rejoicing: no recriminations, no judgment, ultimate safety, the truth of peace. We are then served with peace and joy, and our being served allows us to serve others, sharing those gifts of peace and joy. We can breathe, relax, trust: the Peace which passeth all understanding. And we can enjoy. Joy is the language of the Angels. Joy is the juice of living Large, living powerfully, living our dreams. Again, if you are reading this book, it is no accident; you are on the list for more joy. No matter how it came into your hands, whether as a gift, a find, a favor to a friend, or a falling off a bookstore shelf, if you are reading this sentence right now, this was meant to be. The Angels made me do it—made me write it, made you come across it, made us come together. They organized our meeting in this way to sort out some things together. By the end of this reading/meeting time, we will go our separate ways in the world, more efficiently and effectively living Large, with our angelic Friends in High Places making the way smooth for us.

To be clear, Angels cannot, do not, "make" us do anything; however, they can knock on the door and send us reminders, invitations, and signs. In fact, they do this all the time. The question is whether we are ready to notice those signs, and if we will accept their invitation once we get it.

Angels come to us in many ways. Sometimes they arrive subtly, through the lyrics to a song we hear, a timely hand on the shoulder, or a book we "happen" upon. Other times (with tougher cases and more defended hearts), Angels call to us far less subtly, as in the story I recount at the end of this book, when an Angel walked up to my desk in a bank in Midtown Manhattan to give me an amethyst crystal and a much-needed message (at that time, I needed a rock to open my heart!)

Thus "served," we are reminded of a truth beyond the visible. That we are loved. That we are much more than the person we see in the mirror. That there is no place that God is not, including within us! We are not small; nor are we separate from or forgotten by Source.

(NOTE: For the purposes of this book, I will use the terms "God" or "Source" or "the Universe." Please feel free to insert the Holy Name with which you are most comfortable. God is not rendered small by our naming.) When we remember, we can relax. As with a good friend, when we cultivate that Divine connection through the Angels, we remember that all is well: we have Friends in High Places! So consider yourself served. And relax!

How It Began:
Kona, Hawaii

As I loitered on the hotel grounds in front of the door to the conference space, watching intently as sparkly-dressed assistants were checking in equally sparkly-dressed workshop participants, I wondered what the heck I was doing there. In my cutoff jeans and t-shirt, I was feeling decidedly out of place. I had my bathing suit underneath in case the workshop turned out not to be for me. Plan B was going swimming with dolphins, if they'd have me. It seemed like many of these smiling gods and goddesses knew one another, and I felt both like an outsider looking in and like one who might possibly prefer to stay outside and hang out with dolphins. At that moment, Plan B was looking good.

Finally, I decided to risk it. The workshop was, after all, a significant investment of time and money. I had flown all the way from France to Hawaii for it, and on top of the hotel charges and the substantial workshop fee to come train to learn about Angel therapy, I had taken time off work. The very pragmatic then-banker in me could not walk away from such an investment. Still, when I checked in, I took a seat in the back by the exit (just in case). Better safe than sorry!

As I waited for the workshop to begin, my mind wandered back along the path that had brought me to this unlikely place. It started with a book…

෴

I was at the Paris airport headed to the United States to see my boss in Charlotte, North Carolina (at the time, I was an expatriate banker in France with a large American bank). While I waited for my flight, I stopped at an airport bookstore to pick up something for the coastal Carolina vacation I was planning just after my Charlotte meetings. As I reached for one book, another, different one tumbled off the shelf. It was small, colorful, eye-catching, and odd—a book on chakra clearing by Doreen Virtue.

Huh? I had been meaning at some point to see what the heck this chakra stuff was all about. No time like the present! I took it and the one I had been reaching for (I no longer recollect what it was) to the register and hurried to the departure gate, then forgot about it.

A week or so later, I was officially on vacation, and having a party. A big party! It was at the house I call Attitude Adjustment, a beach cottage in a small town called Emerald Isle on the Southern Outer Banks of North Carolina, a spot of heaven that ironically feels very much like home to this Irish kid from the Bronx. I had invited a bunch of family and friends from the old neighborhood in the Bronx and Inwood in Northern Manhattan, and there was a house full of party going on in my cottage by the sea. It was the off season, so the lack of neighbors meant that my musician friends could play their hearts out, and (almost) all manner of (over)indulgences were taking place amid loud conversation and raucous laughter, smoke, drink, and noise.

Suddenly, it was too much. I needed a break and headed for the door. As I went to step outside onto the deck, something colorful caught my eye: the chakra book. I grabbed it, along with my drink and cigarettes, and snuck out of the party, making my way over the dune walkway to the steps leading down to a perfectly empty beach.

Plopping myself down on a sandy wooden step, I lit a cigarette and took a sip of my Greyhound (vodka and grapefruit juice). Ahhhh . . . peace and quiet! I watched the pelicans flying low in tight formation over the breaking waves, mesmerized by what seemed to me to be their perfectly choreographed flight, then thus situated, I opened the book at random—and almost dropped it . . .

Talk about perfectly choreographed! Right there, on the page I had just opened, I read a list of things that impede our clairvoyance and our connection to Angels. It included everything in which I had just indulged: alcohol, cigarettes, drugs, junk food, noise. The list went on, but I had seen all I needed to. It was a list of what was happening at my house at that moment!

The perfect orchestration continued. At that very moment, in the distance, over a neighboring town called Atlantic Beach, fireworks went off, an ironic "By George, I think she's got it!" applause that I had finally gotten the message the Angels had been trying to convey to me since the day one walked into the Bank on 42nd Street in Manhattan to deliver an amethyst and a message.

From that moment on, I could no longer pretend not to be aware of what was going on. I had been served, and I knew that it was incumbent upon me to walk through the door that had opened and to look squarely at that which had been keeping me playing small and fearful, when we are all meant to live Large, in love.

Thinking back to that awakening, I was glad now that I had dared to enter the conference space. I knew why I was sitting here in this great room at the Sheraton in Kona three years later, after many other paths (shamanism, crystals, pilgrimage) had led me to this one. I was here to go farther, to see more of what the fuss was all about, and to confirm what I already knew in my heart, what I had always known: that I had a job to do here on Earth; that my real life was out there, waiting for me; that the sneaking suspicion I had ignored for 20 years, that I wasn't meant to be a banker, was true; and that there was a whole lot of help waiting for me to give the thumbs up, if I were just willing to risk letting go and letting everything change.

You guessed it: I stayed for the whole five days of the workshop, even when I was pretty sure that I was the only person who wasn't clairvoyant in the room. I stayed, and that is really all we have to do to live Large: accept the invitation, the call, show up, and stay.

PART ONE

TAKE ACTION WITH THE ANGELS

Preparation

CHAPTER 1

Who's Who and
What's What

It is important to note at the outset that the words here are co-created and can be powerful, but that above all, you are the expert on your own life. As you read through this book, see how it resonates with you, perhaps in a way you already knew deep inside. That is the key. These words are not to convince anyone of anything, but rather, to awaken that which already is.

A lot is going on around us all the time that we never see—not with our eyes anyway, not most of us. (Huh? Yep. A lot!) Have you ever found yourself alone, maybe in a very quiet place, and experienced chills or your hair standing on end? Ever had the feeling that someone was in a room with you, only to turn to find no one there?

Even as our heads (trained by a world that knows so little) try to tell us that it's all nonsense, the sensitive instruments that are our bodies are designed to tune in to things not available to our physical sight. In their natural, balanced state, our bodies give us useful information pretty much constantly, but most of us live blissfully unaware of it.

I say "blissfully" because such experiences call into question the foundation of what we so often deem "reality," how we think the game is played. And when our foundation is shaken, everything trembles, generally not a comfortable situation. But in order for life to thrive, things always need to be shaken up. Land needs tilling before planting. Water needs to be boiled for cooking. Muscles of an athlete are torn down before being rebuilt and strengthened. Life grows in us through such shakeups.

The reality that is called into question, however, is our comfort zone, including even the parts of it that are not so comfortable. Like the idea that only that which is tangible and visible is real; or that we are somehow alone and on our own "down here" on Earth; that the world is a hard place; that lack and competition are givens—just the way it is.

Such beliefs—which we soak up from birth—lead to a perception of ourselves and this life that is false, which leads us to "play small," to make choices that favor what we deem safe and conservative out of fear of lack and fear of mortality.

But let's say that none of those beliefs are true.

Let's say that we are not alone, that we are not small, that we are more powerful than ever we imagined. We just forgot, and no one ever told us any better.

Consider your life, right here, today. If you were powerful beyond measure and aided by the Universe itself, what would change? Most importantly, would you be having more fun?

Who We Are

Before moving onto the passionate subject of Angels, let me say a word about an even more important subject: us. Who are we? Who are you?

Let's begin with the obvious: we are human beings: flesh, blood, and bones. Common knowledge teaches us that we have a body that had a beginning and will have an end at some point. That as humans, we don't have a lot do to with those two end points, although we have everything to do with the middle!

But what if there is a part of us, a soul, that does have something to do with those end points? We are humans, yes, and magnificently so. But we are not just humans.

You may have heard as many times as I have the following "There is no place that God is not." (Just a reminder: Although I am using the term God for all instances in this book where I refer to the Divine, if it is more comfortable for you, simply replace one name for another in alignment with your culture. God is not changed by our use of language or our cultural/religious, limiting beliefs, despite some popular opinion. God is bigger than that. There is no limit to God: all that is, is part of God.)

If there is no place that God is not, then God is everywhere, in everything, at every moment, even right here, now, in this moment (especially in this moment), the present with Presence, even in (and thus ever with) all of us, no exceptions.

So we are human beings with a birth day and some future unknown expiration date. The word "expiration" can be taken literally in English as when we expire or die, but we can also look at it in a larger way. In French, "expiration" means to exhale. Life as we know it is carried on breath. The first inhalation of a baby kicks off life, and our life is maintained through breath until our last is exhaled and our life, carried on that last breath, continues on its journey.

I like what John Lennon said: At death, we simply change one vehicle for another—small "life" for Large "Life." But what if we don't have to wait until we kick the bucket to open up to that Large Life? What if we can access our soul and live deeply, right here and now, in this body we refill with life at each breath?

Our Body

In short: our bodies carry our Life, but we are not our bodies. Just as we are not our cars or bicycles, so we are not our bodies. Our bodies are our instruments to play, the vehicle that our soul chose even before our Game (Life) began.

We begin before we have a body, and we continue on after there is no longer Life in that body, long after the instrument we call our body stops playing. This is not to say that the body is without importance: our body is the holder of the breath of Life eternal that lives in and through us for the time of our lifespan: a true temple! As such, it is worthy of honor.

The wonder that is our body enables us to be physically present: to inhabit Earth in a very solid and tangible interacting form with other solid and visible interacting forms. It also, as chills and hair standing on end might tell us, indicates when there is also Life around us here on the earth plane that is not in bodily form.

Angels, guides, ascended masters, as well as energies we sometimes refer to as entities or unfortunate negatively charged names like demons and such also exist around us. (Let us not be so naïve as to imagine a world where Angels exist but lower-energy beings do not.) We will look clear-eyed and fearless at these beings, but it is good to remember always that there is no place that God is not (including so-called entities). Thus we can confidently turn our immediate attention back to us.

If we have a body, but are not our body, what are we? We often hear the phrase "body and soul" or "mind, body, and spirit." These common expressions are rooted in truth. The body is the temple that holds our divine aspect, or Spirit, expressed as soul through us. (Again, there is no place that God/Spirit is not.) The soul is the individualized aspect of that eternal being, thus our soul goes on, lifetime after lifetime, tending toward remembering. The mind is the linchpin between the two: that which allows us (or not) to remember, which accepts (or not) to live the life we were meant for.

If we recognize that our body is truly a temple, maybe we can also see that it is of necessity also a doorway to the Divine, just as a physical temple or church or mosque can be a doorway (not *the* doorway; there is not one doorway, but many) to the Divine, a place where we can more easily connect to the sacred. If and when we see our bodies as holding the Divine, it is time to honor them as such. Would we treat a temple thoughtlessly? Would we cram a temple with too much junk? Would we allow just anybody access? Would we allow it to get dirty? Would we fill it with a cacophony of noise and clanging?

No, we probably would not. Just as we would honor a physical holy place, we are invited by the Angels to honor our physical body, and to recognize that the body is necessary to angelic connection here on Earth. We were never meant to repudiate our bodies but to honor them and recognize them as a conduit to the Divine. Honoring the temple of our bodies inside and out, with harmony and balance and beauty, cleanliness and silence and natural space to grow, allows the breath of the Divine to thrive and our soul's purpose to be realized.

Our Soul

Before our birth, it is the soul, accompanied by Angels, and always within the holding fertile love of the Divine, that chooses to incarnate (take on flesh) with a particular purpose or mission in mind. Along with Angels and our guides, the soul determines the human person/ incarnation that will optimize the chances for the success of that mission. We are perfectly conceived and created to realize or soul's mission. Even our so-called "imperfections" are perfect: they support the greater goal of the soul's mission.

Take, for example, a person who is timid or introverted. In our too-too-busy, too-white-toothed-smile world, it may well be that such a person has a mission that will require a deep inner life. All aspects of our personality, the personality chosen by the soul and aided by our Angels, serve the mission. This is a subject we will explore later on. We are perfectly set up for success, so as we remember during this life, our chances of mission success rise, tending toward 100 percent, as our human will for this life-time and the soul's Divine purpose ("thy will be done") become one.

So how come so many people express regret at the end of their lives (a sure indicator that the mission was left incomplete, at least in part)? Here's the rub: the trick to this Game of Life, the challenge of it, is that we "un-remember." All the pieces of the puzzle are put into place to facilitate mission success, but when we are born and take on a physical body, with rare exceptions, we forget who we truly are and why we've come here. This represents both the challenge and the beauty of the Game. We forget the ineffable beauty of Source/God. We forget whatever lifetimes we may have lived prior to this one, and even what our mission is.

This complicates the task at hand and can be frustrating. We have the sense that we are meant to be doing something, but we are not sure what it is. It's like walking into a room to do something but forgetting what that something is—just on a bigger scale.

Once we are born, the Game is further complicated by the fact that everything supports our new (and patently flawed) reality—that we begin at birth, that we are merely mortal, that we are small—when, in fact, we are so much more; we simply forgot. As we all forget on arrival, the world is not apt to remind us of the truth, but rather, to steep us in the illusion.

Of course, that is also the beauty of the Game, which is marvelously engineered. We must forget! It must be so! The forgetting is imperative. If we remembered all that came before, would we accept the difficulties and hardships that so often mark life on Earth? Or would we spend our time here pining for "there" and skip out early?

As it is, many of us already do just that. Without necessarily being conscious about why, some sensitive people never really come to accept life as it is here on Earth, and instead, wish themselves away or take steps to "away" themselves.

We see around us such steps in the most extreme form of suicide, but can we recognize also the myriad ways in which we humans "take ourselves out" of the Game by sidelining ourselves and numbing our consciousness in various ways?

This can happen in ways we deem "negative," such as drinking, drugging, smoking, or overeating, or ways we deem "positive," where we overdo everything in order to avoid facing what Life is asking us to look at. On the face of it, such escapes can be positive, such as taking exercise, following a diet, watching television, or even reading or meditating, but when we are "lost" in these exercises (and who has never been "lost" in a good novel or film?), we are on a time-out: we (temporarily) lose ourselves in the activity, and effectively cut ourselves off from the vagaries and vicissitudes of this Life, this Game we are playing.

In itself, taking a time-out is not "bad"; it can serve a purpose when done consciously. But often the sidelining of oneself happens unconsciously, and therein lies the danger. It is admittedly counterintuitive to imagine a book on Angels warning against the perils of meditation (we will even plunge into meditation shortly!), but anything that we (consciously or unconsciously) use to take ourselves out of the Game diminishes our chances of living our soul's purpose (living large) in this lifetime. Balance is always necessary: going into meditation to reinforce our strong participation in Life is highly recommended (and why not do it with the Angels for added oomph?), but using quiet times of meditation to hide from our lives disconnects us from any possibility of living our dream in line with our mission.

It is easy to think of situations where such a time-out might be positive, even necessary. For example, in my harsh childhood, books were always my safe port in a storm. I needed a place to hide, as the situation in which I found myself was overwhelming, too difficult for the child "me" to handle. But we know that old habits die hard sometimes, and as an adult, in periods of difficulty, I found a variety of other "hiding places" that lasted a while: drinking and drugs, smoking and eating, extreme exercise, television bingeing—all of which served to hide me from Me for a time.

Thankfully, as we grow more conscious of the role we are meant to play in this lifetime (and of the help that is there for us) we come more and more into consciousness. We find that less and less happens due to the draw of the unconscious. Even today, I still sometimes like to give myself the gift of a "time-out" and fall into the familiar safe haven of a book, or a TV binge (*Game of Thrones* supplanted the game of Life for a time, as I recall), but that hiding from life is now done intentionally and never lasts; it's a strategic time-out during an important game.

To keep the Game moving, then, our forgetting of the soul and the larger picture is important, as it maximizes the possibility of playing the Game fully, hopefully permitting us to remember and align ourselves consciously with our soul and, at our own human rhythm, agree to live in our life and purpose.

Whew! With all this forgetting and remembering, it is undoubtedly a good thing that we are not alone in this pursuit of the fullness of the Game of Life...

The Angelic Realm:
Angels and Archangels

What is an Angel? Is it a wingéd creature that flies hither and thither, doing the bidding of a faraway God? A being who perhaps intercedes on our behalf in Divine communication? Do they really have wings and halos? Is our friend's sainted mother who passed away (as our friend insists) now "an angel?" Are Angels make-believe, as adults believe Santa Claus is (hey!) or the Easter Bunny . . . or even dragons and unicorns (don't get me started!)?

Although popular parlance uses the term "angel" in many ways, in the interest of clarity and for the purposes of this book, I will hold to the following definition:

An Angel is an expression of God that accompanies us here on the earth plane during our lifetime.

Some people "see" wings when they envision Angels. This is deliberate on the part of the Angels; they use it as a way for people who have been brought up believing that Angels have wings to know what they are dealing with. Iconic imagery aside, when we speak of Angels, hushed terms and deep respect are warranted. An Angel is an expression of God; not separate from God, but an expression of God's love and desire to ease the burden that this life can present.

Angels are our get-out-of-jail-free card (jail being the illusion that we are small and alone); an interaction with an Angel rings a bell, reminding us to come back to Consciousness of who we truly are and why we are here, all of which makes it easier to realize our mission . . . and have fun while we're at it! The Game of Life is meant to be juicy; we are meant to be having fun. Joy is the key to remembering; Joy is Angel juice. Where there is Joy, there are Angels!

A Word about Joy

Joy is our intended state of being. Love and Light and Joy are three aspects of the same Divine energy. Joy is not happiness. Happiness ebbs and flows with events, with the tides of our lives; Joy is rooted in the truth of our being, eternal and light-filled, no matter what our current experience is on the earth plane.

When we find our way back to Joy (it took me 42 years to do so; may it be quicker for you!) we anchor in a reality that is more vast than everyday life; we root in Life itself, in God, in Source, in Love. That anchoring allows us more stable access to a higher perspective and an unerringly "strong foundation when the winds of change shift" (thank you, Bob Dylan).

Joy is the essence of Large Life and the fun of the Game.

Angels come in many forms, although I would argue that when we rank them in order of importance (in groups like cherubim, seraphim, angels, and archangels), we miss the point. Our habit of ranking things (and people) in order of importance, often with skewed standards, is a human habit and often influenced by the values of the culture we happen to live in. As we open to Angels, we recognize more easily that there is no order of importance; that all is God, and all is Good, sacred, loving, and lovable—even that which we find harder to love.

It is very freeing when we find release from that habit of valuing and judging; when we see that all things express God's will marvelously; when we release that human tendency to value this over that; when both this *and* that serve.

For the purposes of this book, I will focus upon two angelic groups with differing functions that interact with us actively (if we allow it): Angels and Archangels.

Angels

The definition of Angels I used earlier is simple and perfect: an Angel is an expression of God's love and will to accompany us in the sometimes-harsh density of this life. But an Angel is *not* an intermediary between us and God, and nor is an Archangel for that matter. We don't need one. We are sons and daughters of a loving Creator. How can we imagine that we need an intermediary? We are invited to the table. The Divine awaits our coming home, our remembering. So what's stopping us?

We are stopping ourselves. The imposed original forgetting (that some call original sin) is part of it. Added to that is our willful forgetting, as we consciously plunge into identification with the body and persona we have taken on in this life, including the judgments and beliefs that make up the human being we are, reflecting family and cultural context: religion, country, language, and so forth. This cultural context imbues our experience with values and beliefs, but at some point we opt to adopt; we choose whether or not to make them our own. The judgments we place on ourselves, such as believing that we are small and guilty or somehow unworthy of the Table or our version of Large Life, can keep us from the Joy that is our birthright and the fullness of the Game and our mission.

Furthermore, sometimes we consciously stop ourselves from playing due to fear of what could happen if we were to step out of the mold in which we find ourselves and emerge from our comfort zone into the fullness of Life. It's not called a "comfort zone" for nothing; change *is* scary! The more we have fallen into the trap of routine and habit, the harder it is to leave it behind.

There are also sometimes fears about who we might disappoint or piss off. We forget that those around us are also playing the Game, and that maybe their Game will be shifted into a higher gear when our moves trigger a movement for them and invite their play, too. When we step out of our comfort zone we challenge others, consciously or unconsciously, to do the same, which won't always make us very popular. It's why the world, including many friends and family, might discourage our taking steps to make big changes with their seeming risks. Dreams of living Large are often discouraged by loved ones—the world prefers we stay in our place and live small until the Game is up.

That doesn't sound like much fun, does it?

The true risk lies not in trying out the unknown but in remaining where we are, in stasis, a poor excuse for rich Life. Still, it is an understandable choice, as the world raises us in fear; sometimes we are so afraid of dying that we forget to live.

Finally, we are also sometimes blocked by our inability to comprehend and enter into relationship with the vast power that is Source/God. Imagine, or try to, a God that is everywhere, at all times, outside and yet inside, filling Time and Space, and yet somehow outside of and at the origin of it all. Now, imagine having a chat with that largeness. Does it feel possible? Does it seem easy? If so, does it feel personal? Maybe not;

yet, as we are operating in human form, it is important for many of us that it be personal. That we can enter into relationship, so that our love (and not fear) can flow in that Presence.

We humans find personal contact and relationship important. The tender, human part of us yearns for a nurturing love that is not always easy to find as we sometimes defend ourselves in the presence of another human being. In light of that, how possible is it for us to wrap our minds around the idea of intimate relationship with God, the eternal and omniscient Omnipresence. Yowzer! How can we get close to that? If I want to reach out to God, what assurance can I have of success?

Thankfully, when God reaches out to us (perhaps in the form of an Angel), we cannot miss! Intimate relationship (closer than breathing) is indeed the sacred intention. So, like a loving parent reaching to calm a child experiencing a nightmare, in a gesture of unfettered generosity God reaches down to us, extending a hand into the density of the earth plane through the presence of Angels. An Angel is not separate from God; it is the hand of God—the many hands of God—holding and loving us and helping us play the highest and best version of our Game possible, if we allow it.

Guardian Angels

When we were children, many of us were told that we have guardian angels watching over us. In general, this is seen by adults as a cute story we tell children to comfort them and help them get to sleep at night. But why do children need to hear this, especially at night?

Children come into the world open and fearless, loving and sensitive, then, over time, with experience and conditioning, they often close up defensively, retreating to a safer place within, to protect themselves from the harsh energies of the world that surrounds them. The very young are often so open they can sense and feel invisible presences around them, so the idea (and truth) of Guardian Angels helps them to settle in and sleep.

When children arrive here, open and sensitive, hearts wide open, there is a tremendous difference energetically between them and the human beings around them who have been "around the block" a while. The difference is sometimes palpable, which is why the presence of a baby, a glimpse of pure Light, can bring a tear to the eye of an adult. A child with his or her heart wide open may shout at the top of their lungs, "Hey, Mom! Look at me!," offering their fabulousness to the world and expecting it to be recognized.

It doesn't always happen. Even in the best of families, there is a difference between coming from the Source, from unlimited unconditional love, and being born into a human home. As energy will always seek equilibrium, the lower energy surrounding the pure energy of a child will often cause children to close their hearts (even if only a bit) to fend off the hurt incurred by a response that is less than enthusiastic—a word that at its root means "filled with God"; to whit, "Oh, would you stop yelling? Mommy's got a headache."

As we grow, passing through stages of school and work, many (if not most) of us instinctively learn to close our hearts at times, such as with our least favorite person. We learn that parts of us are socially loveable, but other parts are maybe less so; in this way, we build our defenses experience by experience and learn to hide our treasure—Truth, the beauty of our light within. Angels can help us to reopen, to find and renew our Light, allowing it to shine forth more constantly in a world that sorely needs it. Guardian Angels are meant for just this role.

> *A Guardian Angel is the Divine presence that has been with us since our soul chose to incarnate, and will remain with us until this soul's experience—our life and mission—is complete.*

Imagine, before you were born, your soul raising your hand and saying, "Ooh! Ooh! Ooh! Send me. I'll go!," when it came time to find the right soul for the mission that is yours. Further, imagine your Guardian Angels following up with something akin to "Oh, I would love to accompany this soul! This is gonna be *good*! It will be my honor."

It may sound simplistic, but this is essentially what goes on, even before our parents connect to create the embryo that will carry our soul.

A Guardian Angel, then, is:

- our closest, oldest friend, who we sometimes ignore, but who loves us anyway, completely and without conditions;
- just waiting for us to remember that they are at our side, and always have been;
- God's love expressed, an invitation to intimate connection with the Divine;

- closer than breathing to us;
- here to assist us in daily human life as well as with our lofty soul's mission—one cannot be separated from the other;
- awaiting our invitation; the rules of the Game include respecting the free will of the human beings that we are, so they cannot intercede on our behalf without our asking;
- a personal accompaniment that is there for only you (the human being that you are) and You (the soul that chose to come into the Game, playing the role of you);
- a welcome addition to any team!

A Word about Free Will

In "the Game" of Life, free will plays an important part. We as humans are given this gift (which sometimes doesn't feel like a gift), and we get to choose. The choices we make cumulatively either align us with our soul's mission or distance us from it. The results of such choices greatly impact our lives: our happiness, our joy (or lack thereof), our health in mind, body, and spirit are all impacted by choices, which we sometimes make unconsciously!

And yet, those are the rules, and the Divine order of things is to allow us, like children in a playground, to grow and find our way in the world, sometimes learning by falling, sometimes not falling as we learn, sometimes not learning at all.

Sometimes folks ask, "Why would God allow this to happen?" The answer is God didn't; we did, but a compassionate and loving Universe/ God "allows" us to live through some difficult experiences because it is part of our Game experience, this life. Like that child having a nightmare, a loving parent knows that their child is perfectly safe. Similarly, our Creator is always aware that we, in the truth of who we are, on a soul level, are always and ever safe and secure, unharmed by what happens in the Game. The soul is always safe—we are always safe—in the arms of the Divine.

As Shakespeare said, "All the world's a stage, and all the men and women, merely players." We are soul actors who are playing on the world stage. But it is like the actors we are have completely identified with the roles we are playing, forgetting that the truth of who we are is on the other side of the curtain. The Angels never forget, however; they simply are waiting for us to remember.

Thus, Angels will not intercede on our behalf unless we ask them to, with the sole exception of a situation of mortal risk when it's not our time to go. For the most part, such situations are soul contracts, designed as a "wake-up call," a context for awakening and aligning to the soul's purpose for the human being who survives it. We will speak more of soul contracts later.

Archangels

There is no order of importance in Angels, since all are expressions of and part of God. Thus, the prefix "Arch" before "Angel" is not a reference to a more powerful angel—after all, how can God be more powerful than Herself?—but in fact means "overarching"; as in, more contacts.

An Archangel is an expression of God or Source as a particular quality, such as Power (Archangel Michael) or Healing (Archangel Raphael).

As with the whole of the Angelic realm, Archangels respect our free will and so do not intervene unless we call for their guidance or assistance. As noted above, archangels are overarching; they accompany all of humanity, as opposed to a Guardian Angel, which accompanies us individually. That said, we can develop relationships with Archangels. This can either happen overnight or over a period of lifetimes, as a soul hones a certain quality, such as Healer.

Though Archangels are unlimited in number (how can we enumerate the qualities of Source/God?) for the purposes of this book, we will look at 15 Archangels that are commonly recognized and that have Divine qualities we can open up to and welcome into our lives through these relationships:

ARCHANGEL	DIVINE QUALITY
Michael	Power of Love
Raphael	Healing
Gabriel/Gabrielle	Communication
Jophiel	Creativity
Zadkiel	Forgiveness
Metatron	Understanding
Sandalphon	Gentleness, Music
Ariel	Nature

ARCHANGEL	DIVINE QUALITY
Uriel	Change/Chaos
Azrael	Death
Chamuel (Samuel)	Seeking/Finding
Jeremiel	Dreaming
Haniel	Sensitivity/Natural healing
Raguel	Justice
Raziel	Wisdom

Now here's a trick question. If someone doesn't know, say, that Raphael is the Archangel of Healing, does that mean that God's healing power is not available to them? Of course not! (Hey, you're good at this.) Rather, we ask, and the Divine answers . . . always. We might not always see the answer, or like it, but there is always an answer.

If a person with no knowledge of the Archangels, such as myself years ago, were to call out to the heavens, sending out a plea for healing, Divine Healing (Raphael) would always respond. Raphael is the name given to Divine Healing: that heavenly succor that so many receive but rarely link to Archangel Raphael. We will delve into how this works later on, when we discuss healing with Raphael.

So, you may ask (I would!), "Hey, Kathryn? If I don't need the name of Raphael to call for and receive Divine Healing, what is the use of learning the names of the Archangels?"

To answer, once again, the question leads us back to ourselves, to our human nature. Names are important to us. It was always so. Man gave names to all the animals. In some cultures, the giving of one's name is a weighty thing: the name is not shared with just anyone. Usually, one of the first things we ask of a person we are meeting for the first time is their name. Why?

We are body, mind, and spirit, we humans, and the mind is involved in most of our interactions. Having the name of someone or something, knowing what to call it/him/her, gives us access to them in a way, helps us to mentally connect with them, allows us, in a way, to integrate and assimilate them. The cat meows. The dog barks. Tommy plays guitar, Andy plays keyboards. Anna has brown hair, Kira's hair is red. Shannon's is multicolored. Conner is smart, Steve is kind , Colin is funny. Well, you get the point!

A name allows us to remember a person, to recall them when necessary, and to connect with them more easily each time we meet. We know this to be true from our own experience, don't we? When a person remembers our name, we feel closer to them; we appreciate it. If they don't (even if we think we don't mind), we notice that, too.

So, the naming of the Divine presence of the Archangels is essentially *for us*. The name, like a doorknob, helps us access certain energies and various portals to the myriad aspects of the Divine. Again, too, this all makes it easier for us to know and love (in our very human way) God, and all of it makes us remember who we are and why we came to this lovely planet called Earth.

We will go more deeply into and explore our relationships with each of the 15 Archangels in chapter 4, but let's make a quick detour to learn about other beings that can help and accompany us on our life path, while we are on the topic. Angels are not the only presence that accompanies us through the course of our life, and so, even if this book concentrates on Angels, we would be remiss not to look at, however briefly, the various other beings that are around us as we go through life.

Ascended Masters and Guides

"Jesus, Mary, and Joseph!" I can still hear my sainted (!) mother exclaim, in her very Irish way but with a Bronx accent, these three holy names of Ascended Masters in rapid-fire order, at once calling out an SOS and expressing great displeasure, a neat trick I never fully understood.

Jesus, Mary, and saints such as Joseph, Francis, Claire, Catherine, Bernadette, Theresa—the list goes on—are what are known as Ascended Masters in the Christian (including my Catholic) cultural context. Examples from other cultural contexts include Buddha, Mohammed, Rumi, Quan Yin, Lao Tse, Brigid, Mikao Usui, and so on.

An Ascended Master is a being who reached remembering and ascension in a single lifetime. They completely aligned with Divine Will and incarnated it. They lived large!

The great difference between Angels and Guides (Ascended Masters or not) is the fact that guides have lived through incarnations, while Angels are pure Spirit. Unlike other Guides, such as relatives who have passed or those who inspire us from the beyond, Ascended Masters have, through their incarnations, reunited with Source. Often these beings continue to be a re-Source for those of us still playing the Game, still evolving, still stretching and tending toward that alignment. Like a coach who understands the ins and outs of the Game, because they've been there, Ascended Masters can help us along our path, if we ask them—and due to the free will rule, *only* if we ask them.

Ascended Masters are the highest form of Guide. They offer us a higher perspective, and guidance (when we can receive it) that is infallible. We are drawn to the Ascended Masters with whom our soul has prior ties and contracted support in this lifetime. This explains why one might be drawn strongly to one Ascended Master and not another, even if our cultural context does not explain it fully; for example, when a person who has been raised Catholic is drawn to Buddha. Situations that negatively impact our experience of a particular culture are also organized to align us with the highest form of guidance for realization, so even unfortunate incidences within an institution like the Church will serve the highest guidance in the end, if we allow them to shake us to the core and remake us, both individually or as a group.

In my own Christian culture, the Ascended Master Jesus is recognized to be one with "the Father," God or Source. But Jesus taught us to say the "Our Father" in the Lord's Prayer, and gave us to understand that he cleared the way for us ("that such as I do, ye shall do also, and more"), making it clear that we are one, of the same family. Such is the message of an Ascended Master who aligns completely with the Divine and becomes a conduit for God's Love here on Earth. The mechanisms we will use to open up to Angels will also work to allow us to open up to an Ascended Master to whom we feel drawn, or even to "regular" Guides, such as John Denver!

Other Guides (Such as John Denver)

I'm looking for space and to find out who I am . . . and I'm looking to know and understand —the words of the song that became a mantra for me as a teen echo still in my heart. So many of John Denver's songs stoked a surging spirituality in me back then, and revealed the depth of a singer/songwriter most kids I knew wouldn't admit to enjoying in an era of hard rock and disco. When, as an adult, I reopened to my spiritual side (the whole of me and Life), I searched for and renewed a kinship with this man whose music still speaks of Truth and brings me to tears—except the kinship happened across the Veil, as Denver was already dead when I woke up and came alive. Through his music, he impacted me greatly as I sought to grow. Thank you, John!

But not everyone feels that way about John Denver or his music legacy, which illustrates an important point: Guides are personal! What or who moves me will not necessarily move you. Our Guides in this lifetime are souls that stir the pot for us, souls that push or poke or prod us to grow toward Large Life.

A Guide is any soul with whom we have a soul connection who watches over us or assists us when called to return to or hold to our soul's chosen path, Ascended Masters included.

When our Guides are still living, it is easy. Mentors, friends, teachers—Guides such as these accompany us on our path for a time here on Earth. But it is when Guides are not "alive," per se, when they accompany us from another (nonphysical) dimension, that things can get a bit tricky. They are not here on Earth with us physically, so seeing, hearing or feeling their presence might be difficult, especially if we are only beginning our remembering, but they can help us with that, too!

Those that coach us from the other side of the Veil, the famous separation between eternal reality and the seeming reality of the Game here on Earth, help us to open up and welcome guidance that may seem to come from afar but really is right here and now with us.

Deceased Family Members and Friends as Guides

Certainly, this is very personal terrain, but also perhaps the most accessible for many of us, as the belief that our loved ones watch over us when they have left "this mortal coil" is quite common. We can be moved on a soul level by Guides who are deceased friends or family members. That includes our "sainted mother," a grandparent (even one who passed before we were born), a sibling (even one who passed *in utero* or at birth), aunts, uncles, godparents, and indeed, anyone who formed close bonds with us, either during this lifetime or one prior.

This may even include a grandparent or great-aunt or uncle, or other relative whom we never met, but with whom, we are told, we share much in common: our laughter, or musicality, or even our clairvoyant gifts. When I came out to my mother, finally telling her I would no longer go back to being a banker, and that I was already working in the world helping people open up to their Angels and Guides, her response sent my jaw to the floor.

"Oh, not you, too!" she exclaimed in dismay, shaking her head as if she should have known.

"What? What do you mean, 'not me too'?" I responded, curious, and maybe a little defensive.

"Your grandmother," Mom almost spat the words out. "My mother used to read tea leaves for all the neighbors in our building. I hated it!"

I could feel the pall of shame my mother must have carried as a teen about her immigrant mother with the almost-incomprehensible brogue thick from Ireland, not fitting in and working her "magic" around a neighborhood where tongues flew quickly and not always gently.

Although I was eager to have more details, I saw clearly that she didn't want to talk about it, and so I let the matter drop. Still, it was heartening to know that my Grandma had gifts she shared with others. Even though she had already passed away, I knew her to be in that room right at that moment, both encouraging me and trying to give my mom a hug.

Guides are not always family members. The rough Bronx of my youth includes many friends who passed away too soon, as a result of an overdose, violence, or illness, and since then, many have been the moments when old friends have been able to reach through the Veil and touch me. I am always grateful for those "wink-wink, nudge-nudges" that remind me of the broader Game, and of the fact, that love does not die with the body.

Other Guides

As we open up and begin to live Large, we may recognize that we are accompanied by other Guides. In addition to deceased family and friends, or saints and Ascended Masters from all cultures, one might feel a pull toward other Guides. For those who sense a strong connection with the stars or constellations, such Guides might be from other dimensions or planets. Others may feel a strong connection to this earth, and as such might feel a calling toward shamanic Earth Guides, totemic objects and beings such as Crystal, Cedar, Eagle, Dolphin, or Horse.

We are attracted to Guides only if they will play a part on our path, and none of it is accidental. They may be soul connections from a life lived elsewhere (oh, the chills I get when I raise my eyes to the sky and the Pleiades just happen to be right overhead!) or from an earthbound lifetime tied closely to the earth and shamanic practices. Like my dear John Denver, Guides can also present in the form of individuals who have passed and who inspire us on our journey with what they did while here; for example, athletes who have passed or artists such as musicians, painters or writers who impact our journey and inspire us in particular ways. We can call on these Guides and ask for support in our own endeavors to create, write, or paint, or play a sport or an instrument.

Nothing in our human makeup is by accident: we are perfectly conceived and constructed to realize our mission. Whether the Guides we are attracted to are living or deceased, our attraction to them is never accidental. These are soul contracts. We will discuss this concept further when we come to the preparation exercise on Forgiveness.

Rules of the Game

Though the above suggests that we are not alone, it sure can feel that way here sometimes, can't it? If there is all this help around us, why do we struggle so? Why don't our Angels and Guides just step in and take over, helping us out?

They can't. Or rather, they won't!

As noted earlier, our free will is one of the rules of the Game, like the forgetting we have already discussed and the soul setting the intended mission and choosing the person who is best suited for the job (in this case, you). Human beings are never forced to do something, not even awaken to the mission.

"Oh sure," I laughingly say. "The Angels made me do it." It's more accurate to say, (if rather unwieldy for a catchphrase), "The Angels dropped hints all around me until I caught on and decided, what the heck, I will give it a shot."

Our free will is respected throughout the Universe, just as our brave derring-do here is respected. The Angels will respect our free will until the end, but the moment we willingly choose to enlist their aid, Divine assistance comes flowing from the high heavens.

Here is another story.

When I was finishing my first book, *The Angels Told Me So: A Practical Guide for Lightworkers*, an old habit kicked in, and I began to operate as I would have in my many years as a banker. Even before finishing the project I began to worry about how I would manage to get the book published. But once I remembered, I realized that worrying would get me nowhere, and besides I did not have to do everything myself. Right there and then, I made the gesture of moving my arms upward, as if I were tossing a basketball in the air to the Angels, saying "This publishing burden is too heavy for me. I will focus on the writing (and thank you for the guidance with that, too), but I need you to take on the task of getting our book published. Thank you!"

And then I got back to writing.

And there is the key. When we give a burden to the Angels to handle, we need to leave it up to them to follow through. If we pick up the burden again, we effectively take back the job and take away the request we placed before them.

The very next day, I received a Facebook message from Chris Verbeke, a student of mine who lives in another part of France. She asked, simply (and in French), "Do you have a publisher for your book yet?" Long story short, she had spoken to her publisher about me, and her editor wanted to speak to me. My amazement was compounded by the fact that it was the same publishing house I was going to target when banker Kathryn was gnawing at the problem. I can still hear my Angels laughing every time I recount the story. (Glad I can be a source of amusement!)

To close out this chapter, we are not the first generation who had an idea of all this, not by a long shot. Remember the Shakespeare quote cited earlier? In it, the Bard could have been describing the Game perfectly when he wrote in his play *As You Like It* (act II, scene 7):

All the world's a stage, and all the men and women merely players; they have their exits and their entrances, and one man in his time plays many parts . . .

The master Shakespeare (himself, part of the mysterious Illuminati), through his 30 plays and myriad sonnets, displayed an extraordinary wisdom, one that sheds light on the nature of the Game. This quote is no different. It sheds light on the truth that we are indeed meant to play here: "the play's the thing!"

Our souls choose this incarnation, and the reason why the soul incarnates (takes on flesh or is born) is a mission or objective selected by our soul in conjunction with our Guides and Angels before we are born.

Every single person born on Earth comes for a reason, and the soul behind that incarnation (even if it is only a brief stay of weeks or months in a womb) comes with a purpose, a mission, something to accomplish. We all then forget that purpose and live out that mission more or less fully in our lifetime, depending on how we align with the soul (or not) during our stay.

Our souls are the actors of which Shakespeare speaks, and the human beings we are are the roles we have chosen to play in order to best express the objective set for this lifetime. Those who cross our paths in this lifetime come and go, with their entrances and exits, and sometimes, when we think they have left the stage definitively, they remain close, just at the other side of the stage curtain (the Veil), ready to whisper our lines to us when we get stuck.

Now that the Who's Who and What's What is clearer, let us move on to the Angels, our Friends in HIgh Places.

CHAPTER 2

Your Clairvoyant Gifts: Open the Channel

We have already spoken of the importance of our bodies as temples of the Divine. Each of us, every person on Earth, carries the light of the Divine within us. "This little light of mine" will shine brightly or not, depending on where I am on my life path, and the degree to which I am living consciously, living large in alignment with our soul's mission. Our bodies hold our light and either allow that light to shine . . . or not.

We know this, don't we?

Some days, when all is right with the world, we seem to beam out that light, and folks come to warm their hands by the fire. We can see (perhaps in others more easily, but it is also there, in us) even physically that the faces of some people seem lit up: their eyes shining warmly, a smile mirrored by their lips and the rest of their face. Such people are attractive, not in the worldly sense perhaps, but in a more real sense. We want to know them. We want to get close to them. We want some of what they've got! What they've "got"—and what we've "got" too, though sometimes it may be covered under a bushel—is Love, the unconditional kind, the "God" kind. Light reflects that Love made visible. Joy is that Love expressed.

Conversely, we sometimes might come across folks who are *not* shining, *not* happy—people whose light is dimmed. Though perhaps overused, the adage is no less true: our eyes are the windows to the soul. If we have ventured far from our soul and our mission, the light can seem to go out of our eyes. In such a soul (and I know whereof I speak), it is as if the fear and anguish of the world have grabbed the person by the heart and dragged them down.

Who has not seen someone who looked (and maybe even with a fake smile on their face) as if all hope was lost? Whose light seemed almost snuffed out? Whenever I see such ones, I always want to go give them a hug, because I know how it is. I know that space. I remember the feeling. (I don't always hug them, though—sometimes, but not always, and never without asking permission—free will, and all that.)

We each begin with that light: it is visible in the beauty of an innocent baby, or in the eyes of a child who is loved. But not every child is loved, and even in the best of families, certainly not unconditionally! Human parents tire, and the flow of love can waver and diminish depending on a child's behavior, naturally.

A child comes into the world capable of Large Love, but over time learns to temper that love in accordance with the expectations of the parent, the family, or the adults and others around them. Because they come from a source of unconditional Love, children acclimate to the (sunny or tempestuous) climate in which they find themselves in order to glean the love and attention they desire.

Kids adapt. They learn quickly how to get what they need and what behaviors they need to adopt to ensure that they are cared for and about. Sometimes that means they will pretend to be something they are not: noisy, funny, quiet, polite. Not all children naturally fit the expectations of their parents, but most will learn to adapt to please the people who are the most important to them. Sadly, that habit of people pleasing often becomes the modus operandi for our behavior here on Earth, and (if we get good enough at it) can sometimes lead to us losing a real sense of self and disconnecting from our own needs and desires, who we are, and our Life and our purpose.

A story I like to tell is that when I was a little girl, my father would take me and the brothers who were close to me in age (there were seven of us kids in all) to the park, where we would hike, play ball, or run track. In such outdoor moments, he would occasionally teach me to whistle as he did: a shrill, piercing affair, heard for blocks and blocks (the measure of Bronx distance). When my father whistled for his kids to come home, the whole neighborhood heard it. I practiced that whistle until I got good at it. One day, I decided to show my mother what I had learned and let loose a fierce whistle in the tiny kitchen of our six-story walk-up apartment.

"No!" my mother exclaimed, distressed. "Don't do that!"

"Why not?" I asked, confused.

My mother explained, "When a girl whistles, it makes the Blessed Mother cry."

End of discussion.

I got the picture: either I stopped whistling, or my mother would not be happy; in other words, I stopped whistling for fear of losing my mother's love.

After that day, I would whistle with my dad in the park and never whistle when I was with my mom. Somewhere in there, I lost sight of whether or not I even enjoyed whistling (I have since decided—I do), but back then, what was more important was making sure that my parents were happy with me.

Fear Trumps Love?

That habit of adapting our actions to the expectations of others is how the game (small "g") of life is played—the game in which fear trumps love, where children will torment each other to be accepted and appreciated, where adults do the same, and where admiration is accorded to the one who succeeds, even if such a one steps on others to get there.

Coming out of the institutional schooling that most of us have had, we generally aim to please, whether it be at home, in school, at work, or even in any kind of relationship in which we find ourselves. We learn to put aside anything that makes us stick out from the norm. In the game of life that everyone accepts (at least in the Western world), the weak fall by the wayside; it's dog-eat-dog, or as the saying went in the Bronx of my childhood, "Life sucks and then you die."

But what if that is *not* how the Game (capital "G") is played?

Our natural light begins to diminish when we learn that who we are naturally won't quite do; that we must adapt and change our way of being to fit in, be respected, admired, even loved. We learn to judge, even as we hope to avoid judgment, a sticky habit that clouds our light until we release it. Fear diminishes our light, and as we adapt to pleasing others, we wander far from ourselves, from our own love and light.

All that pleasing others can obfuscate what actually pleases *us*!

When the bank shut down my job in Paris, and I chose not to take the one they offered me in Charlotte, North Carolina, I was faced with a new chapter for which I wasn't ready. But how could I "follow my bliss" when I didn't know what it was? I had wandered so far off *my* path while following the world's path that I had lost sight of myself completely. Depression ensued, naturally. Depression is often the measure of how far we have wandered off our life purpose. When we adapt to please others, we can lose sight of what really makes us happy—and our Light right along with it.

The things that please us (our "bliss") are signposts or markers on the path to our soul's mission. Insofar as we ignore our heart's yearnings, instead doing what is expected of us, our Light dims. But when we renew or remain steadfast in connection with our heart's desires, we align with that Light. This is not true just for some, but for all of us. Each person holds the light of the Divine; we are all beings of Light.

The more we cultivate our own Light (and why not with the help of the Angels?), the more our presence can stoke the flame in those around us, and in those we love. We are here in this moment (and if you are reading this book, this includes you) to open up to our own Light with the help of Angels. We are not only beings of light but also "Lightworkers," souls here with a specific mission.

The Soul's Mission and Life Purpose — Lightworker

We are living during a period of great change, in which humanity has a chance to remember and consciously return to our Light, both individually and as a whole. To support this transformation or en-light-enment, many "old souls" (those who are evolved) have chosen to come to Earth at this time, taking on the role of Lightworker.

The soul's mission in being a Lightworker is literally "to be Light"; that is, to anchor Light in the darkness and transform fear (darkness) into Love. More than these fluffy words, though, the goal of a Lightworker is simply to stay put and courageously hold true to ourselves in the face of a world that will try to shake us. That is where our Light is, what allows our Light to shine. We are here to allow our truth and our Light to shine forth unsullied by a world that understands very little of the Game as it is meant to be played.

The Lightworker lives out the soul's purpose of being a portal for Light into the world, each of us shining in our own way. Each of us—with our unique strengths as well as aspects we may deem weakness—is perfectly composed, created to live out the soul's mission of Light in our individual way.

The mission of the soul as Lightworker has to do with a quality of being: we are called to shine, to be Light. That shining cannot be forced; there is no burden to it.

The more lightly we step or dance through our life, the more of our shining we allow.

This is the soul's movement. In contrast, the life purpose of the human being has more to do with doing: *how will I personally shine my Light? What activities will maximize my joy, and thus, the Light I share in the world? How will I consciously be a portal for the Divine and express that Light in the world?*

The earth is in the grip of fear, and the more things change, the more fear arises. Like a sensitive child who steps back and hides behind a mother's skirts, many of us hide a part of our Light to protect it from the harsh critique of a world that would ridicule Love and sensitivity as weakness and naiveté. Imagine that child stepping back and energetically putting up defenses. They shut doors and windows to ward off the tempest that is this troubling world and hide, afraid of the fray. We often act instinctively to protect the more tender bits of ourselves from the harsh glare of the world's judgment. When this happens to a child, perhaps we can even see the Light dim in their eyes.

It may seem like protection is key to survival—and when we are children and dependent on caregivers it can be. But when we close doors and windows and keep them closed, when we put up walls and defenses against the harsh world to protect ourselves from the judgment of others, those same protections also limit our access to guidance and accompaniment from above. How often have I transmitted a message from someone's Guardian Angel to the effect that the Angels had been with them all the times they had felt so alone as a child but the defenses they had constructed had also prevented their Guardian Angel from making its presence known. This book—and specifically, this chapter—is about reopening those doors and windows, reopening (or widening) our ability to communicate with the Angelic realm, in order to receive assistance in our daily lives and with our life purpose.

Opening Our Channel

We have already spoken about the body as being our temple. An equally interesting way to view it is as our instrument, the means by which we more lightly play our solo, our role, here on Earth. It is up to us to become more aware of how our instrument works and reach toward its mastery. The body can be an instrument in the sense that we are invited to play it—to practice until we understand how our unique instrument works, and then put it to good use creatively to support both who we *are* and what we *do* in alignment with our soul's mission and our life purpose.

You are perhaps already aware that you have clairvoyant gifts. In fact, we all do. Sure, some are more developed than others, but each of us has gifts that are both personal and clairvoyant.

Our personal gifts are those that are more easily recognized by the world, such as athletic ability, leadership skills, musicianship, ability to write (or even leap tall buildings in a single bound!). The talents we are born with and those we have cultivated along the way all serve us in life. Our confidence, or lack thereof, is often linked to the recognition we have received for our gifts, from others and/or from ourselves.

Most of us know that we have five senses—sight, smell, hearing, taste, touch. They can be called "gifts" as they are free, and (at least by those who do not have them, or for whom they are diminished) are deemed priceless. These senses give us information that helps the vehicle that is our body efficiently and effectively navigate the waters of our lives.

In addition to the five senses above that are deemed "normal," we may enjoy the benefits of other senses, forms of clairvoyance, that can also help us to navigate our way through this life, and perhaps even come to live it Large. Our body and its specific senses form the basis for clairvoyance: it is through our instrument, the body and its senses, that we communicate with Angels, and indeed, all that is beyond the Veil, included our Higher Self or soul.

Clairvoyance

In the large sense, clairvoyance is defined as "a capacity to see/understand things in an extraordinary way, over and above what is deemed 'normal.'" In our clairvoyant experience, we "see" or "get" something that someone else standing right next to us might not "see" or "get" at all.

Clairvoyance, then, can be rightly seen as remarkable and extraordinary; very often, however, it is also considered "not normal." But it is not because it is an underused muscle that we should question it or call it abnormal (even if the majority of people don't use the muscle); rather, it would be better to explore how we can put a muscle to use that we never knew we had? As with developing the muscles of the physical body, in order to develop our clairvoyance "muscles," we will need to use them.

The Angels around us can help with that!

*The extraordinary knowing, seeing, and understanding
that is clairvoyance can be expressed in four different ways:
clairvoyance, clairaudience, clairsentience, and claircognizance.*

Clairvoyance, as noted above, is the capacity to see images that allow us to understand things in an extraordinary way. This would include capabilities that are often deemed rare or even odd, where human beings like you and I see dead people, or auras, or Angels, and so on. Such "seeing" may be experienced with our actual eyes, though that form is more rare. It may be our experience since birth, or we may decide (as with sport or music) to cultivate it consciously, through practice "playing" our instruments: our bodies and our gifts.

That said, any message that our instrument captures that includes an image is a form of clairvoyance ("clearsightedness"); thus, images associated with our clairvoyance may indeed be seen with our physical eyes, but more often they come in other ways: in a dream or in our mind's eye (our "inner screen," most easily accessed when we close our eyes).

Inner Screen Example

Close your eyes. Think of someone you love: their eyes, their nose, their hair. The way you "see" that face is on your "inner screen," or the mind's eye. This is where and how we often perceive or "see" flashes of clairvoyance, in visions.

It is good to know our terminology when we engage with clairvoyance:

A Word about Visions versus Visualizations

A vision is not the same a visualization. A vision comes to us unbidden, by grace; a visualization is an exercise we undertake on purpose, with intention, like the exercise invoking a loved one's face, above. Both visions and visualizations can be useful on the path to living Large, but it is interesting to note the difference: We move forward in life both by following guidance (visions) and by exercising our free will (visualizations). Both are important, and the practice of visualizing can cultivate our capacity to receive visions.

Extrasensory Perception (ESP)

We clairvoyantly see something either with our physical eyes (an aura, for example) or with our internal sight on our inner screen, as in a "flash" or a vision in a dream (such visions will often be recurring; the information keeps knocking at our door until we open it).

Each experience is a unique one: someone standing or sitting right next to us will not see what we "see." This form of clairvoyance is sometimes called ESP, or "extrasensory perception," as it is a form of receptivity that goes beyond the five "normal" senses of sight, hearing, taste touch, and smell that we all recognize, or what someone right next to us would also be able to capture.

Sensory Perception – "Extra" (SPE)

There is also another way we can experience clairvoyance, which is much more common. This is when we experience clairvoyance (the capacity to receive information and understanding beyond the "norm" through images) with actual physical things we see with our own eyes, i.e. signs.

When we are open to it, this is a true form of clairvoyance that relies on our natural, "normal" sense of sight to receive messages and understandings from beyond the Veil, as Angels or perhaps loved ones try to get a message through to us. Receptivity to signs is often the precursor to the more extraordinary forms of clairvoyance, at least it was for me, as you'll see in the following story.

Here's an example from my own life:

I left the driveway, sand and stones crunching under the tires as I backed out onto the street in front of the beach cottage on Emerald Isle, NC, which I fondly and aptly call "Attitude Adjustment." It is a place that I co-own with a bank, and during the vacation season it is rented, which satisfies the requirements of the bank. In the off-season, when the island is deserted, sometimes I head there myself to oversee maintenance work, walk the beach in the company of dolphins and pelicans, and write.

As much as I like to stay put when I am writing, from time to time I find myself leaving the house to do the small errands that life requires. As I pulled out that day, I scanned the area under the house, the pylons that kept the house safe from flooding, the retaining wall, the dunes beyond, and sighed. It was just perfect. I ran my errands quickly, as is my wont, always eager to come back to the haven of stillness that is this place, but as I pulled up only 15 minutes later, I noticed right away that something was different.

There, leaning against the retaining wall under my house, was a can. A soda can (or as some friends would say, a can of pop) had somehow found its way under my house, balanced neatly despite the windy day on the retaining wall holding back the dunes. At the time, Coca Cola was printing names on cans, and I was somehow both surprised and not surprised to see the name on this one: Buddy.

My dad's name was Buddy, or at least that's what friends and family called him. I have the habit of signs from dear old Dad, including a sweatshirt story I tell in another book. Well, this kind of topped it! Not a person on the beach, the houses on either side empty, and somehow a soda can with my Dad's name on it appeared under my house during the mere 15 minutes I had run out to the store and back!

Now let's remember our definition of clairvoyance: The capacity to understand something in an extraordinary way through "seeing," through an image. Another way we can experience Large life is to recognize that we are not alone, that we are accompanied, and when we receive messages from the other side of the Veil, that becomes more clear. Soon, we come to see that these types of messages are both "normal" and "extraordinary."

If someone had been standing right next to me as I got out of the car and walked over to the can, they would have seen what I saw: the Coke can marked with the name "BUDDY." Yet they would not have "seen" what I saw; they would not have "gotten it." The message was for me alone, a sign from my dad, a wink-wink from beyond, reminding me that he loves and watches over me, and all of my family.

Whether the messages come from dearly departed ones or Angels (which is our main objective here), our willingness to be receptive to signs is a strong point of departure for all manner of clairvoyance: cultivating our SPE opens the door for our ESP, both with clairvoyance and with our next topic, clairaudience. It would have been great if in schools they taught us that we have not only our five traditional senses, but also other ways of seeing, feeling, hearing and knowing. When we decide to open up to our (spiritual) sight, it is as if someone who had been walking around with their eyes closed, thinking they were blind, suddenly decided to open them. It can be that simple!

Clairaudience

Clairaudience is the capacity to hear or understand beyond the norm by means of sound.

What I would call the Hollywood version of clairaudience is what we see often on TV or in the movies: the burning bush that speaks; the Long Island medium receiving messages for the woman scooping ice cream for her; Whoopi Goldberg as a fake medium suddenly finding herself transmitting messages from the dead-but-ever-beautiful character played by Patrick Swayze for his tearful wife played by a young Demi Moore in the cult film *Ghost*.

That common understanding of a medium as a person who receives messages from the dead for the living is quite limited. In fact, a medium is any person who bridges the worlds, who acts as intermediary between our earthly experience and the other side of the Veil, the invisible. This includes people who hear (and possibly transmit) messages from the dead but also from other domains as well: Angels and Archangels (what we are about here), as well as Guides, Ascended Masters, and so on.

The ESP or special version is where one person "hears" messages that someone right next to them may not hear. This "hearing" creates an understanding (I hear you!) that is extraordinary, and it can happen in the form of hearing with our physical ears or our "inner ears."

A Word about Inner Hearing

Close your eyes (closing our eyes to hear better is effective as it allows for less "input" and thus, fewer distractions, permitting a concentration that will be both more subtle and more powerful). Imagine the person in the exercise above, or someone else you care for very much.

Concentrate on that person until you can remember the sound of their voice, maybe through things they would often say, or the sound of their laughter or singing (or yelling—whatever works). In this way, use your imagination to "hear" their voice or a sound you associate with them.

Our inner hearing can be cultivated by doing exercises like the one above. Like a muscle, the more we use it, the more access we have to that capacity, and the more our inner hearing becomes available to us—not just in facilitating similar "recall" exercises but, over time, as a way to receive messages from our Angels, Guides, or loved ones. As we begin to notice what is going on internally, we may also begin to notice songs that pop into our heads, or key phrases that seem to crop up in a repetitive manner. This kind of clairaudience can happen either in the ESP (Hollywood) way or in a very down-to-earth SPE way: imagine a car passing by, windows open, and suddenly a song spills out. Instantly, our body reacts: hair stands on end or our eyes fill with tears. This is a typical and extraordinarily ordinary experience of clairaudience.

As with clairvoyance, the more we pay attention to and listen and hear the world around us, exercising our will to hear with the inner ear (using exercises like the one above), the more we flex our clairaudient muscles and open up to our gifts.

Clairsentience

Clairsentience is the capacity to know and understand things through the feelings of our bodies, to include our senses of touch, smell, and taste.

"I feel you!" A phrase often used these days lets another person know that we understand where they are coming from, we "get it." We can imagine being in the other's shoes and how they feel at that moment. This capacity for empathy is one expression of clairsentience, one that we all take for granted and thus, don't see as anything special.

But what else do we feel?

Perhaps we walk into a room and feel welcome, or not? Perhaps we feel physically uncomfortable in certain spaces (a hospital, a cemetery) and, conversely, feel great in others (at a friend's house, in our favorite place in Nature, or perhaps a spa). The difference between these places, which logically should impact on our sense of well-being, is their energy.

Clairsentience is about responding to energy; our bodies are sensitive instruments that capture, "read," and react to energy. This is true not only for some of us but for all of us!

All of us are more comfortable, happier, in some places but not others, with some people not others. This has a physical impact on us and may include changes in heartbeat and breathing (for example, the instinctive holding of the breath), hair standing on end, goosebumps, feelings of warmth, feelings of coldness, butterflies or knots in the stomach, and weak knees. Each of our instruments "plays" in its own unique way, and it is up to us to pay attention in order to decipher how our body communicates messages and their meanings.

For example, who has never had goosebumps? If you have, then you probably know that there are "good" goosebumps and there are "bad" goosebumps. Right? "Good" goosebumps come when something wonderful and maybe fortuitous occurs; they bring feelings of joy and peace. "Bad" goosebumps, however, bring neither joy nor peace but rather, anguish and foreboding. In both cases, the same physical phenomenon occurs, but instinctively we know which is "bad" and which is "good."

We Already Know How to Play Our Instruments

In future, these sorts of things will be taught in school, but for now, most of us learn these things late, if at all; yet, it is crucial information to be able to play the Game with an instrument able to communicate with Friends in HIgh Places and live Life Large!

Throughout this book, we will continue to do a number of exercises together that will augment your sensitivity to energy and/or your capacity to strengthen so that your sensitivity becomes an asset not a liability.

But for now, let's simply recognize that our bodies respond to energy in the form of clairsentience. In addition, it is this clairvoyant gift that allows us to transmit energy to others in various forms of healing, such as Reiki or Angel Healing, which we will discuss later in the book.

Other forms of clairsentience include the capacity to capture information through our body in other ways, such as through our sense of smell or sense of taste. Sometimes, for example, a loved one who has passed will communicate with us by leaving the scent of their favorite cologne or perfume behind, allowing us to know of their presence even after they have physically left the earth plane.

Claircognizance

Claircognizance is essential, inner knowing. It is also called intuition and is revealed at those times when "we know." We don't know HOW we know, but we know!

The telephone rings, and you "know" who it is. Your friend talks about an interview they went on, and you "know" that they will get the job. A woman is pregnant, and you "know" if it will be a boy or a girl. You are traveling to a new place, and you somehow "know" the turns to take before the GPS says anything.

Here's my tale of claircognizance.

Lost in Japan

I sat in the passenger seat of the car that Saturday with a colleague from the bank who was as lost as I was. In my twenties, I didn't even have a driver's license (that sometimes happens when you grow up in a big city in a family without a car), so there had been no question of me driving.

This normally meant that I could relax . . . not that day. We were working in Japan and had rented a car to take in some sights on our one day off that week, driving far out of Tokyo to try to get to the seaside (I always want to go to the seaside). But we were lost. Back then, all signs were only in Japanese, and neither of us brilliant banker types spoke Japanese. My colleague in the driver's seat was starting to get stressed out.

We came upon a crossroad then, and though there was no way to know which way to go as the signs were in Japanese kanji, I said, quietly, "Take a left here."

"Huh? What do you mean? How do you know?" asked my incredulous colleague, a tad annoyed and peering over at me.

"I don't know. I just know."

I shrugged as I watched him say, "No, I think it's this way," and turned right.

I hadn't offered the information that weird things had been happening to me since I got to Japan: people giving me gifts on the subway, and me somehow understanding some Japanese in conversations here and there, when really there was no logical explanation for it. I was considered "unbankerly" enough already, and generally decided not to share too much information, but this time I tried.

Almost two hours later, we found ourselves back at the same crossroads, and this time my colleague turned left, spitting out a "Don't say a word" through gritted teeth.

I didn't have to.

As this story indicates, claircognizance, also known as intuition, is quite helpful . . . when we listen to it! Contrary to the old wives' tale, it is not the singular domain of women, though one could argue that it is our feminine aspect (the quieter receptive side, as opposed to the more active, masculine side) which is the center for intuition in all of us.

That inner knowing is subtle, but it is simple to determine if we have had intuition in the past. Have you ever had the experience where (in frustration) you have exclaimed, "Darn (or some other epithet)! I *knew* it!" when learning something after the fact that we had felt within but had not acted on. Those are *always* moments when there had been an intuition, a clairvoyance in the form of claircognizance . . . but we didn't listen.

Sometimes, trained by a world that brooks little that is intangible or seemingly illogical, we ourselves become our own colleague in the driver's seat, stubbornly refusing help, simply because it comes from a source that is not "normal." But what could be more "normal" than Source, which is within all of us?

The following exercise is designed to put us consciously in touch with the (very normal) part of ourselves that is intangible and sacred. By trying (and repeating!) this and other experiences like it, we "muscle up" spiritually. We begin to realize that the world which teaches us from young to shut our eyes to clear sight, to ignore energy and angels and sacred moments of ineffable connection, and to abstain from all help which such accompaniment can afford us... is itself anything but normal!

Channel Opening

There are exercises we can do to awaken and cultivate these gifts, some of which I propose in other books and others I suggest here. But the best thing we can do to open up to all our clairvoyant gifts is to ask for help: to allow the Divine to help us to open our "channel."

The doors that we closed as children when we landed on the harsh terrain of this earth will need reopening if we are to fully embody the Light that is ours and live our unique mission fully. The sensitivity that was rejected in favor of self-protection will be invited to reopen, but this time with strength behind it, as we step into the power that is ours, as adults and as souls that are here on a mission, and with an (Angelic) entourage to boot!

When we stand in our power, our body, our instrument, stretches naturally from earth to sky. Our feet are planted on the earth and our head (including the fontanelle, that soft place between the cranial bones on top of the head that closed last and can seem more or less open) is surrounded by sky. Our spinal column represents our verticality between earth and sky, and this position invites us to recognize both our human nature (with our feet planted firmly on the ground) and our ethereal nature, our spiritual side (which some derisively but with splendid imagery call "head in the clouds"). It is by honoring and recognizing *both* who we are as human beings (the "roles" we play in this lifetime) *and* Who We Are, Truly (the spiritual Truth of our Light and Power) that we play this Game most fully.

To do that, we start by carrying out a simple and effective practice now, and in the preparation phase of all exercises in this book: channel opening. The steps for the channel opening are listed below in the exercise. Take time to read through the whole exercise first before working your way through the steps with clear intention. We create with our thoughts and with our words on the energetic plane just as we do with our actions in the physical. As such, intention will be the key to all that we undertake here, with clear intention and the help of our Friends in High Places!

NOTE: If you become lightheaded during this or any of the exercises in the book, a quick fix is simply to open your eyes, even slightly. As this exercise promotes a higher frequency and density of energy, one might become a bit dizzy if we are not yet accustomed to such powerful energy; opening our eyes diffuses the energy by opening us up to other stimuli.

A well-known energetic law can be stated as "where our attention goes, energy follows," and so when we open our eyes, our attention is diluted by the numerous other stimuli all around us, thus diminishing the energetic concentration, and rendering the experience less intense.

EXERCISE Channel Opening

1 **Prepare by breathing**

Find a quiet space where you won't be interrupted. The exercise can be done sitting or standing, but in the beginning, it is best not to try it lying down, unless necessary.

Now close your eyes and breathe! Breathing is something we do about 10,000 times a day, mainly without thinking about it.

We want to do it consciously here. Recognizing that breath carries Life, we quickly come to see that this exercise can enrich our life to Large size, enliven it so that we realize all that we are meant for in this lifetime!

To that end, breathe *in* life at this moment, and breathe *out* anything that has been distracting you or weighing on your mind, diminishing your life, your light, your joy, your shine!

Repeat until you begin to feel clearer and lighter.

Once you feel ready, breathe *in* your intention to open your instrument to your Divine gifts and Angelic assistance, and breathe *out* anything outside of that intention that might distract you.

Remember, breath centers us in Life: our Life in this moment, the only time intention work like this channel opening is possible. Stay present!

2 Ask your Angels for help

Ask your Angels for help. Never mind, if you don't know anything about them or are not even sure they exist yet. Leave it to them to show you over the time to come, more and more each day. For now, all you have to do is ask, so that the free will requirement is met.

Your words are always perfect. Speak whatever comes from your heart. It can be something simple like *Hi, Angels. I have the intention to open my channel to communicate with you (more and more clearly). Please facilitate this opening. Thank you.* (It is always good to include both a clear intention and a word of thanks when doing such work; gratitude, a high-frequency energy, greases the wheels.)

3 Fill your body with Light

Since you now have Angelic assistance, this will be easy. Just imagine that with each breath you breathe in, you are also breathing in Light: the Light of your soul, of your Divine flame, of "this little Light of mine" fame. (If you know the song, you can sing it!)

With each breath, breathe in Light, sending that Light down to the tips of your toes and fingers, lighting up each cell, and even the space between your cells. With each in-breath, bring more Light into the body, and, with each out-breath, exhale anything that has diminished your Light in the past.

In: Light!

Out: Anything that blocks your Light! Continue until you feel ready for the next step.

4 **Light up your spinal column**

Concentrate the light with which you have filled yourself all along your spinal column by simply imagining that all that light within you begins to concentrate around your vertebrae, densifying and lighting up, creating a path of light from your neck to your coccyx. This path or ribbon of light will form the base of your channel as you are creating (or reinforcing) it with intention today, with the help of your Angelic entourage.

5 **Connect with the earth**

Follow your light ribbon down the spinal column from the neck to your coccyx, and, upon reaching the coccyx, with your clear (and powerful) intention, send or imagine the end of the ribbon moving down to the center of the earth.

Imagine or just allow that the ribbon makes its way easily to the center of the earth, as if the earth itself is opening up to receive you! Layer after layer opens and allows the descent of your ribbon of light until finally you arrive at the center of our planet, the heart of life on Earth.

In an ambiance very rich and nourishing, you are invited to *breathe in* that strength and power and *breathe out* anything that blocks your ability to live Life Large: anything that blocks your power.

In that space, notice or simply know that you are not alone, but that the presence or consciousness of Mother Earth is here present. She sees you arrive and holds out her arms to give you a great hug, holding you close to her heart. This is *perfectly normal*, as the moment you, as a soul, chose to take on flesh and blood of mortal existence, you became her child, as she is Mother to all who are present physically on Earth at this time.

A good mother, she offers to fill you with her tenderness and love, knowing all that you have already had to face in this life, and aware of how great your life purpose is. She intends, too, to fill you with every force and capacity you will require to fulfill your life's mission. Will you accept it? Will you open now your channel to receive this reinforcing energetic boost from Mother Earth? (Your free will precludes this happening without your accord.)

If so, it is time to simply set the intention to open up—to the help and support of Earth, to the strength and power of your instrument, to your unique expression of light through the body that you inhabit in this lifetime. Your own words from the heart are always best, but it can be something simple like:

I open my channel to stand strong upon the earth, grounded and ready to live my life's purpose—Large. Thank you, Gaia, Mother Earth.

With that, in your mind's eye or with your imagination (strengthened by your powerful intention), take the end of your light ribbon and affix it here at the center of the earth in whatever way comes to mind: a pretty bow, a sailor's knot, the roots of a tree, even (as with mine) a plug going into a socket!

Before moving on to the next step, *breathe in* the love, tenderness, strengthening, and confidence-building on offer from the earth and *breathe out* anything that has shaken your strength and confidence, and perhaps at times your will to live on this planet! Continue the breathing to fill your whole body (instrument) and prepare for the next step.

A Note about Earth

As we recognize that there is no place that "God" is not, no space not filled with the energy of Life, and certainly when we see the fruit both intentionally planted and naturally growing each year, we can recognize that Earth (at least when left to her own devices) provides a rich abundance of all that we require: Life in abundance! As we connect to Earth here (and again in each exercise in this book), we may come to feel more and more intuitively that Earth (sometimes called Gaia, or Mother Earth) has a consciousness.

That "she" too has a mission, and that she recognizes us and respects our movement. She sees us as we are truly and supports our path as (more and more) loving and powerful sons and daughters of the Divine. She patiently and eagerly awaits our awakening and remembering that we are (co)-guardians (with the elementals, but that is a conversation for another time) of this marvelous blue marble we inhabit. She waits for humanity to remember that we are intimately connected to her, and so, to end the exploitation and avarice that threatens her, and us as well.

6 Fill the body

Thanking Mother Earth for her generous filling energy, and maybe offering her a kiss on the cheek and a quick "See you later!" (because we will), it is time to take your leave of her, to move back to and through your channel, which is now strongly rooted in the earth, the ribbon of light that stretches already between the earth and you.

Go up.

With your intention, it occurs easily, and besides, as you have opened the gates, the strong nourishing energy of Mother Earth flows and follows, lifting you, carrying you upward as if on a geyser, up and up. All the layers of the earth pass easily as you travel with the assistance of Earth's flow to return to where you began: traversing the earth, the foundation of any structure where you now stand, then into your body and up the spinal column as a path to your heart.

When you arrive at the level of your heart, pause a moment, allowing that strength of love and tenderness to fill you—first, your heart to overflowing, then your physical body, then your mental and emotional bodies, and finally, your energy field, your spiritual body. Once filled, your base connection with the earth and the filling and grounding of your instrument for the channel opening are in place, and it is that stable foundation that allows the following opening to occur.

7 Connecting to the Angels

From the level of your heart, follow your light-filled spinal column up through to your neck, where you will come to the other end of your ribbon of light. Set your intention to send forth that ribbon to the heavens—to Source, God, Origin, or the Holy Name you like. With your intention, the ribbon will rise through your neck, crossing your head, and out of the soft spot at the top of your head where the crown chakra is located (more on chakras later).

The Angels around you carry the ribbon (since you asked)

directly to the heavens, up and up and up. Arriving, you may feel an expansion or lightheadedness. If so, simply open your eyes again. *Breathe in* the light and love and joy of the Source. *Breathe out* anything that in the past may have diminished your joy, your light, your Large Life!

The Angels welcome you to the space; here you are known and celebrated. Here, at the Source, that part of you that never believed that you are separated from God dwells eternally. Here, in this space, you can cultivate connection with Angels and Archangels, your Guides, Ascended Masters and your Higher Self, at the soul level. But we are here today to connect with your Angels. Are you ready to open and accept the help and guidance of your Angels? If so, this is best facilitated by opening your channel to Source now.

In your own words, set your intention to complete the opening of your channel to the highest planes of being. Something simple and heartfelt is always best, maybe something like this:

I am ready and willing to open up to the Light and Love and Joy of the Divine now. I set my intention to do so with the help of the Angels and Archangels from this moment forward.

Then, with your clear intention, decide to connect your ribbon here at the Source. Making sure to leave it here in the way you wish, you can hand it to your Guardian Angel, or you can hand it to your soul/Higher Self, or simply allow it to remain here with Source, so that your channel opening is complete. Remember that we are sons and daughters of Creation/Creator, and as such, we create all the time. Our expectations or intentions create in almost as solid a manner as our physical actions: where our attention goes, so goes our energy—energy that creates.

So, wide open to your angels now, *breathe in* and notice how it feels as you are filled. Allow the Light and Love to fill you, the Joy to overflow. *Breathe out* anything that comes up in mind or heart to distract or block this.

Keep *breathing in* that Light and *breathing out* to release all blocks to your Light, to your Angelic connection, to your living Large until you feel replenished and ready for anything!

8 **Return and integrate**

Once filled, when it is time to come back "home," to your heart, ask your Angels to accompany you henceforth, and they will. Allow them to accompany you as you descend along your channel/ribbon to return to the Earth plane, your physical dimension. Slide along the path you have created (the channel will become wider and more fluid with each use) to return to the physical body.

In the company of your Angels, come back into the space where you are, and follow down into the body through your head, neck, and spinal column until you reach the level of your heart. At the heart, place your hands at the center of your chest (where the heart chakra is located, the energetic center of your human being).

Breathe in to bring your consciousness to your heart within your chest, beating between earth and sky. Know that you are on your way, that any doors that had been closed are now reopening, with the help of the Angels. Gratitude!

Aftercare

When you complete the exercise you may feel tired, so rest, if possible. The physical body, particularly if we are not used to energy work, may be easily fatigued by working with our channel, especially at first. In addition, it is a very good idea to help our instrument—just as a master violinist will care for his Stradivarius—each and every time we reach out energetically to our Angels for help and healing.

When we do an exercise like the channel opening we just experienced, it allows us to expand energetically: we become bigger, more powerful. It aligns us with our soul and our mission more each time, but our physical body is aligned with the energetic footprint we had *before* the exercise, so it will try to attune with our new energetic footprint. The frequency of our cells will rise, which will often tire our physical vessel. There are things you can do to assist your body in adapting to the "new you":

- Drink water. This helps with the evacuation of anything that no longer serves, and helps the instrument, which is mostly made of water, to acclimate to your new, expanded energy footprint.

- Go for a walk (or sit) in Nature, which helps you ground further and integrate the work. Do this barefoot, if possible.
- Eat nuts or fresh fruit. Organic is preferable, and/or blessed.
- Sing or chant, as the vibration facilitates the integration.
- Relax. Take a nap, sleep, daydream, and generally, find the downtime necessary for integration.

These are only a few of the organic, simple techniques that can help us to integrate expansions as we go along the way to living Large, completing our life's mission with the help of the Angelic realm. We will look at others as we move forward.

CHAPTER 3

Angels and Archangels:
A Little Help Here?

The class had gone well, and I smiled, as I was getting ready to leave Attitude Adjustment, the house/sacred space on Emerald Isle, North Carolina, where I had been teaching a Reiki Master Teacher class all day.

It had been a special class, with only one student: Father Everett Thomas, the local parish priest of St. Francis-by-the-Sea parish, a lovely church with lovely people and an outdoor labyrinth that is well worth visiting if you ever find yourself in the area.

We were finishing early. Father Everett's lovely wife Phyllis was terminally ill, and he was hurrying back to her side. In fact, Phyllis, also a Reiki teacher, had insisted that Father Everett do his Master level training with me at that time, probably the only reason he was there.

The day had gone well, and I was very relaxed, so when I saw that my keys were not where I thought they should be, I simply called out, "A little help, here?"

"Of course," Father Everett said kindly. "What can I help you with?"

Oops!

Before answering him, my head turned (that is usually how it feels— as though my eyesight is being directed, either physically or in my mind's eye, to where the lost object lies), and I saw the keys sitting exactly where they should *not* have been, where I would never have thought to look: resting on the tank in back of the toilet in the guest bathroom. Got it! I sent out a grateful thought of *Thanks!* before turning again to face the music, trying to decide what to tell the curious elder priest standing in my living room waiting for an answer.

I decided to simply tell him the truth.

"Well, thank you, Father, but I wasn't asking for your help. I couldn't find my keys and was asking the Angels for help." (More specifically, Archangel Chamuel, the St. Anthony of the Archangels, but I felt no need to divulge anything further.) This piqued his curiosity, and I found myself explaining as we left that I live alone and have the habit of speaking out loud to the Angels around me. I had simply forgotten that he was there, or I would have asked for help silently.

The priest was intrigued, as Angels are often left out of church worship, except at Christmas time. A year later, he came back to Attitude Adjustment and began to do the work outlined in this book, joining the Angel workshops I teach on the island.

No Job Too Small for Angels

Sometimes people ask, incredulously, how I can ask Angels for help with small things like finding lost keys or parking spots. They feel (some, strongly) that we shouldn't be "bothering" Angels with such things.

Nothing could be farther from reality!

First, Angels are expressions of the Source and as such have no limitations: nothing is too taxing for them. Furthermore, they yearn to be in connection with us and ease our journey in support of our life mission.

Second, remember our exercise at the very beginning, the one about paying attention to those with whom we are relaxed? Angels want to serve as that safe haven for us. With no judgment, they seek to help us to relax and shine. Are we relaxed when we can't find our keys? Are we shining when we can't find a parking spot? Not really! So, when the Angels assist us in such seemingly small things, they are really lightening the load of stress and increasing the peace in our lives and on Earth. It is important to note, too, that there is no order of importance in miracles. One gift of grace is not greater than another (although we humans do love to rank things).

Finally, for us, it is often easier to entrust the small stuff to the Angels as we begin our relationship building. Then, as we develop the reflex to pass our burdens over to the Angels ("A little help, here?"), our confidence builds, and we relax.

Imagine if we have a neighbor whom we never talk to and then one day we have a big crisis and need their help. Do we feel comfortable going over and knocking on the door just like that? Probably not. However, if we have a conversation going with our neighbors, if there are already small favors rendered and received, we will feel much more confident in asking for help, *non*?

Similarly, in the event of a big need, it is easier for us (Angels are thankfully not like us and do not judge or withhold love from us for not reaching out sooner) to reach out and accept Angelic assistance if we already have the habit of doing so. The more we work with our Angels and reach out to them for little things, the more things will flow easily when it is time to reach out to them for the big things. Again, the judgment around what is big or little is ours alone; to the Angels, both are big, as both are experiences that allow us to bond with them and remember.

How to Connect with Our Guardian Angels

Continuing with the example above, we know how to cultivate a relationship with a neighbor, don't we? We call, stop by, spend time together, and with the accumulation of these experiences, solid ties of friendship (and perhaps some relaxation) is put into place.

But how do we do this with Angels?

Basically, we do it in the same way. That is, the same principles apply: where our attention goes, energy follows. The more attention (positive or negative) we give to our neighbors, the stronger that relationship (positive or negative) will be. But let's stick to the positive, and talk about our Guardian Angels.

As mentioned in the first chapter, our Guardian Angels are here with us from the beginning of our journey (when the soul agrees to incarnate as the person you are in this lifetime) until we draw our last breath, at which point Archangel Azrael takes over (more on that later). In general, relationships with Guardian Angels are sadly often relegated to fairy tale status, and most of us allow ourselves to be convinced by a world that knows nothing that Angels only exist in stories for children or in a distant past.

Society often will encourage us to tell small children that they are accompanied by a Guardian Angel that loves and protects them, yet people who encourage this belief in a child of five may roll their eyes when a woman, say 55 years old, expresses the same belief. This may lead us to the conclusion that there is some sort of expiration date on Angelic assistance.

It appears to be the norm that some time in our teenage years, we are encouraged to drop our belief in Angels as somehow childish and foolish. How silly! If we follow that logic, that would mean that our Guardian Angels abandon us at about the time that we actually begin to need them.

Most children don't much need Guardian Angels, as their parents watch over them and protect them. But teens are in that critical phase of development that sees them both detaching (at least to a degree) from the watchful eyes of parents and human guardians and opening up to a wider, wilder world.

Yikes! Anyone who's ever been a teenager knows that teenagers (and adults) need Guardian Angels much more than children do. But the Game is perfect, and our lack of understanding of the Game as a society does not change that perfection. Angels never leave our side and though they cannot intervene unless we agree to it, they are ever attentive, waiting for that first opening, that first moment when we will allow them to pierce our defenses to perceive their presence around us.

But I am not asking you to believe me. Try it for yourself!

We build angelic relationships as we would any relationship: by according time and attention to it. We share experiences and honor these exchanges; we value them.

That being said, how exactly can we cultivate a relationship with a being or beings that are not living in the house across the street and are not physically present in our lives?

Well, anyone who has a Facebook account can answer that one! We don't need to be physically together to create relationship, to put in place the ties that bind us together. It's all about attention, intention, and energy.

Energy Connection

Imagine we meet our new neighbor for the first time and decide to grab a cup of tea together (it can be coffee, if you prefer. I am Irish and like my cuppa). You find it easy to talk to the person, time flies by, and you chat about anything and everything, then suddenly notice that two hours has elapsed. When saying your goodbyes, feeling quite close, you decide to meet up again in two weeks, and off you go.

Now imagine it is two weeks later.

SCENARIO ONE: For two weeks, you have each lived your own (busy) lives, with no contact. When the time to meet up comes, you may feel odd about the meeting, wondering perhaps why you had felt the desire to see that person again so soon when you really are so very busy. Or perhaps just a kind of shyness comes over you, as, you don't really know the person.

In this case, the ties that were put in place during the two-hour gabfest evaporated during the two weeks without contact. (As attention goes, so goes energy.) In such a circumstance, it is normal to feel much more distant from the person at the beginning of the second meeting than you did at the end of the first.

SCENARIO TWO: Imagine that right after the first meeting, the two of you began to message each other virtually, by text or email or Facebook, or whatever. ("How did it go?" "What did he/she say?" "How are you feeling?") The exchanges continue daily for the intervening two weeks, steadily. When the time comes to meet again, the difference is clear: you are excited and happy to see your new friend again!

The reason for that difference is simple: since energy (and the ties that bind us are made of energy) follows intention/attention, when we focus on another person, it builds relationship.

If we do not, the relationship is not "fed" and not cultivated. This is why after a breakup, one is often told to avoid the person completely, with no contact, virtual or physical, because a virtual contact can be as powerful energetically as a physical one.

When we know this, the answer to our original question is clear: how to build a relationship with our Angels? Remember, they have nothing to build, as they are an expression of God's pure love and support for us. The way is shown by how we as humans build relationship: we send our attention their way!

So here are some simple ways to invite or cultivate a more solid relationship with our Angels:

- Think of them
- Ask them for help
- Do energetic rituals, e.g., the channel opening from chapter 2
- Sing with them ("He who sings prays twice," as St. Augustine said)
- Dance with them
- Share a laugh with them
- Invite them along whenever you do anything you are passionate about
- Invite them along whenever you do anything you are nervous about.

. . . Wait, what? How can I do something with the Angels? Let's step back a moment and return to our neighborly example above.

As your friendship grows, there will likely come a time when you and your neighbor will plan an outing or activity together, rather than a simple coffee klatch. A trip to a museum, water skiing, sky diving, a visit to a library, attending a concert together—all activities that are shared create a foundation of shared experience upon which a relationship can be built.

The idea of sharing a pastime comes directly from a truth about our relationships with other human beings: when we share experiences, positive or negative, work or play, the ties between us solidify more quickly than by simple chatting. In the same way, we can invite our Angels to accompany us as we go through life, whether it be in our typical or daily activities, such as food or clothes shopping, or in our more unusual endeavors, such as hiking or expressing our creativity through writing, singing, dancing, painting, and so on.

In the beginning, we may not feel or sense the Angels' presence, but as time goes by, we become more and more aware of it—when we are nudged to foods that will support our emerging higher energy, when we are directed to an article of clothing that suits our uniqueness to a tee, and when the words flow in a rush, and we realize that the book we think we are writing is more like a dictation than anything else.

Fun Stuff

As Angels are all about the Joy, one way of connecting with them that I find very effective is creating a morning ritual that allows for their input every day. Opening your underwear drawer, you can ask, "Okay, Angels, what do I wear today?"

Act quickly, and don't overthink it or let your head get in the way of the answer that comes. Whatever comes—maybe the first item of clothing your eyes fall upon, or you think of a particular undergarment when you pose the question, or maybe even something falls out of the drawer—whatever it is, go with it. The longer you stand there, the more your head may confound things.

Move quickly (good advice for doing card readings too), before your analytical mind, trained by a world that doesn't "get it," steps in and gums up the works! You can confidently go fast, as the Angels do. They are ever ready, waiting to get in the Game, waiting for your question, so once you ask it is answered. Don't agonize over it; don't analyze it. Accept. Over time this exercise (which can be elaborated to include "What outfit should I wear today, Angels?" or "What vegetables should I choose, Angels?") allows us to build a relationship and recognize how our body/instrument reacts to Angelic guidance (tears, goosebumps, flows of energy around the body). All of this feeds, supports, and nourishes the reopening of our clairvoyant gifts as discussed in chapter 2.

A Word about Intention and Ritual

Often, on a spiritual path, we humans can become fairly rigid about ritual. Just think of all the religions who declare (and they're sure of it) that their rituals are the only potent ones, that their religion is the only "right" one!

But religion is a cultural expression of man's quest for God. All of the major religions include many of the same main bases, including ways to ascend or connect to the Divine: good works, good thoughts, prayer, and meditation. Although they all recognize that man will strive for God in these varied ways, they all also have precluded (at least before the ecumenical movement) the validity of the other's striving.

But the key to all striving is the intention, which carries our energy with it. It is always our intention that creates; the ritual simply serves to strengthen and reinforce that intention. As such, we can un-deify ritual perhaps, and step into the power of our own conscious intention. In this knowledge, we can understand that we really have free rein in coming up with ways to connect with our Angels.

EXERCISE Guardian Angels Connection

This is but one example of an energetic exercise that helps us to intentionally cultivate our relationship with the Angels around us.

1 **Fix your intention**

You can set your intention either out loud or within, but a clear intention is the key to the success of this ritual and all others. Using your own words, words that come from the heart, is always best. In a pinch, something simple like this works well:

I set my intention to open my channel further and connect to my Guardian Angel, now. Thank you!

(For steps 2 and 3, refer to the Channel Opening Exercise in chapter 2.)

2 **Connect to the earth**

Follow your channel/ribbon of light down to the center of the earth creating the foundation that will later permit connection to the heavens, to your Angels. Every time you use the channel, every time you relive this experience, these connections become more fluid and powerful.

Find the ribbon of light you have put in place illuminating your spinal column. Begin at the level of your heart and, with your clear intention, descend the length of the channel to the center of the earth, where the energy of the earth—vast, stable, loving, supportive awaits. Decide to welcome all forms of energetic support from our Mother Earth: love, tenderness, respect, gratitude (yes, she is grateful: she knows that your mission will lighten her load!). *Breathe in* that strength and *breathe out* anything that would diminish your full experience of that love and power.

Then (maybe with a kiss on the cheek), thank Gaia for this reinforced grounding and power before taking up your channel, upward, toward yourself and the heavens.

3 **Connect to the heavens**

Follow the energetic path you have already put in place, and note that as you go upward, there is a strong flow of energy from the earth that is supporting your movement upward, like a geyser or a fountain, lifting you upward, across all the layers of the earth.

As you come back into your body along the spinal column, continue up to the heart level, and pause a moment to allow all that you have received from the earth to fill your heart to overflowing, then your physical body, to every cell, down to the tips of your fingers and toes, then overflowing to the etheric levels—the mental body, the emotional body, the spiritual or energetic body—until you are filled and well grounded, stable and prepared for opening up to the Angels of the Source in and around you.

Find your ribbon of light and this time set your intention to the heavens. With the clear intention to connect with your Guardian

Angels, rise along your channel, traveling through the neck and the head, then rise on the wings of your Angels, carried easily along the path you have already (with Angelic assistance) put into place in chapter 2.

Up, and up and up . . .

You arrive at Source, in the Presence of your Higher Self (the soul, the Player of the Game who chose you for this lifetime), and the Angels and Archangels are delighted, because you have returned, and this time, consciously.

We all return to Source frequently, most often when we sleep, or re-Source. Those visits are not conscious, though, so have less of an impact on our instrument than a visit such as this one. Each time we make the journey consciously and intentionally, the path becomes that much easier, both for us and for those who may follow us. Each conscious visit lightens our energetic footprint and also lightens the load carried by Gaia, Mother Earth.

4 Opening your hands to energy

Rub your hands together briskly, until you feel a certain amount of heat rising. When you do, separate your hands, holding them, palms facing each other, just a couple of inches apart. You may sense or feel what seems like a ball of energy between your hands.

If so, play with it a moment, move your hands closer or farther away to see how the feeling shifts and changes.

If your hands grow cold or you do not immediately feel or sense the energy, you might try repeating the brisk rubbing, but not to worry; it is normal not to have a direct physical experience this first time.

However, if you engage in this exercise each day for, let's say, seven days in a row, you will certainly see, feel, and sense a difference. Our doors reopen easily with Angelic assistance!

A Word about Healing and Our Hands

We work with our palms because our palms are truly made for energetic work: not just the hands of those known as healers among us, but all of our hands! Think about it: what do you do when you have a headache? A stomach-ache? Or a sharp pain in the elbow, a hip, a toe? In each instance, we put our hands where it hurts, and it feels better! All of us do this, every human being on the planet. We do this because that is the natural expression of our being: we each can transmit energy and healing through our hands and, more specifically, through the palms of our hands.The palms of our hands are (like the top of our skull) a point of great opening where energy passes easily once we activate our natural capacity to do so.

5 Inviting Angelic connection

When your hands are warmed up, *breathe in and out,* coming wholly into this space and time with the express intention to connect with your Angel.

Extend your arms out in front of you, palms facing upward, and invite your Guardian Angel to come and connect with you at the level of your palms, wide open and primed for contact.

While in that space and holding yourself open at the hands for Angelic connection, stay present, and notice any sensations you may have in your body, or any thoughts images or sounds that may come to you.

It is common when we are opening to the Light that darkness comes in, trying to hinder the movement, but we are in Source space and in the presence of Angels, so there is no risk, nothing to fear.

Yet our head (trained by a world that knows so little of Love) may try to pull a fast one, throwing ideas at us, such as *This is ridiculous!,* a sly move indeed, as shaming is a very effective tool for darkness and fear, keeping us small instead of living our heritage of Large Life! (As a general rule of thumb, if the head is telling you a certain experience is ridiculous, it is likely very, very interesting, energetically, so stay with it.)

This first time, just stay a few minutes, noticing any sensations you may have, or anything you may notice. What you notice in a context like this is always important. No need to analyze it; just remember and use that experience as a baseline for the next time.

While in that space, feel free to ask for a name.The according of the Angelic name is a sacred experience, and with so much new going on here, it may not come right away. If it doesn't come immediately, keep your eyes and ears open in the days to follow.

Ask for a name simply, and note what arises in you. Do not reject whatever name comes, no matter what. If it is the name of someone you know, or perhaps it doesn't sound "Angelic" enough for you, don't worry about it! The name that comes through can be used to call your Angels, and as the relationship grows there may be other names that are added.

Remember that the name is *not* what is important; it is simply there to facilitate the connection for us. Angels are expressions of Source; all names are thus expressions of the One, the I Am.

6 Completion and gratitude

When the work feels complete, or when your attention has dissipated, it is time to complete the work. Thank Source, the Angels, the Archangels, all Guides, and also your Higher Self for this moment of sacred reconnection, remembering.

Then follow your channel/ribbon down to return into the body. Your Angels will accompany you. As you connect more, you will come to see/sense/feel/know this, but for now, simply descend inviting that accompaniment, returning to the body and the heart.

Place your hands at the level of your energetic heart (at the center of your chest). They carry Angel energy. *Breathe in* that Angelic connection and *breathe out* all that no longer serves. Energy seeks equilibrium (the second Law of Energy, which we will discuss later), and so with the entry of Angel energy, there is always darker, heavier, less Joyful energy that will be released. Hallelujah!

Lastly, find words from your heart to express *gratitude,* or perhaps simply use something like this:

Thanks be to the Source in all expressions, earthly and celestial.
Thanks be to Mother Earth, to my Angels, to the Archangels,
and to my Higher Self, that the doors that were closed be reopened.
Thy will be done.

And so it is!

NOTE: the techniques for Aftercare suggested on p. 56 are excellent for integrating and grounding this Angel opening work.

PART TWO

OUR FRIENDS IN
HIGH PLACES

The Archangels

CHAPTER 4

Archangels Michael, Raphael, Gabriel, Jophiel, and Zadkiel

The following three chapters introduce you to the 15 Archangels, with five Archangels in each chapter detailing how they can assist us in our lives, crystals or stones that carry their frequency, and unique exercises for you to try if you should decide to connect with them.

The five we will work with in this chapter are, arguably, the "Big Five," or perhaps "The Big Three" (Michael, Raphael, and Gabriel), that is to say, the Archangels who are the most well known, as well as two with whom we really need to work in order to get free of what is holding us back from Large Life!

ARCHANGEL	DIVINE QUALITY
Michael	Power
Raphael	Healing
Gabriel or Gabrielle	Communication
Jophiel	Creativity
Zadkiel	Forgiveness

Some Notes about Connecting to Archangels

As we saw at the beginning of chapter 3, our lives can become easier when we have Friends in High Places, as when I called out to Archangel Chamuel ("A little help here?") to help me find my keys—admittedly not a rare occurrence; Archangel Chamuel is an ally on whom I have come to rely. This chapter sets forth the information I share in my Angel classes—information that is part common knowledge and part uniquely my own. As with everything in this book, I invite you to see what resonates with you, what attracts you, and what you feel called to put into place, letting go of anything that doesn't speak to you at this time.

Developing these relationships is often not an instantaneous thing, as we humans generally don't work that way, and for the most part, our relationships are cultivated through shared experiences. So simply notice to which Archangels (if any) you feel attracted, then, if you feel so inclined, try the connection exercise you just learned for Guardian Angel connection in chapter 3 with the Archangel(s) of your choice, or the specific exercise noted for the Archangel in question.

You cannot choose wrong. Our choices are not haphazard, and there is no such thing as coincidence; rather, there is a choreography to Life that, like an elegant form of inner GPS, allows us to dance with the Universe at the level where we find ourselves at this moment. Your desires and the fact that you are reading this book signal that, on a soul level, Angelic and Archangelic connections (and help!) are on the menu for you in this life, if you want it. Your free will precludes any intervention without asking for assistance, but when we do ask, well, watch things move!

Why 15 Archangels?

The 15 Archangel relationships described in the following three chapters are those that I have worked with since I began working as an Angel Healing Practitioner in France and the United States, and then as a teacher all over the world.

I work with these 15 Friends as *they* came looking for *me*. They came into my experience thanks to my initial training back in Kona, Hawaii, and the evolution that has been mine since that time. Since you are reading this book, you may say that they have now come looking for *you*!

In my experience, over time, these relationships have grown more and more solid, each one distinct, and those connections are still growing stronger. Like any relationship, the more we feed it, the more it grows.

It is a very human mind that asks "Why 15?" as we humans like to enumerate and analyze everything, even the Divine. But in accordance with the definition of Archangels as set forth herein, it is useful to remember that "all are one." Each of the Archangels is part of the Divine, an expression of the Source. Each one represents a particular frequency, quality, or energy of God: for this reason, it is clear that there are not only 15 archangels, because God is not limited to 15 qualities! But these 15 do cover most of what we may require in this lifetime.

Divine Healing, Power, Communication—each of these Archangels is a portal to a particular Divine quality. When we need more of that particular quality in our lives, it is a good idea to cultivate the habit of asking for (and receiving!) help.

A Word about Asking for Help

It is highly probable that you who are reading this book already participate in life here on Earth as a Lightworker. Probably all through life, you have been a re-Source for people. You likely have a habit of helping others, of giving to others easily. This is a talent you have cultivated: you may recognize that service, that giving, is right up your alley!

That said, the question is: Have you also cultivated the capacity to receive?

So often, an evolved soul who arrives here on terra firma to live out a particular Light-filled mission learns quickly that not everyone here on the Earth is the same; that many know very well how to take but are not gifted with the talent for giving.

Additionally, those who are tasked with a life purpose of service to others and to the whole often find themselves surrounded by "takers"; "givers" and "takers" find each other. This is neither positive nor negative, but simply is: energy seeks equilibrium.

So, it behooves a "giver" to learn to receive, and to balance our energetic patterns so as not to attract only/largely "takers." Learning to receive is tricky if our life experience has taught us that people are not reliable or trustworthy, that we are better off doing it for ourselves.

If that has been part of your experience, one way to balance our giving and receiving is to do it with the Angels. Becoming accustomed to receiving from these highly placed Angelic allies, our energetic fields find more balance, and we, more health and happiness.

So, maybe start with these 15 Archangels, or pick one Archangel to begin with. It is up to you. Each Archangel can both offer their particular quality to a situation on our behalf or help us to cultivate that quality for ourselves. (For example, Archangel Michael can either walk before us in protection or aid us to step sufficiently into our power to no longer require that protection.)

Let's get started! It is my honor to introduce . . .

ARCHANGEL MICHAEL

QUALITY: The Power and Protection of God

Archangel Michael, or "He Who is Like God," is the Archangel that expresses the quality of the Power and Protection of God. This power of Michael is not at all the power of the world, which is concentrated in force; rather, it is the power of relaxing, the power of Love, the power of God that melts hearts open. This is the power so sorely needed at a time when there is an epidemic here on Earth of hearts closed and hardened by the brutality of the world. Michael also assists us with protection when we feel we need it. Until our power is in place and stabilized, it is very helpful to request that Archangel Michael (often pictured with a large sword) walk before us, clearing the path to our highest purpose, warding off our foes and any obstacle that doesn't serve our purpose.

Many people who walk a spiritual path talk about a need for protection. While it is true that we must not be naïve and speak of Angels without recognizing the truth of darker energies that impact our path greatly in this life, I am not suggesting we be fearful here. Respect, recognition that evil exists, yes; but when we walk in the company of Angels and Archangels (especially Michael—this chick from the Bronx loves walking with a Friend with a sword!), there is nothing to fear.

When we come to Earth as children we know only Love, then we learn to fear and hate. These are learned behaviors, not innate ones! But so often, we learn them all too well, and it is our fear of others that brings us to close our heart and diminish our love. It is when we are hurt by others after we offer Love that we learn to temper our loving, to reduce it, to "hide our love away," until we are all hiding our love away and the world has become a cold place indeed!

As Lightworkers, we are here to reverse that trend.

These days, my goal is to keep my heart open, no matter what. As a human being, I can tell you that it is certainly easier with some people than with others, but I see progress! It is now easier for me to love others—all others—than it was in the past, and I have some neat tricks up my sleeve to help me do it . . . like remembering that the other person was a child filled with only Love and seeking only Love once, too, and that their particular habits rub me the wrong way because they are sore points for me, personally. Nothing is personal; they are in my life to teach me something, and the sooner I learn that something, the sooner I can move on to something else!

All these understandings are part of what stepping into our power looks like. But until we get there, until we can relax around everyone, Archangel Michael can walk before us to protect and support us.

COLOR: Blue or Purple

Not all Archangels are recognized to show up energetically in a specific color. Here, I will note colors only when there is a color that is generally accepted by people who "see" colors. Remember that our instruments are all different, so you may not "see" a color, or you may even "see" a different color. No matter! Your instrument is unique, and when you call Archangel Michael, Michael responds. You will, over time (if you haven't already), come to experience the presence of Archangel Michael in your own way, and it may not be in the color blue or purple. (Note: the color purple here carries energy akin to that which you may know as the Violet Flame of St. Germain. The two are closely linked. Remember: *all are one*.)

ENERGY SIGNATURE: Heat

When Archangel Michael is around, things heat up! In general, people who "feel" energy will say that they feel heat when Michael is present. Again, this does not mean that you will experience that heat as well, or that you will feel it right away. Remember: your instrument is unique, and the only way to determine how you experience connection with Archangel Michael (or any other Angel) is to notice what happens for you when you practice calling upon him.

CHAKRA: Third Chakra–Solar Plexus–Power

Archangel Michael is known for helping us to step into our own power with confidence, both in ourselves and in the Divine. When we are connected with both our soul level and Higher Self and firmly grounded in our bodies and human aspect, that Light which is ours can shine forth powerfully. If we ask, Archangel Michael will walk with us, affording us protection, until such time as we stand; shining in our own Light and power, by grace. Michael can assist us with all of our chakras, as each chakra contributes to the overall wellness critical to stepping into our power.

CRYSTAL: Sugilite

Sugilite is the crystal most associated with Archangel Michael. The stone of Lightworkers, sugilite helps us to stand in our power and face the challenges that inevitably come when we dare to step out of the norm and shine.

Other Attributes

Lightworker Boss

If you recognized yourself in the earlier description of a "Lightworker," then you may be interested to know that in a very real sense, Michael is your boss. The "mission" that is Michael's is to transmute fear so that human hearts can reopen and Love can flourish here on Earth. (The opposite of Love is fear, not hate; hate is simply fear amplified and expressed violently.) It follows logically, then, that the mission of a Lightworker—to bring Light into darkness— would be one that underpins Michael's mission.

The more we open to our mission (and the more we open our Heart), our life's work supports Archangel Michael's objective.

In a sense, we can (if we will it) decide to be the hands and voices and physical presence of Archangel Michael here on Earth. When we do that, it is not surprising that our "boss" ensures that our mission flows smoothly.

Technician and Plumber

Much has been written about Archangel Michael assisting folks who ask for help with situations like technical problems with cars, computers, phones, and other electronic glitches. But in my experience, he has always been (and was again today) a Divine Plumber! I kid you not. I love sharing Angel experiences but always feel a bit discomfited when I speak to this aspect of my experience with Archangel Michael. In fact, this afternoon as I was beginning this section, I was thinking perhaps that I wouldn't even include these stories!

But then something happened that told me I needed to speak to this aspect of his Power as well. Archangel Michael has come to my rescue three times when plumbing problems threatened the smooth movement of my work: a few years back in Paris, more recently in New York City, and then today in Emerald Isle, North Carolina. You can't make this stuff up!

A Toilet in Paris

I was teaching an Angel workshop for a group of deaf people. As they were a small group, I decided to teach it out of my apartment in Paris. After the second day, I fell asleep exhausted, until I woke up to the worrying sound of a toilet running.

Apparently, someone had pushed instead of pulled to flush the contraption, and now it would not stop running. Gloom-and-doom thoughts ran through my head (It was Saturday night. How could I find another venue for the next day? Lord knows, no French plumber would show up on a Sunday! Even if I found one who would, it would break the rhythm of the class . . . You get the idea).

I fell into the panic mode that had been my default system for so long. I worked and worried at the problem and at the toilet, pulling and pushing and swearing (I admit it. LOL!). Nothing worked.Arrrgghhh! Basically, I freaked.

Until I didn't . . . Suddenly, I remembered what I teach, recalling that Archangel Michael helps with machines, and decided that a toilet was kind of a machine.

I left the bathroom, which I had charged up with negative panicky thoughts, and instead, walked into the kitchen and opened my channel by connecting to the center of the earth, then up to the heavens. Then I asked for help: I called my Boss.

I asked Archangel Michael to help me with this small problem so that the good work could continue. I asked my Angels to help me calm down. Once I felt peaceful again, I went back into the bathroom and just jiggled the flushing mechanism once.

The toilet flushed easily.

The New York Bathroom

A couple of years later, I was teaching a small group out of an apartment in the Riverdale section of the Bronx. I had just finished recounting the story of the Paris nightmare and Michael rescue, and we were getting ready for the lunch break, when one of my students informed me that there was a problem with my toilet.

I called the lunch break, and when they had all left (you can't say I don't learn from my mistakes!) I opened my channel right away and called on Archangel Michael for assistance. Just then came a knock on the door.

"Wow, that was fast!" I said jokingly, thinking that a workshop attendee had forgotten something.

But no. A man was at the door dressed in the garb of the permanent staff who kept the building running smoothly.

"Sorry to interrupt ma'am, but we got a call that there is a problem with the bathroom in this line. Do you mind?"

Dumbfounded, I nodded and stepped aside, but not without noticing that the name stitched on his work shirt was—you guessed it!—GABRIEL. (Close enough—the Angels have a sense of humor!)

Plumbing Emergencies in Emerald Isle, North Carolina

This afternoon, as I was trying to explain to Archangel Michael why I didn't want to include these "toilet stories," as I like to call them (why don't I get elegant sacred stories like other Lightworkers?), I had another plumbing emergency.

I am at this cottage on the beach, and it is not made for freezing temperatures, but that is what is going on here, has been for a day, so both the heating and the pipes are acting up.

The plumbers were here for a good while this afternoon, and after a bit, the chief plumber came up to me to say that they had gotten one side of the house working but the other side was still blocked and it would take too long to find which pipes had the problem, so they were leaving, as they had many emergency calls that day.

Astonished (and not happy), my Bronx side rose up, and I reminded him that the side where there was water was where I had no heat, so he needed to stay put and finish the job he had started. A third party (Andy, with the management company) arrived then to propose a compromise: he would lend me a space heater for the bathroom that was working, and that way I would avoid paying a big fee for the plumbers' time, as they were on emergency scale today.

Grumbling, I accepted, but I should have known that everything was under control! As I started writing this section on Archangel Michael in earnest, suddenly I heard water flowing (I had left the spigot on, just in case). What the plumbers said would take hours for them to fix happened by the grace (and good sense of humor) of God. Archangel Michael to the rescue again! All toilets and showers are now in working order. I include this story in gratitude, as now I can stay put on the island as planned. Hallelujah!

Our relationships with Archangels (like with our Guardian Angels) are personal, unique, and intense, but also can be fun—even with a powerhouse like Archangel Michael!

Connecting to Archangel Michael

For each Archangel, it is possible to use the exercise for supporting connection to our Guardian Angels as outlined in chapter 3, and simply replacing the intention with that of connecting to a particular Archangel. But remember: it is our intention, not the ritual we employ, that allows these connections. In this chapter you will find different practices, simple and efficient to use, to connect with each Archangel.

There is no one way to connect with an Angelic presence; the practice that speaks to your heart, the one that makes you want to give it a try, is always the right one in any given moment. It is a good idea to avoid rigidity in these practices, and to let spontaneous guidance come into play. The operative word is PLAY!

Connect with Archangel Michael

1. Connect with your breath, and come into a peaceful place of quiet. Set your intention in order to cultivate your connection and to play with Archangel Michael. (Yes, we can play with Archangels. The highest energy is Joy, and we are most aligned with God/Source and the Angelic realm when we are creative and at play.)

2. Use your channel (opened in chapter 2), and anchor (ground) yourself, following your ribbon of light into the center of the earth, then open to the highest, tracing your channel of Light from the center of the earth through your heart, with the intention to rise and connect to the heavens. Return to your heart in order to set your intention both as the human being you are and on a soul level. (If you are undertaking this exercise, you can be sure that it is the will of your soul.)

3. Stand up, if you are sitting, feet shoulder-width apart. Stand tall, shoulders pulled back, so that your spinal column—the bridge you create between the earth and the heavens—is straight. Place your hands on your heart, and invite Archangel Michael to connect with you. *Breathe in* the presence of angels and archangels all around you; *breathe out* anything that blocks opening to them. Allow yourself to fill with Light, with a sense of the Love that is there for you, and to feel, perhaps, the Joy that your presence brings in this space. Take three or four deep breaths at least before continuing.

4. With your eyes closed, imagine that Archangel Michael stands before you and awaits your signal to begin. Salutation: Place your nondominant hand along your body, palm facing outward, in a position of energetic openness. Slowly, with intention, raise your right hand in a gesture of salutation, one warrior of Light to another. Your palm will be facing forward, your thumb, at the side of your head, at the level of your ear.

5. Imagine (or "see," "feel," or "know") that Archangel Michael mirrors your movement, saluting you, too, in recognition of the mission you have accepted in this lifetime and the degree to which you already bring Light into the lives of those around you.

6. When the salutation/connection feels complete, bring your hands again to your chest in a gesture of gratitude for this sacred moment of sharing and relationship building.

The Aftercare as noted on p. 56 is a good way to help yourself integrate this important work when connecting with the individual Archangels.

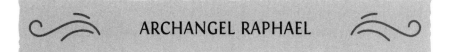

ARCHANGEL RAPHAEL

QUALITY: The Divine Healing of God

The Archangel whose name means "God heals," not surprisingly, is the Archangel of Divine Healing, but healing in the Divine sense is not always what you might expect.

Some years ago, in the center of Paris, at an esoteric shop/center called l'Univers d'Esther, I was holding an Angel Party (a series of conferences I have been doing all over the world for about 10 years). The theme that night was "Healing with Archangel Raphael," and some of the information that follows was presented then. Before we got to the energetic work, I asked if there were any questions. A hand shot up in the last row and to the left, and I somehow knew right away this was trouble.

"Yes? Madame in the last row?" I said, feeling that somehow this exchange was going to be important, if not particularly pleasant.

I was right. The lady was irate.

"I was very sick recently and called on Archangel Raphael for healing, as you suggest, but I he did *not* heal me! I got sicker! So how can you teach this?" The woman pointed an accusatory finger at me, jabbing it in the air.

As she was speaking, I called silently for guidance in responding. Hers seemed a fair point, and as she spoke, I received the response and understood, thanking Raphael for his rapid assistance before transmitting what I had learned. (I love when people ask questions to which I don't know the answer. That is how I learn. As the person asks the question, I "hear" the answer. Thank you, Angels!)

Then I went on to tell her what I had just learned, thanks to her helpful question—that there is a difference between our human concept of healing, which has a lot to do with symptoms, and the Divine concept of healing, which is more about the truth of who we are and the expression of that truth as we currently live it (or not): physically, emotionally, mentally, energetically. For us humans, so often we see healing only as a relief from symptoms, expressed physically or otherwise. But the definition of Divine Healing is quite different. It is "the realignment with the truth of what is."

Human healing can include treatments that ease symptoms until they diminish or disappear. Often treatments mask or control the symptoms, rather than going to the root of the problem. But since, generally, we are happy to no longer suffer the symptoms, often we deem that a small price to pay.

Divine healing, on the other hand (as in the case with the lady in the Paris conference), does *not* always ease our symptoms or suffering, at least not initially; rather, it is an energetic movement that shifts something within us so that we are once again more aligned to our soul and our purpose.

Many maladies, such as depression, can result from having wandered very far from our life's mission. The deep sadness that accompanies it is more than human sadness; it is a soul-level sadness that is designed to wake us up, to push us to make some changes.

Imagine a pimple, and how it is healed. For the root of the imbalance to be healed, the pimple will have to come to a head, explode, then truly get cleared out in a deep healing that erases its imprint from our being so that it won't need to return to make its point.

This was the case with the healing that the lady had eventually received. She confirmed that all trace of that malady was gone.

If healing does not occur at the root of the problem, even if the pimple "goes away," the root will likely resurface at some future point. The healing is temporary and superficial, unsustainable on its own. This is often the impact of pharmaceutical solutions.

Be Careful What You Wish For

As I explained all this to the Parisian woman, the phrase "Be careful what you wish for" came to mind. The kind of healing of which we speak with Raphael is life-changing; it is meant to shake things up—not a Band-aid, but a radical transformation and wholeness, by the grace of this presence of God's healing.

A friend of mine who is a Reiki Master had a friend who was dying. She regularly did Reiki treatments for her friend, who was also being treated by the traditional medical community.

One day, she was complaining to me that she was doing all she could, but that her friend wasn't getting better. I reminded her that Divine healing (and Reiki, or spiritual energy, is aligned with Raphael and Divine healing) does not always "cure" the seeming malady of the person, but that it always allows the person to align further with the truth of who they are, with the soul, "curing" the imbalance the world has caused. So the external efficacy of healing work depended on whether the soul was aligned with external healing. If a malady persists, it is of service to the soul's purpose.

As hard as that can be to hear, I have seen it in action, and maybe you have, too. Imagine a child who is ill. What happens around him? I am thinking of a specific Danny, who in his too-short time on Earth brought adults closer and inspired those around him with his courage and Love. Such souls are not small souls; their impact continues long after they leave the Earth plane. Aligning with soul means that someone may get well or pass on—another way of "getting well"; it depends on whether the soul is slated for departure or not.

If the soul is meant to depart, Reiki or any Divine healing with Raphael will allow the person to leave Earth more peacefully. If the soul is meant to stay, the healing work will reestablish a balance that will allow the person to release symptoms and thrive. For this reason, Reiki or any form of Divine healing (Raphael) is excellent for accompanying people who have begun their transition between the worlds; that is, it is supportive in palliative care.

Healing for All

We may call upon Archangel Raphael for healing for ourselves (and we will, in later chapters), for others, for animals, and even for the earth. Everything tends toward realignment with the highest good. Each time we call on Raphael for healing, everything realigns further. Helping ourselves thus also helps the earth, as we are part of the earth through our physical presence.

ENERGETIC SIGNATURE: Cool

The consensus from people who feel energy is that the energy of Raphael is cool and refreshing. When we do some healing work with Michael and Raphael, perhaps the contrast will lead you to understand how your particular instrument perceives that presence.

CHAKRA: Sixth Chakra–Third Eye–Clairvoyance

Archangel Raphael is known for helping us with the reopening of the third eye, or sixth chakra, which impacts our clairvoyant gifts. Other Archangels can also assist us in the cultivation of our clairvoyance, most notably Jeremiel (who helps us with visions in dream form) and Gabriel (who assists us with Divine communication). It is logical that Raphael, the Archangel of Divine Healing, helps us with clairvoyance, which aligns us with our souls, so we might see as our soul would see.

COLOR: Green

For those who "see," the consensus is that the presence of Raphael is most often expressed in a green light. The green is vibrant and rich, like the green of fresh new grass, a sign of new life.

Of course, if you call Raphael and see another color, do not call your experience into question. Our instruments are unique, and there is no "right" color or "wrong" way to experience the presence of an Angel.

CRYSTAL/STONE: Malachite

Malachite is an excellent stone to support healing and also to support those transitioning from this life to the next, and in palliative care. They say that the stone allows angelic presence to slow down enough to be felt more deeply, and that includes Raphael. I gave my (very Catholic) mother a malachite as she was transitioning, and she passed gripping the stone in her hand. That was all the confirmation I need.

Connecting with Archangel Raphael

Play with Archangel Raphael!

1. Connect with your breath, and come into a peaceful place of quiet. Set your intention to cultivate your connection (and for healing!) with Archangel Raphael.

2. Use your channel (created in chapter 2), and anchor (ground) yourself, following your ribbon of light into the center of the earth. Open to the highest good, tracing your channel of light from the center of the earth, through your heart, and upward, with the intention to connect to the heavens. Return to your heart in order to set your intention both as the human being you are and on a soul level. (If you are undertaking this exercise, you can be sure that it is the will of your soul.)

3. Stand tall, feet shoulder-width apart, shoulders pulled back, so that your spinal column—the bridge you create between the earth and the heavens—is straight. Place your hands on your heart, and invite

Archangel Raphael to connect with you. *Breathe in* the presence of Angels and Archangels all around you; *breathe out* anything that blocks your opening to them. Allow yourself to fill with Light, with a sense of the Love that is there for you, and to feel, perhaps, the Joy that your presence brings in this space. Take three or four deep breaths at least before continuing.

4. With your eyes closed, imagine (or "see," "feel," or "know") that Archangel Raphael stands before you and awaits your signal to begin. On the inner screen of your mind's eye, imagine a tall form, with flowing garments of light, and hands illuminated with that light, perhaps in a cast of green which reminds us of fresh grass in springtime. This is the energy of healing and renewal.

5. Heart healing: open your arms wide, palms facing forward, energetically opening to the beautiful presence of Archangel Raphael just in front of you. *Breathe in* to permit a preliminary expansion as Raphael prepares the connection that heals and aligns you with the highest good and best for your being and your mission; *breathe out* any tension you might feel in the body.

6. Extend your hands in front of you, palms upward (like we did with the Guardian Angel presence), inviting Raphael to connect with you and activate and/or amplify the natural healing power of your hands.

7. When you feel ready, place your activated hands in the center of your chest to allow Archangel Raphael to do a heart alignment, through your hands. Keep your hands at the energetic heart center unless and until you feel a desire to move them to another spot, anywhere on your body. If you feel the impulse to move your hands, allow it. Do not second-guess yourself. Allow for spontaneity, and permit the grace of healing, knowing that Raphael is responsible for the healing, and not you. This is incredibly freeing, as the burden of efficacy is transferred from your shoulders to the very capable shoulders and wings of the Divine!

8. When the healing work feels satisfying, and you feel relaxed and complete, bring your hands again to your chest, a gesture of gratitude for this sacred moment of sharing and relationship building.

The Aftercare noted on p. 56 is a very good way to help integrate this important work.

ARCHANGEL GABRIEL/GABRIELLE

QUALITY: The Divine Communication of God

Archangel Gabriel (sometimes spelled with the feminine spelling of Gabrielle, as this is a strong feminine or receptive energy, though we are clear that Angels do not have a gender), aka the Messenger of God, is the Archangel who expresses the energy of Divine Communication.

Whether for personal or professional reasons, all who seek to communicate better would be well served to seek the assistance of Gabriel. Writers, speakers, peacemakers, and all for whom communication is a key element to their life and work can find inspiration with Gabriel.

In today's world, where there is an emerging emphasis on nonviolent communication, as well as an acceleration of exceedingly violent communication (especially around religion), there is a dire need for the energy of Gabriel.

Oddly enough, though religious rhetoric is at times among the most contentious forms of communication in our world, this Archangel is recognized by three of the main religions of the world involved in such fear-mongering and hate: Judaism (Gabriel appears to the prophet Daniel in Jewish scriptures), Christianity (Gabriel appears to Mary and Elizabeth, foretelling the births of Jesus and John the Baptist) and Islam (Gabriel dictated parts of the Koran to Mohammed).

Thus, one finds in Gabriel hope that, like the angelic realm, we humans may find language that will allow for peace and unity, with a higher level of communication that will promote just that.

Gabrielle and Mothering/Parenting

Perhaps thanks to the role the Archangel played in announcing the births of Ascended Masters like Jesus and John, Gabrielle is sometimes spelled with an "le" at the end, as noted above. This is because the energy of this Archangel is said to be feminine, receptive, soft, caring, and nurturing, like the language of peace. She is a strong ally for people who would like to become parents or who are parents already, to exercise that important role with compassion and benevolence.

With this strong mothering energy, no matter how you spell this Archangel's name, Gabriel or Gabrielle can help us when we look to mother/love/heal the child within, the inner child. This is very important work for all who seek to live Large, as the child within holds the keys to both our creativity and our Joy.

Gabriel and Clairvoyance

Since clairvoyance is fundamentally about communication, Archangel Gabriel can help us with opening to and cultivating our gifts. We can call upon Gabriel when we undertake the communication exercises here.

CHAKRA: Fifth Chakra—Throat—Clairaudience

Archangel Gabriel is known for helping us with the reopening of the fifth chakra, located at the throat, which impacts our clairvoyant gifts, especially that of clairaudience. As the Messenger of God, Gabriel is well suited to aid us in releasing anything that blocks our authentic self, our ability to speak and hear truth. This is particularly of interest in situations where we need help in speaking our truth on an earthly level, and to assist us in opening our channel to Divine communication at all times.

Gabriel and Color

There is no consensus around the color one might see when Gabriel is present. I have seen blue (like the blue so often painted for Mother Mary's cloak) and have heard of gold, but there is simply no consensus. For the rest of the Archangels, where there is no consensus, no discussion of color will be presented.

CRYSTAL/STONE: Rose Quartz and Blue Topaz

An ideal stone for connecting with Archangel Gabrielle is rose quartz, the lovely and soft heart energy. However, a nice blue topaz can also be effective, as it allows all forms of just and noble communication to flow.

Connecting/Communicating with Archangel Gabriel/Gabrielle

Play with Archangel Gabriel/Gabrielle!

1. Connect with your breath, and come into a peaceful place of quiet. Set your intention to communicate with and cultivate your connection to Archangel Gabrielle.

2. Use your channel (created in chapter 2), and anchor (ground) yourself, following your ribbon of light into the center of the earth, and open to the highest good by tracing your channel of light from the center of the earth with your intention to the heavens. Return to your heart in order to set your intention, both as the human being you are and on a soul level. (If you are undertaking this exercise, you can be sure that it is the will of your soul.)

3. Seated, feet are planted solidly on the ground, shoulder-width apart, legs and hands uncrossed, shoulders pulled back so that your spinal column—the bridge you create between the earth and the heavens—is straight. Place your hands simply on your lap, palms facing upward (open energetic position) and invite Archangel Gabrielle to connect with you. *Breathe in* the presence of angels and archangels all around you; *breathe out* anything that blocks your opening to them. Allow yourself to fill with Light and peace, to be filled with a sense of the Love that is there for you, to feel, perhaps, the Joy that your presence brings in this space. Take three or four deep breaths at least before continuing.

4. With your eyes closed, imagine or "see" or "feel" or simply "know" that Archangel Gabrielle stands before you and awaits your signal to begin. (Thinking of someone, or imagining them with us, has an energetic effect and acts as an invitation. This is why people we are thinking of will sometimes contact us out of the blue or we happen to run into them on the street.)

5. Once you are ready and your intention is clear, open your arms wide, palms facing forward, energetically opening to the beautiful presence of Archangel Gabrielle just in front of you. *Breathe in* to permit a preliminary expansion as Gabrielle prepares the work of communication to come, aligning you with the highest and best for your being and your mission.

6. *Breathe out* any tension you might feel in the body, and as you do so, bring your arms from the sides in a semi-circle first in front of you, then closed in around your body in a sort of a hug, a loving embrace you give yourself. You can imagine the child you once were within and decide to hold that child preciously to you, but as you begin to hold yourself, allow your head to drop to your chest until your forehead rests on your arms. This position of receiving allows the following step to occur.

7. Invite Archangel Gabrielle now to enfold you in her wings, creating a haven of Love and security where you feel perfectly safe and loved, where you can see clearly what is, and where you can speak your truth in a loving way with no holds barred, always perfectly relaxed knowing you are so held. *Breathe in* that Love, and allow that Light to fill you and that peace to calm you fully on every level. *Breathe out* any stress or tension, any fear of speaking your truth. *Breathe in* again, and allow the Love for you that is there to be mirrored within you and to help you cultivate a healthy, loving respect for yourself. Recognize how hard things have sometimes been. *Breathe out* again to release any judgment of yourself that you have been holding (judgment blocks Divine communication), and let go of any situation that you feel you should have handled differently. *Breathe in* again, and embrace the you that is here right now, loved and held by the Divine. *Breathe out,* and let go of the version of you that was. Continuing the breath, allow yourself to be held for as long as you feel comfortable. If you receive any messages, take time afterward to write them down and mark the occasion. If not, simply notice any difference in how you feel before and after the exercise. Each time it is undertaken, there is an energetic shift. After only a short time of practicing this exercise, you will begin to notice a difference.

8. When the healing work feels satisfying, and you feel relaxed and complete, thank Archangel Gabrielle, and bring your hands again to your chest, a gesture of gratitude for this sacred moment of sharing and relationship building.

The Aftercare noted on p. 56 is a very good way to help yourself integrate this important work.

ARCHANGEL JOPHIEL

Quality: The Beauty of God

Archangel Jophiel, whose name means "Beauty of God," is not surprisingly the Archangelic Presence that can help us see the beauty around us and within us.

A receptive feminine energy, Jophiel can help us see and appreciate the beauty that abounds here on Earth— so we can stop and notice the beauty of the roses but also accept and value the beauty that is our own.

Not surprisingly, the Archangel most connected to our creativity, Jophiel is of course an excellent mentor for artists of every ilk—painters, sculptors, poets, and so on—but not just for those who the world deems "artists"! We are all sons and daughters of the Creator and, as such, we participate in Creation. We are all creative, even those who perhaps think they are not!

In fact, we create all the time; it is impossible *not* to create. Our actions, words, even our thoughts influence and create the world we inhabit. The only question is whether we create consciously or unconsciously, whether we create intentionally. The fact that so many of us are not even aware that we create our earthly experiences tells us that most of us create unconsciously. If there are elements of your life at this moment that you do not appreciate, it is quite likely that (at least in part) you are currently creating unconsciously.

When we are ready to undertake this (highly recommended!) transformation from unconscious to conscious creation, working with Jophiel can help us to render conscious that which has been (at least in part) unconscious, to take responsibility for our "being" and "doing" in the world, and to add Beauty to the creation of the work of art that is our lives.

She helps us understand that we create not just with our actions but with all we put forth, which includes energy; thus, our thoughts and words (which express certain energetic vibrations) affect the reality of what we draw to ourselves every day.

Here's a simple example from my childhood.

Oh, No!

When I walked back home after school as a child, there was only a city street for me to walk down—"down" being the operative word. It was a hill, and as it was in the Bronx, not surprisingly, it was concrete, and in winter months, it would become slick and icy.

Often, when the hill was icy, I would be nervous, certain that I would slip and fall (I'm gonna fall, I'm gonna fall, I'm gonna fall!), followed by my feet slipping out from under me and SLAM! I would find myself yet again on the ground, my derrière in the snow and ice.

I could never understand why it was me who fell. I was in general a tomboy and pretty athletic, and friends who were perhaps less so would navigate the hill just fine. It was only years later, when I began to work with Jophiel, that the mystery cleared up. I was sabotaging my descents with the worried thoughts of falling.

Other ways in which we sabotage ourselves is by holding gloom-and-doom thoughts about areas of our lives that are important to us. If we are sure that something (a job, a creative project, a relationship) is going to fail, it is quite likely that we will be right. Remember the Law of Energy we previously discussed: Energy seeks equilibrium. This is the rule that underpins the famous Law of Attraction; that is, we can only attract what we are emitting energetically. So if gloom and doom is going on within, then we attract gloom and doom in our experience without.

Once we begin to pay attention both to the words that fall from our lips and the thoughts that wander across our minds, we may want to rein in and redirect this powerful force of creation. We will look at this more in depth later, but with the exercise that follows, we can allow Jophiel to help us begin to move toward more consciousness, more mastery of what we create in our lives and in the world.

The good news is that the lives we lead right now reflect our prior actions, thoughts, and words. As we become more conscious of our words and thoughts, what we attract into our lives begins to shift fairly quickly and in surprising ways (such as being offered a transfer to Paris after living much of one's life in the Bronx!).

CHAKRA: Second Chakra—Sacral—Creativity, Body Acceptance

When we seek her assistance, Archangel Jophiel's energy stirs and enlivens our second chakra, found below the naval and connected to our creativity as well as our sensuality and sexuality. Stepping into our creativity rests on our recognizing that we have such power. Expressing that power through the physical form, sensually or sexually, brings harmony to our being. Thank you, Jophiel!

COLOR: Pink

There is some consensus around Jophiel showing up as pink light, although variations occur regularly. Stay open in order to see how this Divine Beauty reveals herself over time, should you decide to cultivate this relationship.

CRYSTAL/STONE: Quartz (Clear or with Rutiles)

Quartz is the master stone that amplifies all intention (whether conscious or unconscious), thus reminding us of the call of Jophiel to step into our role of responsible, conscious creation.

The quartz may be clear, echoing and amplifying our clear intention and reminding us we create with every thought and word, or we may choose a quartz with an inclusion of some kind, to give us an object of focus to create very precisely specific intentions (as long as the intentions respect the free will of others, of course).

Conscious Creation with Archangel Jophiel

This is an excellent exercise to begin the day, if you decide to take on the task of changing what you create by rendering your creation conscious.

Play with Archangel Jophiel!
1. Connect with your breath, and come into a peaceful place of quiet. Set your intention to communicate with and cultivate your connection to Archangel Jophiel.
2. Use your channel (created in chapter 2), and anchor (ground) yourself, following your ribbon of light into the center of the earth, and open to the highest good, tracing your channel of light from the center of the earth through your body, with the intention to

connect with the heavens. Return to your heart in order to set your intention, both as the human being you are and on a soul level. (If you do this exercise, you can be sure that it is the will of your soul.)

3. Seated, with your feet planted solidly on the ground, shoulder-width apart, legs and hands uncrossed, sit tall with shoulders pulled back so that your spinal column—the bridge you create between the earth and the heavens—is straight. Place your hands simply on your lap, palms facing upward, and invite Archangel Jophiel to connect with you. *Breathe in* the presence of angels and archangels all around you. *Breathe out* anything that blocks your opening to them. Allow yourself to fill with Light and peace, with a sense of the Love that is there for you, and to feel, perhaps, the Joy that your presence brings in this space. Take three or four deep breaths at least before continuing.

4. With your eyes closed, imagine that Archangel Jophiel stands before you and awaits your signal to begin. (Again, imagining or thinking of someone has an energetic impact and acts as an invitation, which explains why people we think of sometimes will contact us out of the blue.)

5. Once you are ready and your intention is clear, open your arms wide, palms facing forward, energetically opening to the beautiful presence of Archangel Jophiel just in front of you. *Breathe in* to permit a preliminary expansion as Jophiel prepares the work of conscious creation to come, aligning you with the highest and best for your being and your mission.

6. *Breathe out* any tension you might feel in the body, and as you do so, bring your arms from the sides in a semi-circle, first in front of you, then direct your open hands to touch your forehead, palms toward your head, fingers pointed toward each other, meeting at the center of the forehead. This position prepares for the following opening/healing to occur.

7. Invite Archangel Jophiel now to enfold your hands in hers. Allow her to take your hands and move them in a gentle caress, from the center of your forehead toward the outside, again and again, hands moving in rhythm, as if you were gently brushing off crumbs of stale ideas that no longer serve, clearing the space for new, conscious creation. *Breathe out* to expel any old "stinkin' thinkin'" as your hands move outward, then *breathe in* your power reset to conscious

creation through beautiful thoughts and words, as your fingertips come back together again. Continue the motion until it comes naturally and you feel satisfied that it is complete. (You cannot make a mistake here: it is your intention and the request for assistance of Jophiel that renders the exercise effective; the length of time you remain in that space is training your instrument over time.) Know that you are being held in grace and your clear intention that it be so, makes it so, with the help of the Divine Beauty, Jophiel.

8. In the days ahead, ask Jophiel to support you as you make an effort to stay present and notice your thoughts and words. If you find a thought or word not apt for your conscious creation (an old habit cropping up, for example, saying something like "Oh, I'll never be able to do that!"), erase it and replace it ("I can easily do it!"). This works because conscious creation is always more powerful than habitual unconscious creation.

9. When the healing work feels satisfying, and you feel relaxed and complete, thank Archangel Jophiel, and again bring your hands to your chest in a gesture of gratitude for this sacred moment of sharing and relationship building.

The Aftercare noted on p. 56 is a very good way to help you integrate this important work.

ARCHANGEL ZADKIEL

Quality: The Just Forgiveness of God

As a child, I was sexually abused by two people who should have been my protectors. This is a weight I bore heavily for many years and, in the main, unconsciously, the weight of that anger and mistrust played out again and again, as I would not or could not engage in a committed relationship with a man, no matter how good he was to me.

But all of that was unconscious until much later, when my spiritual path opened up and I sat in a workshop much like the ones I teach today and heard it suggested that I should forgive.

"YOU'VE GOTTA BE FREAKIN' KIDDING ME!" was my reaction, and the anger that flared up did not clue me in to the fact that there was something going on there. All I could see was red, even as I was told that it would be good *for me* to forgive them.

Over time, though, I recognized that the actual traumatic circumstances had happened years (decades!) ago, and that it was I, not the original perpetrators, who chose to hold onto those experiences and relive them again and again. Remember the other energy law? "Where our attention goes, so goes the energy" clearly indicates that if I continue to go back to the past and any ugliness buried there, then *that* is where my energy will remain.

1. Let go of the weight of the past

The first reason to forgive anything, no matter how egregious, is to let go of the weight of it—to free ourselves for the rest of our lives, instead of dooming ourselves to relive the past again and again, to give ourselves the gift of happiness, the possibility of Joy . . . and of Large Life!

When I was finally able to release all of the low energy tied to the trauma of my youth, my energy was freed up to allow me to react differently to others and to myself.

2. Forgive because we are actors on a stage (soul contracts)

The second reason to forgive is more esoteric—it has as its foundation the idea we explored earlier that the truth of who we are, at the soul level, is not the role we play in this lifetime, the human beings we as souls came into this world to play ("All the world's a stage . . ."). The idea is that no matter how dramatic the hurts of the past might be, the *truth* of who we are is untouched; the actor or actress is unscathed by any seeming attacks during the play.

Similarly, we can perhaps imagine that though free will exists, certain experiences (especially the setting at the beginning of our lives) are put in place by our soul to "nudge" us in the right direction, like choosing wisely the currents at the put-in that will impact a boat trip. As we go on, events will occur that will continually offer adjustments to the path; Life will continue to give us opportunities to come back home to our soul's direction.

Big events of our lives—positive or negative—are such adjustments. Everything does happen for a reason, and the Universe is set up for your success. The people who interact with us in those *big* moments are souls with whom we have contracts: agreements put in place before we were born to optimize each soul's growth and chances for success on our respective missions.

I am sometimes asked, "Well what good could ever have come from being abused?"

Good question! And one that I have (as you can imagine) pondered many times. The value of that experience is that it forced me to close my heart (joining in the epidemic of the planet); much later, I learned to reopen it. That particular trauma (sexual or child abuse) runs rampant in society, so I am able to help those who cross my path who have lived through similar experiences. The experience for me (once I cottoned on, reopened my heart, and accepted my mission) has enhanced every aspect of my work and created in me a compassion that nourishes all my personal contacts as well.

Zadkiel is the Archangel who expresses God's justice, not Man's. And God has the benefit of the larger view, the soul level view, which facilitates forgiveness.

3. *We are all doing our best*

The idea here is that we always do the best we can with what we've got. I don't know about you, but when I first heard that phrase, something in me rebelled against it. It seemed too easy, like letting everybody off the hook, even for the most egregious of sins, as if there was no sense of responsibility at all.

When I teach it now, someone will almost invariably throw out the example of Adolph Hitler, expecting me to concede the exception. But no, even Hitler was doing the best he could with what he had—and what he had was a belief system that truly believed that the Jewish people were a threat and needed to be extinguished. Now, we know he was a sicko, a nut job, and wrong, but with that set of beliefs, it is not surprising the lengths he went to to extinguish a whole people. In his madness, he considered himself a sort of savior.

Another refutation might arise if we think of something we may have done in the past of which we are ashamed, the shame stemming from the certitude that we could have done better. But could we have?

I find it funny (funny strange, not funny ha-ha) that many of us will judge ourselves much more harshly than we would judge someone else. We may cut others some slack, try to understand where they were at in their lives that promoted a particular action, but are we as generous with ourselves? The person you are today is not the person you were back then. We change all the time. Even if you knew an action was "wrong" back then, your belief structure at the time made that choice, your choice. It is as patently unfair to judge another person using your belief structure today as it is to use it to judge your past actions.

That is not to say that we do not make amends or pay any corresponding debts, but carrying around that lack of forgiveness of ourselves is weightier than any anger we may harbor toward another person, as it pits the self against the instrument, a no-win situation. No Large Life is possible there!

Zadkiel, the Archangel of God's Justice, and (thus) of Forgiveness, is the ideal ally to help us *let go* of the small past and open our wings and fly, to open up to Large Life!

Forgiveness is *always* available from God, who sees past our earthly performance to the truth of who we are. Judgment is of the earth, not of the heavens. The Divine knows only Love.

For those who might rebel at the idea of there being no Divine punishment for evil, know that a lifetime of evil, far from the Light and Love of God, is punishment enough. After death, the rehabilitation of souls is a whole process, when the weight of such a life has been heavy and the fear of punishment lingers.

Zadkiel offers us the Light of Freedom through forgiveness long before we get to that point.

CHAKRA: Seventh Chakra–Crown–Alignment

Given the above, it is no surprise that Archangel Zadkiel is known for helping us with our realignment to the eternal truth of God, helping us to see beyond the limitations of perception here on Earth. As such, Zadkiel helps us at the level of our seventh chakra, whaich opens and aligns us to our soul's expression of that eternal truth, helping us to release the weight of the world from our shoulders and aligning us with our soul's path and mission.

CRYSTAL/STONE: Obsidian (Especially Rainbow Obsidian)

The ideal stone to do the kind of deep releasing work we may want to undertake with Zadkiel is obsidian. The black stone is known to absorb lower energies, transmuting them to higher ones, similar to the effect of forgiveness. The rainbow version of Obsidian is particularly interesting if you decide you would like to work with Zadkiel to release anger and judgment you may be harboring against *yourself.* Just as the rainbow is "hidden" in the depths of the stone, revealed only in the light, the truth of Who You Are Truly, and your innocence and purity as a beloved child of God can be revealed to allow your light to shine for Large Life here and now.

Connecting/Releasing and Forgiving
with Archangel Zadkiel

Play with Archangel Zadkiel!

1. Connect with your breath, and come into a peaceful place of quiet. Set the intention to cultivate your connection to Archangel Zadkiel to facilitate a release of any anger or judgment that might be weighing you down or dimming your light, consciously or unconsciously.

2. Use your channel to anchor (ground) yourself, following your ribbon of light into the center of the earth, then open to the highest good, tracing your channel of light from the center of the earth with your intention to the heavens. Return to your heart in order to set your intention, both as the human being you are and on a soul level. (As you are undertaking this exercise, it is certain that this and any exercise undertaken with the Angelic realm is the will of your soul.)

3. Seated, feet are planted solidly on the ground, shoulder-width apart, legs and hands uncrossed, shoulders pulled back so that your spinal column—the bridge you create between the earth and the heavens—is straight. Place your hands simply on your lap, palms facing upward, and invite Archangel Zadkiel to connect with you. *Breathe in* the presence of Angels and Archangels all around you. *Breathe out* anything that blocks your opening to them. Allow yourself to fill with Light and peace, with a sense of the Love that is there for you, and to feel, perhaps, the Joy that your presence brings in this space. Take three or four deep breaths at least before continuing.

4. With your eyes closed, imagine that Archangel Zadkiel stands before you and awaits your signal to begin. (Imagining has an energetic effect and acts as an invitation, in accordance with the energetic law that says: "Where our attention goes, so goes the energy." This, by the way, is why people we are thinking of will sometimes contact us "out of the blue.") In your mind's eye, see Zadkiel before you; feel him shining brightly and kindly upon you, ready to accompany you in this sacred work.

5. Once you are ready and your intention is clear, open your arms wide, palms facing forward, energetically opening to the powerful presence of Archangel Zadkiel just in front of you. *Breathe in* to permit a preliminary expansion as Zadkiel prepares the work of conscious release, aligning you with the highest and best for your being and your mission.

6. *Breathe out* any tension you might feel in the body, and as you do so, bring your arms from the sides in a semi-circle, first in front of you, then direct your hands to your chest, pointing your fingers toward your chest until they touch the heart center. In this position, your two hands will be touching each other at the backs of your fingers as your arms create two circles anchored in the body where your fingers touch your chest, the heart center. This position prepares for the following opening/healing to occur.

7. Invite Archangel Zadkiel now to enfold your hands in his. Allow him to take your hands and to move them in a gentle pulling motion, as if each of your hands were grasping and removing veils covering your heart Light. Alternating one

hand after the other, *slowly* pull away any layers that shadow your Light—judgment, anger, hate, fear, shame, guilt, whatever. Do not analyze this! No need to determine what is leaving. Just know that with Zadkiel's help, all layers that are ready to be removed will be released. *Breathe out* to expel any old "stinkin' thinkin'," as your hands move outward to release the veils you remove. *Breathe in* your freedom and light, more and more, as your fingertips come back, seeking further release.

Continue the motion until it comes naturally and you feel satisfied that it is complete. (You cannot make a mistake here—it is your intention and the request for assistance from Zadkiel that renders the exercise effective; how long you remain in that space is training your instrument over time.) Know that you are being held in grace and your clear intention that it be so, makes it so, with the help of the Divine Justice, Zadkiel.

8. When the healing work feels satisfying and you feel relaxed and complete, thank Archangel Zadkiel, and bring your hands again to your chest in a gesture of gratitude for this sacred moment of sharing and relationship building.

The Aftercare noted on p. 56 is a very good way to help yourself integrate this important work.

CHAPTER 5

Archangels Metatron, Sandalphon, Ariel, Uriel, and Azrael

I n the following chapter, we continue our connection to helpful Arch-angelic relationships by exploring connections with five more Arch-angels: Metatron, Sandalphon, Ariel, Uriel, and Azrael. Though these Archangels are perhaps less well known, they are strong Allies in our movement toward Large Life, Life with a capital "L," where we are so *relaxed* our Light shines forth and our highest and best path lights up before us. As before, we will look at each Archangel and their *raison-d'être*, that is, why they are active on the earth plane and what Divine quality they express; any unique signatures such as color or energy (only included where there is some consensus around the question); and unique exercises to connect with each one—an invitation, if you will, to Large Life with the aid of each Archangel!

ARCHANGEL	DIVINE QUALITY
Metatron	Understanding
Sandalphon	Gentleness, Music
Ariel	Nature
Uriel	Change/Chaos
Azrael	Death

THE FIRST TWO ARCHANGELS: Metatron and Sandalphon

Even the names of the next two Archangels, Metatron and Sandalphon, are different from all the others. You may have noticed that the other 13 Archangels all have names that end in "el," which at its root means "God" or "of God." The "on" at the end of the names Metatron and Sandalphon both marks a difference from the others and reminds us that we are all finally "on-e", as there is no place that God is not.

Another specificity is that Metatron and his "twin brother" (the Greek roots of the name Sandalphon) are the exceptions to the rule: both are known to have lived human lives that culminated in illumination, or enlightenment: a complete realignment with the Truth, with the soul, with the Divine. In their case, that illumination permitted (as with Mary and Jesus from the Christian tradition) "ascension," a rising, leaving human life behind without passing through the normal doorway of death, but rather, a transformation by grace.

Furthermore, each one is said to have lived their last lives as well-known characters from the Hebrew tradition and the Old Testament of Christianity.

ARCHANGEL METATRON

QUALITY: Divine Wisdom

Archangel Metatron expresses the quality of Divine Wisdom and adds the specificity of having had personal experience as a human being to his offering as an Ally (making him one of the best Friends in High Places to have). Since Metatron understands the human experience completely, he is uniquely able to help us connect to Divine Wisdom and understanding, and to release anything that blocks our access to our own innate wisdom.

How Archangel Metatron Can Assist Us
Students and Tests

Metatron is an excellent Ally for students, and for anyone who seeks to learn and understand. During the stressful period of exams or tests, he can come to our aid with the calm that is critical to understanding and learning.

Procrastination

Metatron also can help us with procrastination, allowing us a deeper understanding of that phenomenon, often judged as weakness in a world that understands so little. In the Western world, we are encouraged to go fast—very fast!—and so we may judge ourselves when certain projects or objectives seem to take longer than we (or others) think they should. We may be tempted to be hard on ourselves (that old judgment that will weigh us down!) when days, weeks, or maybe even years slip by without a particular goal coming to fruition.

Instead of judging our procrastination, Metatron can help us to understand it. Behind all procrastination we usually find either fear or a state of unreadiness created by fear.

Let me give you an example from my own life.

My first book (already published in French), *The Angels Told Me So*, had a gestation period of about seven years, during which time I successfully changed my life completely, began teaching and touring, and accompanying individuals and groups. I even wrote, produced, and acted in a short film!

Clearly, it was not a barren period of laziness, but I noted that from time to time I would (the habit of a former banker) judge myself harshly because I had not yet produced "the book."

What became apparent with time was that I was not seeing clearly. Later, when the time was right, the form of the book had changed completely from my original idea, and with an astonishing fluidity, it was written in about two weeks!

To get to that point, I worked with Metatron, who helped me understand that a fear of being seen was operating behind the scenes for me (being "seen" was not always a positive experience in my childhood, earning me the occasional smack in the head or kick in the pants or other discipline). Once I realized that the limiting belief/fear "being seen is dangerous" was holding up my book, I was able to work with the Angels to release it.

So fear was holding me back, but not only that! In addition, the project was simply not ready (even though I thought it was). When it had evolved into its final form (teaching tool rather than autobiography), the project, my "baby," was birthed easily, painlessly, and quickly. Before it was completed, I was even contacted by a French publisher for it!

With regard to the "readiness" aspect, the following is now clear: No matter the project, if it were ready, it would have already come to light.

The image of a cupcake in the oven always helps me, or that of an apple still on the tree. In both cases, it makes no sense at all to force it: the taste and richness of the experience to come is commensurate with the time it takes.

Metatron/Enoch and the Akashic Records: Life Lessons
In the Bible, before ascension, Metatron walked the earth in the form of Enoch, the holy man from scripture. It is said that Enoch walked so closely with God that one day, God simply asked him, "Enoch, we are closer to my place than yours. Why don't you come home with me?" I always loved that story.

In his human life as Enoch, Metatron was a holy man and a sage, a true Lightworker. In those days, the few people who could read and write held an important role in the community, as custodians of the culture and history of the people. Once ascended, Enoch aligned to become Metatron, and continued to play the role of custodian for all humanity as guardian of the Akashic records.

The Akashic records are the treasury of all that has ever been and all that will be. Many people use the Akashic records to obtain information about their past lives, previous lifetimes that may have marked us deeply enough to have an impact on this life.

A Word about Past Life Reviews

I am sometimes asked if past life regressions are a necessary part of a spiritual path of reawakening. My answer (less than satisfying for some) is "Maybe." If we feel compelled or strongly drawn to have a reading done (or to do one ourselves, with Metatron, for example), then it is likely that it serves the soul's purpose to have those specific clarifications, but if you do not feel so inspired, then it is not necessary; there is more than one way to undo a karmic knot!

If there are "karmic knots"—issues from past lives that need balancing—the life we are in right now will provide us with "echo situations," opportunities in the here-and-now that allow us to face and heal them. An example of a situation where we might turn to a past life regression analysis is the case of a debilitating, unexplained fear that limits our freedom to live fully in this life.

For example, since childhood, I have had an inordinate fear of walking on rocks, and also a very strong fear of heights. I had no physical experience that would account for any of this, at least none that I remembered in this lifetime.

At one point on my journey, during the time I walked the Camino (the St. James Way, a pilgrimage across Spain), this fear was limiting my freedom and Joy. There were times when we had to cross shallow creeks using flat rocks that provided easy footing—easy for most, that is . . . I found myself in a few instances frozen and unable to go forward or retreat. Determined to free myself of this constraint, I asked Archangel Metatron to help me to understand the fear so that I could release it. I saw a vision where, in another lifetime, I had been pushed off a cliff to die on the rocks below.

That understanding freed me to a great degree, although I will probably still not be the first to get on a roller coaster.

COLOR: Rainbow

Many people say that they see all of the colors of the rainbow, like a prism, when Archangel Metatron is present.

CHAKRA: Sixth Chakra—Third Eye—Wisdom

Archangel Metatron is known for helping us to open to our claircognizance or inner wisdom, one of our clairvoyant gifts. This gift is closely associated with the sixth chakra, governing the energy around our beliefs and understanding. This chakra is located at the forehead, in the area known as the third eye, between the eyebrows in the center, and is central to our knowledge of Angels.

CRYSTAL/STONE: Opal

The opal in its many variations is consistent, in that it always allows the light and colors of creation to shine through. Metatron also promotes this, as he helps the Light of Understanding to pierce through the density of the illusion, allowing us to align further with the will of the creator, the mission of our soul.

Connecting to Wisdom with Archangel Metatron

Play with Archangel Metatron!

1. Connect with your breath, and come into a peaceful place of quiet. Set your intention to communicate with and cultivate your connection to Archangel Metatron.

2. Use your channel to anchor (ground) yourself, following your ribbon of light into the center of the earth, then open to the highest good and with your intention, trace your channel of light from the center of the earth through your heart/body to the heavens. Return to your heart in order to set your intention, both as the human being you are and on a soul level. (If you are undertaking this exercise, it is without a doubt the will of your soul.)

3. Stand, feet planted solidly on the ground, shoulder-width apart, with your shoulders pulled back so that your spinal column— the bridge you create between the earth and the heavens— is straight, arms relaxed at your sides, palms facing forward, in a position of energetic openness. *Breathe in* the presence of Angels and Archangels all around you. *Breathe out* anything that blocks your opening to them. Allow yourself to fill with Light and peace, with a sense of the Love that is there for you,

and to feel, perhaps, the Joy that your presence brings in this space. Take three or four deep breaths at least before continuing.

4. With your eyes closed, imagine that Archangel Metatron stands before you and awaits your signal to begin. Raise your arms to the sky, palms facing one another. Invite Archangel Metatron to connect with you, facilitating the work that is to come.

5. *Breathe in* to permit a preliminary expansion as Metatron opens the flows of Light and Understanding for you, aligning you with the heavens and the highest and best for your being and your mission. With your eyes closed (or open, if it is more comfortable), "see," "sense," "feel," or "know" the flow of pure golden light from the heavens that is streaming down through your hands along your channel/ribbon of light, filling you.

6. *Breathe out* any tension you might feel as you release all blockages to deeper understanding.

7. Invite Archangel Metatron to now enfold your hands in his, increasing the flow and the release process. *Breathe out* in order to expel that which no longer serves you, as your hands, which have ushered in this new Light, move downward, settling on your energetic heart at the center of your chest. *Breathe in* all that light, delivering it to your heart, the seat of your inner knowing and your cosmic GPS. Continue until you feel satisfied that it is complete. (You cannot make a mistake here: it is your intention and the request for assistance from Metatron that renders the exercise effective. How long you remain in that space is training your instrument, over time.) Know that you are being held in grace and your clear intention that it be so makes it so, with the help of the Divine Understanding and Wisdom of Metatron.

8. When the healing work feels satisfying and you feel relaxed and complete, thank Archangel Metatron by bringing your hands to your chest again in a gesture of gratitude for this sacred moment of sharing and relationship building.

The Aftercare noted on p. 56 is a very good way to help yourself integrate this important work.

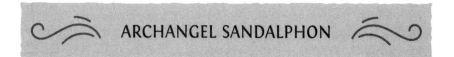

ARCHANGEL SANDALPHON

QUALITY: Music and Gentleness

Archangel Sandalphon expresses the quality of Gentleness, and he is the Archangel of Music. As with Metatron, Sandalphon's having had experience as a human being allows him to be tender in his approach to us, teaching us to approach ourselves and each other in a softer, gentler way. Much of what limits us from living Life Large, in alignment with our soul's purpose, is simply the harsh judgments (others' or our own) that are pervasive here on Earth—limiting beliefs that a Large Life is not possible, and that our dreams are "only dreams."

Only by softening our approach to ourselves and calling into question the way we dismiss our dreams can we really move strongly into and along our highest path, to the fullness of Large Life. Sandalphon, the Gentle One, is an ideal Ally for children (of all ages), as we humans (of all ages) blossom when surrounded by the safety of Love and gentleness.

Music

Sandalphon is an excellent Ally for musicians, both for those who seek to play music as well as those who love to listen to it. Furthermore, he helps all those who ask to open the doors to their own more vast form of "musicianship": our body is our instrument, and it behooves us to learn to play it.

Understanding how our instrument plays is compelling work, learning to recognize its language and the specificities of its vibrations. Chanting or singing can aid us in getting in contact with our instrument in ways that nourish all of our creativity. If we do it with that intention and with Sandalphon, we can endeavor to achieve mastery of our instrument: taking back not only our voice but our Voice with a capital "V," our capacity to speak our Truth.

An exercise like the one at the end of this section can help us reopen the doors to our clairvoyance in all forms, facilitating our capacity to communicate in the "extraordinary" ways we discussed earlier and recognizing that we are entitled to such high-level communication in all its forms: seeing, hearing, feeling, sensing intuitively, or knowing innately.

A Word about Our Voice

When I receive people for individual Angel sessions, as a follow-up, each one is invited to connect directly with their Angels in particular ways that will create wholeness and healing and facilitate Angelic communication. Very often, I am prompted to transmit the Angelic invitation to sing: the Angels around the person suggest that he or she sing (with angelic assistance) to take their voice back (and not only their singing voice).

There are a lot of people whose singing voices (and thus their Joy) have been silenced or quieted by things they heard about their voice when they were young. The rule "No singing at the table" came into being in our apartment in the Bronx because the urge to sing was too strong in me for my parents' taste. (I took to singing into a pillow when that rule broadened to "No singing in the house.")

And how many voices have been silenced because a choirmaster somewhere did not know what to do with the particularities of a child's voice? (I remember the joy of singing "I Won't Grow Up" in our parish play as Peter Pan—my short hair allowed it! – and know first hand that singing is an expression of joy in children and in adults.)

But people who have been told that they are tone deaf or have voices that annoy others will often shut down that doorway to Joy completely; yet it is a necessary element, that Joy, if we are to live Large. In such cases, the Angels around a person, and Sandalphon, in particular, may propose a healing of those wounds so that a person might find and express Joy through song once again.

Sometimes, however, it is not our singing voice that was taken away when young, but our Voice altogether.

"Do not speak unless spoken to." "Be quiet!" "No one asked you!" Such phrases and others, more hurtful, effectively stunt our ability to express ourselves, to speak our truth. They can be at the root of why we don't feel comfortable with some people (as we saw in the very first exercise of the book). When we don't feel "safe," we cannot speak our truth. We lose our authentic voice, perhaps instead adopting words that we hope will be acceptable to those around us.

If life has either shut down our singing or our speaking voice of authenticity, working with Sandalphon and the Angels around us is a great aid for healing and will support us in expressing our truth and taking back our joy and our power.

CHAKRA: Fifth Chakra—Throat—Gentle Authenticity

Archangel Sandalphon is one of the Archangels known for helping us with the reopening of the fifth or throat chakra, which impacts our daily life as well as our clairvoyant gifts with gentleness and authenticity. The Archangel of music helps us to sing our song, speak our truth, and to communicate gently and harmoniously.

COLOR: Sky Blue

Many will see a sky-blue light, wide and open, in the Presence of Sandalphon.

CRYSTAL/STONE: Larimar

Gentle as the sound of waves softly lapping at the shore, larimar perfectly embodies the energy of Sandalphon, which recognizes that Love has the power to transform, like water that carves rock not with violent force, but with the power of constancy and intention.

Connecting to Joy and Authentic Voice with Archangel Sandalphon

Play with Archangel Sandalphon!

1. Connect with your breath, and come into a peaceful place of quiet. Set your intention to communicate with and cultivate your connection to Archangel Sandalphon.

2. Use your channel to anchor (ground) yourself, following your ribbon of light into the center of the earth, then open to the highest good with your intention, tracing your channel of light from the center of the earth to the heavens. Return to your heart in order to set your intention, both as the human being you are and on a soul level. (If you are undertaking this exercise, it is without a doubt the will of your soul.)

3. Stand, feet planted solidly on the ground, shoulder-width apart, with shoulders pulled back so that your spinal column—the bridge you create between the earth and the heavens—is straight, arms relaxed at your sides, palms facing forward, in a position of energetic openness. *Breathe in* the presence of

Angels and Archangels all around you. *Breathe out* anything that blocks your opening to them. Allow yourself to fill with Light and peace, with a sense of the Love that is there for you; to feel, perhaps, the Joy that your presence brings in this space. Take three or four deep breaths at least before continuing.

4. With your eyes closed, imagine that Archangel Sandalphon stands before you and awaits *your* okay before he gives the signal to begin, like a Divine conductor of the orchestra. Place your hands on your diaphragm, and on the in-breath, open your arms wide with palms facing forward. On the out-breath, invite Archangel Sandalphon to connect with you, facilitating the work that is to come.

5. *Breathe in*, this time breathing deeply into the diaphragm, and at the same time, place your hands on your diaphragm so you can feel the vibration your instrument creates as you hold and support it in this way. As you breathe out, deeply chant the *OM* used in so many traditions, connecting us with the Truth of the Unity of all things and the Power therein. As you chant, permit an expansion as Sandalphon opens the flow of the Energy, Power, and the Sound of Love through you, filling every cell of your being, aligning you with the Joy and Power that is your heritage. With your eyes closed (or open if it is more comfortable for you), "see," "sense," "feel," or "know" the flow of pure golden sound that is the Light from the heavens streaming through your instrument, as you breathe it in and sound it out intentionally, coursing through your instrument along your channel/ribbon of light and filling you.

6. *Breathe out* any tension you might feel as you chant the *OM*, releasing all blockages to your voice (little "v") and your Voice (capital "V") and to your Joy and Power.

7. Invite Archangel Sandalphon now to place His hands over yours on your diaphragm, as you *breathe in*, increasing the Power and the process. Then *breathe out*, each time chanting *OM* on the out-breath to expel any blockages as through the Grace of God/Source (and with gratitude to Archangel Sandalphon), your voice (and your Voice) opens and strengthens, moving and vibrating your instrument, through the diaphragm center in the region of the solar plexus or seat of power. Continue until you

feel satisfied that it is complete. (You cannot make a mistake here—your intention and the request for assistance from Sandalphon render the exercise effective; how long you remain in that space is training your instrument over time.) Know that you are being held in Grace, so your clear intention that it be so makes it so, with the help of the Divine Gentle Strength of Voice and Music, Sandalphon.

8. When the healing work feels satisfying and you feel relaxed and complete, thank Archangel Sandalphon and your Guardian Angels by bringing your hands to your chest in a gesture of gratitude for this sacred moment of opening and sounding and Joy and Power.

The Aftercare noted on p. 56 is a very good way to help yourself integrate this important work.

ARCHANGEL ARIEL

QUALITY: Support and Love for Nature

If there were an Ecology Archangel, it would be Ariel. In fact, Ariel is not really here to aid humans, at least not primarily; Archangel Ariel is here for the fairies! Whereas the other Archangels we see here are bade to directly support human life forms here on Earth, Archangel Ariel is here to support other life forms—those that need both *less* help and *more* help than we do.

Huh?

Ariel is here to support the elemental kingdom, and all aspects of Mother Earth that live harmoniously with our planet. They need *less* help than humans as they are already aligned with Divine Love and Harmony (look in the eyes of a beloved pet, for example), but they need *more* help, too, as they are subjugated to the folly of humanity during this period of transformation. Ariel is here to support the natural kingdoms, and as such, she is a worthy Ally to such humans as would seek to support the earth as well.

Note that I refer to "she," as the energy of Archangel Ariel is said to be feminine in Nature, even though, as discussed earlier, Archangels do not have a sex, just as God does not. However, not unlike Mother Nature herself, or the volcano goddess Kali, or Diana the Huntress of folklore, Archangel Ariel is no shrinking violet feminine energy but rather, a force to be reckoned with.

Jealously protecting the earth and the elemental realm, Ariel extends her aid only to humans who work to reestablish the harmony and balance between humanity and the earth. As such, she is an excellent Ally (a Friend in High Places) for anyone who works in ecology, or with the earth, or who works to wake up humanity to our natural (and sadly, often forgotten) role of co-guardian (along with the fairies or elementals) of the earth.

A Word about Fairies

Since the dawn of storied time, human beings and the fairy folk have walked the earth together as co-guardians. At one low point, we humans turned our backs on the role of guardian, choosing instead to exploit the earth for our own benefit. The birth of greed heralded the beginning of imbalance. At that time, the fairy folk chose to raise their vibration so as to no longer be visible to humankind, as the latter fell quickly into the temptation of greed and selfishness.

Competition and self-centeredness continue to reign supreme during this period of history, but fairy folk can still be seen and heard—by those who can get still enough, by those who are deemed worthy of that communication, and by those who have not forgotten the balance and the sacred duty of the guardian.

In so-called "uncivilized" societies where mankind still lives in close connection with the earth, often the respect and harmony and balance remain, and the peoples continue to walk together. But in the Western world, this treasure and sacred trust has been lost for millennia and is only beginning to be reborn. In places like Findhorn, an eco-spiritual community in the north of Scotland, which I proudly represent as a Resource Person, that respect and partnership has been rekindled and human beings work together with the fairy folk and the Angels and devas of the land, deciding, for example, what to grow, and how and when to grow it.

Harmony and balance between humans and the fairy folk, elemental energies of the earth, is still possible (and perhaps the source of redemption that we will need in order to avoid destruction.)

Archangel Ariel, then, is the Archangel that accompanies our fairy co-guardians as she protects the earth and her lands and waters, as well as all manner of elemental beings that inhabit, embody, and give life to the various expressions of life that make up the amazing blue marble we inhabit. She is known to help humans insofar as our intentions are pure and support the awakening of humankind to step back into our natural role of honoring the earth as guardians.

For some Ariel is associated with witchery and white magic, Harmony and balance between humans and the fairy folk, elemental energies of the earth, is still possible (and perhaps the source of redemption that we will need in order to avoid destruction.)

CHAKRA: First Chakra—Root—Groundedness

Archangel Ariel helps us to keep our feet on the ground, literally. The Archangel most connected with Nature and the earth not surprisingly is connected to our root chakra, the first, located at the base of the spine at the level of the coccyx, between the legs. This chakra helps us to handle the material aspects of daily living as well as to accept this incarnation and live it fully... and Large! As she assists with positive manifestation, she can also help with first-chakra aspects of money, shelter and food... all ecological of course!

COLOR: Gold and Green

Though there is no simple consensus with regard to the light that expresses Archangel Ariel, some will see a strong golden hue when Ariel is present, and others will see more of a emerald or light-filled green when she is present. This may be seen either with the actual eyes of one whose clairvoyance is of the ESP kind, or on the inner screen of our inner vision if our clairvoyance if of the SPE variety.

CRYSTAL/STONE: Red Jasper, Garnet, Larimar

There are many stones which facilitate making contact with the Archangel most connected to the earth. Certainly Red Jasper or Garnet, with their powerful grounding energies are very naturally linked to the power of Archangel Ariel. But also water stones like Larimar or a crystal quartz with a water inclusion can easily facilitate an Ariel connection.

Connecting to Balance with Archangel Ariel

Play with Archangel Ariel!

1. Connect with your breath, and come into a peaceful place of quiet. Set your intention to communicate with and cultivate your connection to Archangel Ariel.

2. Use your channel to anchor (ground) yourself, following your ribbon of light into the center of the earth, then open to the highest good with your intention and trace your channel of light from the center of the earth through your body to the heavens. Return to your heart to set your intention, both as the human being you are and on a soul level. (If you are undertaking this exercise, it is the will of your soul.)

3. Stand, feet planted solidly on the ground, shoulder-width apart, with shoulders pulled back so that your spinal column—the bridge

you create between the earth and the heavens—is straight, arms relaxed at your sides, palms facing forward in a position of energetic openness. *Breathe in* the presence of Angels and Archangels all around you. *Breathe out* anything that blocks your opening to them. Allow yourself to fill with Light and peace, with a sense of the Love that is there for you; to feel, perhaps, the Joy that your presence brings in this space. Take three or four deep breaths at least to fully experience this sense of peace before continuing.

4. With your eyes closed, imagine that Archangel Ariel stands before you, laughing and joyful at the prospect of the moments to come, another human being willing to work with Her to restore balance and harmony. She awaits your accord before the work is to begin. With an in-breath, place your hands on the center of your chest, the energetic heart of your being, and on the out-breath open your arms wide, palms facing forward. Invite Archangel Ariel to connect with you, and to do the same.

5. Keeping your eyes open, begin to slowly turn, allowing your arms to swing wide around you as you spin. Feel the power of your movement, even as you ensure (by keeping your eyes open and watching your speed) the well-being of your person, keeping balance at the forefront of your movement. With the assistance of Ariel, allow the Joy and movement to lift your arms, and continue only as long as you feel it safe to do so. Like a child, perhaps, laughter will bubble up; allow it. It may be, too, that your head (the mental aspect of your being) will judge this activity harshly, labeling it "silly" or even "ridiculous"—GOOD! When our head tells us that something is "ridiculous," we can be sure that it is powerful, and that it is our fear that is trying to stop us from growing.

    When you have completed the turning, place your hands on your solar plexus, your seat of power in the body. Drop your gaze to the ground and allow your ribbon of light to strengthen in its connection to the earth. With the help of Archangel Ariel, it will become more clear that your presence here on Earth during this shifting period of transformation is no accident, and that you have a mission to accomplish that will aid in the restoration of balance and harmony here. *Breathe in.*

6. *Breathe out* any tension you might feel in your body as you release all blockages to your Presence here on the earth plane.

7. Invite Archangel Ariel to now place Her hands over yours on your solar plexus as you breathe in again, increasing the Power and the process. Then *breathe out* again to expel any blockages to your innate balance, as by the Grace of God/Source (with gratitude to Archangel Ariel) your presence (little "p") and your Presence (capital "P") strengthens in Authenticity and Light, moving and vibrating your instrument, through the heart center and in the region of the solar plexus, or seat of Power. Continue until you feel satisfied that it is complete. (You cannot make a mistake here: your intention and request for assistance from Ariel render the exercise effective; how long you remain in that space is training your instrument over time.) Know that you are being held in Grace, so your clear intention that it be so makes it so, with the help of the Divine Strength of Tempest and Earth and Power by Grounding that is Ariel.
8. When the healing work feels satisfying and you feel relaxed and complete, thank Archangel Ariel and your Guardian Angel by bringing your hands to your chest in a gesture of gratitude for this sacred moment of healing and recognition, balancing and Power.

The Aftercare noted on p. 56 is a very good way to help yourself integrate this important work.

ARCHANGEL URIEL

Quality: Change/Chaos/Fire of God

Archangel Uriel, whose name can be translated as "the Fire of God," is as one might surmise with such a name perhaps not the Archangel who is the most mild-mannered. Known by some as the "Archangel of Catastrophes" (not the most flattering of titles), Uriel is at hand to assist us when we face situations that test us in trial-by-fire moments. These can include natural catastrophes, such as hurricanes and fires, earthquakes and tornadoes, or personal game-changers like the "Big Four": moving. losing a job, a romantic breakup, or a death.

How can Uriel help?

In both cases (natural or personal "disasters"), Archangel Uriel helps us to cope: before, during, or after the crisis in question.

Natural Disasters

Before a Natural Disaster: Uriel will connect with persons who are open to receiving this kind of information to warn of impending traumatic events; for example, it is said that it was Uriel who warned Noah of the floods. If you or someone you know is gifted in that rare way that receives warning messages, Uriel is behind them. He can thus also aid the person to utilize the information to prepare for and aid the overall situation.

I often meet people who receive warnings in dreams, and who, frustrated, ask me, "Why give me the vision if there is nothing I can do about it?" As ever with my channel, when a person asks a question, I hear the answer, and what I have been given to respond in most cases is this: People who receive premonitions (hearing messages, seeing visions, having a certain feeling or intuition) about impending disasters are being trained. For many, it takes a few experiences to understand that what we are seeing or hearing are true prescient experiences. Experiencing the confirmation of our "hunches" or visions or dreams builds up confidence that we truly have this gift. It was confidence in the truth of her experience that made Joan of Arc unshakeable in her faith, so much so that she, a teenage girl, got an audience with the king. That (I am told) is the kind of confidence that will be necessary when the time comes to share your gift, if you fall into this group of souls.

So here is the message: do not worry if you lack an outlet to warn others if you are one of the few people who receive a message about disasters. When (not if) you have a role to play utilizing your gift, you will be presented with the opportunity and guided to share the announcement. Just remember to call on Uriel to prepare your instrument to be "played" in this way.

During a Natural Disaster: If we call on Uriel during a natural disaster, he will help us to keep calm, guiding us with effective inspirations to handle any crisis in the best possible way for all concerned. When the world around us falls into the trap that is panic, Uriel, with his perspective that allows a broader view, helps us to keep a cool head and clearly see the best actions to take.

After a Natural Disaster: Again, Uriel can help after a natural disaster, providing (when asked) clear-sighted inspiration for rebuilding in the best way possible. Although no one welcomes a natural disaster (or a disaster of any sort), it is true that space and time are created to rebuild in a more positive and constructive way, often those structures whose time had come anyway.

Personal Crises

The "Big Four"—changing homes, jobs, relationships or letting go of a loved one who passes—are experiences that, for better or worse, can rock our life down to the core and are recognized as some of the most stressful times in our life journey.

When we decide to opt for Large Life, it is certain that one or many of these "Big Four" will come into play. For me, it was all four: a change of country, followed by being let go of the job that moved me to France, a divorce, then the death of my dad, all in short order.

When we hit a trifecta or quadrifecta like that, it is in no way comfortable. But when any of the "Big Four" occur, singularly or in unison, we can be sure that our soul has stepped in to straighten us out, to align us with a path that is more likely to allow for the success of our mission. It usually means that something big will shift: we will need to find new work to do, let go of the past, to open to a place or relationship more aligned with the mission our souls set forth before even we were born.

When our job goes away, even if we were fed up with said job, it shakes us to our foundations, especially if we are of the ilk that identify with or as what we do for a living.

In the United States (I notice now what escaped me before I came to live in Paris), one of the first questions a person will ask you in conversation is "What do you do for a living?" That is much less the case in France, although Paris is beginning to catch up to that unenviable situation.

As a result of this identification with what we do for a living, even if we don't particularly like our job, losing it can be a blow. I remember when I was a banker, during one of the many "weeding out" periods where so many were let go, being terribly sorry for one colleague who had lost his job. I felt sure that it was the end of his life.

When my turn came a few years later (the bank in question doesn't exist anymore), it felt the same: I felt panicky and so was not in the best position to find another position—which, it turned out, was all for the best. If I had not lost my job and refused the replacement job they found for me, I would never have found my Large Life.

Whether or not we recognize such an uprooting event as being "for the best" (it always is), Uriel can help us during those periods of transition, which often occur because the soul is "calling an audible," that is, as in football, calling forth a change from the original plan in order to facilitate a movement toward our purpose in this lifetime.

Similarly, events that wreak havoc in other areas of our lives, such as moving house or a change in relationship or even the death of a person near and dear to us, can all bring us more in line with the opportunity to live Life Larger, more in line with our soul's mission, that is, if we don't fight against the changes that are occurring and breathe enough to *let go*.

Nothing happens by accident; everything happens for a reason. Life always invites us into situations that will provide the context for our greatest growth and our largest life. Sure, the experience might be something we never wanted; it might rock our world. But what is built after such upheaval is most often even better than what came before.

A Word about Allowing

When I receive people for individual Angel sessions, often the person is living through, or has already lived through, tumultuous change. Even when things in life are not hunky-dory, we humans often will often stay put until the pain of staying where we are outweighs the pain of allowing change.

Even when we do dare to take steps to change, we may often look back in regret, as change is often uncomfortable for a long while, and the more our stretch is toward our Large Life and our Light, the more opposition to that change will appear. We may second-guess our brave step and seek to go backward, trying to curl back up in the hole we left. But we can't. Once we step out of our comfort zone we grow, so we cannot fit back into the footprint of what was in the past. If other people are concerned with these decisions, they, too, have changed, and our fickle behavior prolongs the pain for ourselves as well as all concerned.

The image that comes to mind is that of a whitewater kayaker—now that is Large Life! But imagine the fear becomes too great for a first-timer, or worse, imagine we fall out of the boat! This is no exaggeration; that can be the level of panic or discomfort we experience when we step into the deep waters of our lives.

Imagine, then, that we have fallen from our kayak, and are boat-less. Like a good kayaker, we know to breathe and relax our body in a seated position, allowing the water to take us down the whitewater rough patch until we get to the calm pool just beyond. But one can easily imagine that the level of panic or fear might be just high enough that we do not "allow" the change, and instead, spy and then reach out for a low-lying branch that seems to be within our reach to try to save ourselves. Ouch! The water is carrying us too fast, and the arm that grabbed the branch is nearly yanked out of its socket; the reach made out of fear in such a case actually hurts us instead of helping us!

Uriel can help us to sit and let the waters carry us back to a new stillness, a new stability. Safety and beauty beyond our imagining await if we can only allow ourselves to be carried. For Large Life to emerge, we must let go of our past and go beyond our fears to the wonders that await us. If we cultivate relationships with our Angels, and Archangels like Uriel, we will be able to remain stable and confident even during situations that turn us upside down, knowing that everything that happens is always for the best. If we do not allow, if we reach for a branch to stop our flowing, we only hurt ourselves and others.

There is a story from scriptures, in the Old Testament, in which God sent Angels to help Lot and his family escape before the destruction of Sodom and Gomorrah. It is said, in Genesis 19, that they ran toward safety "but Lot's wife, behind him, looked back, and she became a pillar of salt." Uriel reminds us that Life is always in front of us no matter the crisis behind us. Juicy Large Life cannot happen to a pillar of salt, so don't look back!

CHAKRA: Third Chakra—Solar Plexus—Calm

Archangel Uriel is one of the Archangels who can help us to cultivate and balance our third chakra, the solar plexus, or our seat of power in this human lifetime. The fire of God can help us to stoke the fire within us so that all unnecessary worry and fear is burnt away. This helps us to remain calm in difficult situations so we may act from our solar plexus, calmly, from our seat of power.

COLOR: Steel Gray

There is no consensus around the color of the light of Uriel, but some (including me) have seen a steely gray, as if black was penetrated by white or light.

CRYSTAL/STONE: Snowflake Obsidian

Obsidian is a stone that is recognized for its protective capacities. The snowflake variety, which has white flecks on its surface, carries that protection, along with a capacity to see the Light within every situation. This is aligned with the energy of Uriel, who helps us to keep a cool head to effectively handle all manner of crises that arise in the movement of our lives.

A Word about Calm Allowing

With all the Angels, it behooves us to create and cultivate these connections before we find ourselves in need of them. Imagine if we have a new neighbor who never comes by or says hello until they have an urgent situation and need a favor! We do the favor (non?), but there may be a part of us that grumbles, or at least notices, that they only come around when they need us.

Fortunately, the Angels are not like us! Uriel will not hold it against us—won't even notice!—that we only call when we are in crisis, but we will. If we are not already in the habit of communicating with the Angels generally, and Uriel specifically, we won't have the habit to go to Uriel for help when a crisis arises. In a stressful situation, we humans tend to do the tried-and-true and we may also feel uncomfortable or doubtful about anything new, not sure of the efficacy of our connections or the power of our Friends in High Places. Creating the habit of going to the Angels in times of calm—as we do in the following exercise with Archangel Uriel—will make the SOS button easier to push in case of emergency.

Calm Allowing with
Archangel Uriel

Play with Archangel Uriel!

1. Connect with your breath, and come into a peaceful place of quiet. Set your intention to communicate with and cultivate your connection to Archangel Uriel.

2. Use your channel to anchor (ground) yourself, following your ribbon of light into the center of the earth, and then open to the highest good with your intention, tracing your channel of light from the center of the earth through your heart and up to the heavens. Return to your heart in order to set your intention, both as the human being you are and on a soul level. (If you are undertaking this exercise, it is without a doubt the will of your soul.)

3. Sit, feet planted solidly on the ground, shoulder-width apart, shoulders pulled back so that your spinal column is straight. Allow the arms to relax at your sides, palms facing forward in a position of energetic openness. *Breathe in* the presence of Angels and Archangels all around you. *Breathe out* anything that blocks your opening to them. Allow yourself to fill with Light and peace, with a sense of the Love that is there for you; to feel, perhaps, the Joy that your presence brings into this space. Take three or four deep breaths at least before continuing.

4. With your eyes closed, imagine that Archangel Uriel stands before you and awaits your okay before he undertakes to free you from the burden of any difficulties you are currently facing.

5. *Breathe in* again, this time deeply into the diaphragm, and on the out-breath, place your hands in front of you, *as if you are holding a heavy package.* Imagine that the package is whatever you are currently experiencing in your life as a burden, such as troubles at work, with a relationship, health, or other issue. No problem is too small, and none too large. If it comes to mind for this exercise, it is weighing on your mind and so obfuscating your Light. Get ready to let it go, to give it over to Uriel. Feel the weight of the burden you are holding before you. Decide— definitively!—to give it to Uriel, knowing that He will resolve the issue for the highest and best of all concerned. *Breathe in* once again, feeling that weight, and on the out-breath,

throw your arms—and the burden—high into the air, in a heave-ho gesture. Watch it rise, and "see," "feel," or "know" that Archangel Uriel has captured it and will carry it and resolve it from now on. *When you release something to Uriel, let it go.* Do not go looking to take it back. If you do, you will have it back. Free will rules!

6. *Breathe out* any tension you might feel as you release any vestigial weight associated with the burden that you have let go.

7. Lift your hands, now free, over your head in the gesture that the deaf use for applause, shaking your hands to and fro, like leaves twirling in the wind. Invite Archangel Uriel now to place His hands with yours in a mutual celebration of the alliance that has just been solidified through this exercise, the connection between you increasing in Power through the process. Continue until you feel satisfied that it is complete. (You cannot make a mistake here: your intention and the request for the assistance from Uriel render the exercise effective; how long you remain in that space is training your instrument over time.) Know that you have been freed, and that you are being held in Grace. Your clear intention that it be so made it so, with the help of the Divine Calm and Power of the Fire of God that is Uriel.

8. When the healing work feels satisfying and you feel relaxed and complete, thank Archangel Uriel and your Guardian Angels by bringing your hands to your chest in a gesture of gratitude for this sacred moment of opening and sounding and Joy and Power. In the days to come, notice any thoughts that come to you about tangible steps with regard to the burden you have given over. Enact such steps, taking action with Archangel Uriel, and then *let go!*

The Aftercare noted on p. 56 is a very good way to help yourself integrate this important work.

ARCHANGEL AZRAEL

QUALITY: Angel of Death

Archangel Azrael, whose name can be translated as "Friend of God," is also known as the Angel of Death, a name that, as you can imagine, does not make him the most popular of the Archangels. First of all, Azrael does not come with hood and scythe, nor does he come to take away our life; rather, he comes to aid us in receiving and living the fullness of Life! Azrael is the Divine Grace that comes to our aid as we pass from this life to the next. He *eases* our transition; he does not hasten it!

For any who have ever called out to God to help them pass through the portal of death, the answer is and always has been the Presence called Azrael. (Remember that an Angel or Archangel is an expression of God, not separate from God.) It stands to reason, then, that Azrael is somewhere in the vicinity whenever the Veil that separates this world from the next becomes thin.

Specific situations where we can benefit from this Friend in High Places would be:

- helping ease the suffering around death, ours or someone else's
- a mentor for those who do palliative care
- a mentor for those whose gift is to "see" beyond the Veil (an aid to mediums)
- a mentor for those who practice dying, who train for death
- aid for difficult "small death" passages.

Death

The most obvious role Archangel Azrael can play as an Ally pertains to the many facets of what is often considered (above all, in the West) the most difficult period in anyone's life: death. He can help the person who is dying or those around that person, before, during, or after death.

Before Death: Azrael can help the person who is dying prepare for death. John Lennon likened our passing from Earth's mortal coil to moving from one vehicle (automobile) to another, a definite upgrade. Azrael can help a dying person find peace with the departure by clarifying the unknown and easing the pain of that passing on all levels: physical, mental, emotional, and spiritual. He can also help family members prepare for the loved one's passing, peacefully taking care of what needs doing in advance of the impending death. Additionally, he can help those who help the person who is dying and their family: doctors, nurses, therapists, those who do palliative care, and so on.

During Death: Archangel Azrael is the Light that one famously sees when we leave the body. In essence, He comes to guide us from this realm to the next in a positive and uplifting way. He also organizes the appropriate welcoming committee that some people see even before they pass on. For example, my father was talking to my (deceased) Uncle Joe from his deathbed a day before leaving to join him. My mother saw Mother Mary. They may have seen others, but that is what I witnessed. Azrael also organizes who will be with the person as they depart, and who won't be, so it is no use feeling guilty about not being there at the end; if you weren't there, you weren't meant to be. Sometimes the people who are closest to the dying cannot be physically with them as they pass, as their presence might delay or block the departure.

When my dad passed, my mother and sister (a nurse) had been with him during the hours preceding his demise, all night. I had begun with them but grabbed a nap on the couch at one point. At around 7 a.m., my mom decided she wanted a cigarette, and my sister went with her to keep her company. Seeing them go out, I went in to my father, held his hand, gave him some Reiki, and he died. Although my sister and mom had assured my father that he was free to go, my mother's presence had stopped him from leaving. And as if to confirm the intentional aspect of it all, my dad passed at 7:07 a.m. on 7/7/07. His favorite number was 7.

When my mom passed, she had been cared for at a health care facility where my sister worked, so she got great care. Each night, one of us kids (there are seven of us) would stay with her, in case it was "the" night. The night that it was my turn, my mom passed. I was able to accompany her peacefully, walking her to the door, as it were, easing the movement with Reiki and a crystal. In the end, my mother passed holding tight to a malachite, with her rosary at her bedside. I share this not to call her faith into question, but rather, to suggest that perhaps there is something we sense innately about the expressions of the earth we call crystals.

Interesting, *non?* Out of seven children in my family, it was the one who lives on the other side of the planet that was with both of my parents at the moment of their passing. And grateful am I that I had at those moments the tools to calm their fears and facilitate their movement with the help of Archangel Azrael.

After Death: After someone passes, Archangel Azrael takes the deceased to their next stop—let's call it a debriefing, not a judgment—with Archangel Jeremiel, who is "up" next. That is the easiest part of his responsibilities after a death. When asked, Archangel Azrael can also help those who cared for the dearly departed with the mourning process and letting go. If we do not let go, we cut short our own life and in part die with our loved one, which makes as much sense as if an actor in a Broadway play were to quit a show mid-performance just because his actor friend exits definitively during the first act. No sense at all!

A Word about Mourning

Sometimes people equate how much we mourn—how loudly we cry, how many tears we shed—with how much we loved the person who has died, or how much we will miss them. But often, this is far from the truth. In addition to those who mourn privately, there are also those who do work with Azrael, and who recognize the truth that our loved ones are not gone: they have simply exited the stage (for a better one). They know our loved ones can sometimes be counted on to prompt us from the other side of the Veil as we continue to act onstage.

When we become used to the idea of death—when we begin to "see," "feel," or "know" that life goes on after we leave this body—the situation of a loved one's passing simply doesn't hurt as much. We feel calm, knowing that our loved one is never far. But our friends or family members might read a lack of tears or sobbing as being "cold" or "inhuman."

In one way, you can say it is not inhuman, but maybe superhuman; that is, we access a perspective that is exceptional—we see things both from the human's perspective but also from Azrael's, and from ours at a soul level.

It can be disappointing if those we love judge us for remaining cool-headed in such a situation, but remember that we can always be of more help when we remain calm than we can if we descend into the dark drama of the death scene as it so often plays out in a world that really doesn't believe we go on.

Palliative Care

Archangel Azrael is a mentor and ally for anyone who works around death and dying. He can help therapists find the words, and healers ease the pain of those that are passing, as well as their families and friends.

A Word about Healing

As in the story mentioned earlier of the Reiki Master friend of mine who bemoaned a situation where his friend was dying ("No matter how much Reiki I give her, she is slipping away") the "higher" Azrael perspective can help both the dying and those who accompany them avoid the trap of despair. At the time, I had to remind him that the intention with a Reiki session is always the same: that the person receive what they most require. This means that we do not control the outcome, which is how it should be! The free will of the person and their soul path are both respected with such an intention. The trick is to keep our own human feelings in check so that we allow the highest and best healing to occur, including, perhaps, the person's passing!

In such a situation, we can rest assured (and sometimes we receive the Grace to experience and know it) that the person has benefitted from a Reiki or other healing session, and their passing was rendered the more peaceful for it. A Reiki healer always and only creates the context for healing; it is the person who heals themselves within that space. This optimizes alignment with the highest good and keeps ego out of it.

Remember the broader definition of healing: a realignment with the Highest Truth of Who We Are, Truly—with the soul and its mission. It may be that the soul is set to depart, and we can only facilitate and ease that passing. Archangel Azrael can greatly help us in this regard!

Mediums

"We go to the island to talk to the dead; we go to the island to get out of our head." The lyrics to a song I wrote during the mediumship training I did in Hawaii with Doreen Virtue years ago still pops into my head now and again. And yes, in order to surpass the limiting beliefs of our society around receiving messages from the dead, it behooves us to "get out of our head." The idea of mediumship is one that is becoming more recognized in a world where the media has begun to make stars of the well-known ones, such as John Edwards, Sylvia Browne, and the Long Island Medium, as well as the increasing presence of the role of mediums in television and film. The definition of a medium is less narrow than what we normally consider a medium to be, thanks in part to that media exposure:

- *A medium is anyone who can cross the Veil between this world and the invisible one.*
- *He or she acts as intermediary, a go-between, between the worlds.*
- Using this definition, not only folks who see dead people but also anyone who transmits messages from the invisible serve as mediums, including people like me who transmit messages from the Angelic realm to those who seek that contact. That said, Azrael assists mediums in the stricter sense, those who are intermediaries with the realm of the Dead (a Lightworker role that is becoming increasingly important). If the transformation that has begun is transmuting darkness to Light, fear to Love, then the work of a medium is essential, as a real medium can calm the greatest fear of all: the fear of death.
- A person who has a credible mediumistic experience "knows" beyond any doubt that their loved one is still alive, albeit "differently" than before. In Western society, we sadly separate the dying from the living and generally block exposure to dying, certainly from children. As a result, we have stigmatized death and created unnecessary trauma around it.

In societies that are considered (laughingly) less "civilized," children are there when Grandpa dies, and might even see him off as he leaves the body, since children often still have access to their clairvoyant gifts and "see clearly." In such a society, death is seen as a natural movement toward something else, a new beginning. Much less fear is stored up around it.

Sadly, in the West, such an open and enlightened view of death is rare, so many people fear death. That fear can be so great sometimes that it even limits how much living we do. Certainly, living Large is not possible when a person is always haunted by the specter of the Grim Reaper hunting them down (Azrael laughs, saying that He is more afraid of *us* when we are in such a state!).

A true medium can provide relief from grief over a loved one's passing and an easing of our fear of death, as they provide proof of the afterlife. For such wonderful Lightworkers, Azrael is the perfect mentor.

A Word about True Mediums

A true medium (not the shysters that fly after desperate mourners like ambulance-chasing lawyers) can ease fear of death because they bring proof that life continues. Sometimes the bereaved are so desperate for news of their loved ones that they turn to "off-road" solutions like mediums for comfort. Shysters of little integrity who take advantage of these people are bottom-crawlers (at least in this lifetime, when they do that). But how to know if a person is a "real" medium or not? Every "real" mediumship reading should contain three things, at a minimum, though there may be more information.

WHO: The medium should have enough information to allow the person receiving the reading to figure out about whom he or she is talking. A name, an initial, a description, a cologne—no matter how it is done, the dead will convey the information necessary to let their loved one know they are there within the bounds of the gifts of the medium. Some mediums "hear," some "see," some "smell," some "feel"; the dead will proffer that which is necessary for identification. Dead people who can come back to pass on messages are not new souls; they are sufficiently evolved to be able to work with the medium to whom we have been drawn.)

PROOF: The medium should be able to offer information that no one else could possibly have ("Your grandmother gave you a hummingbird broach, and she says you never wear it." "Your Dad likes the new man in your life, except for his moustache." "She is showing me that she passed due to choking."). These are just some examples one might run across in doing or receiving this kind of reading, but there is always proof. If you don't have proof, might as well let it go.

A MESSAGE OF LOVE: If you are in front of a medium who has already transmitted the first two points, you are likely in for a treat with this third. Although sometimes the messages of Love are not what we might want to hear (speaking of a need to diet, exercise, or quit drinking, for example), they are always Love-based. Our loved ones have passed beyond the fear of this world, and their messages will reflect that. There will not be scary messages. If there are, it may be that a trickster is at work. How to avoid such an eventuality? If you are a medium, it is critically important to ensure that you limit access to your channel to the highest of energies. Sometimes, especially in the beginning, we are so excited that we are receiving messages that we don't much pay attention from whom we might be receiving them, kind of like a love-starved person on Valentine's Day or someone dying to sell their house on Open House day. Be careful!

An open channel is like leaving the door to your home wide open for all to enter. I don't know about you, but this Bronx girl prefers to allow entry only under conditions with which I am comfortable. Therefore, setting a clear intention to open our channel only to the highest of vibrations is a good way to begin. As we become more comfortable, we can begin to permit other vibrations to come in (like dead people) but staying attentive and clearly blocking the lowest of vibrations to come in by remaining strong in that intention and transmitting only messages of love. It is always a good idea to ask Azrael to accompany us in this endeavor, and thus pass the burden of that "channel sentinel" role to Azrael, so we can relax and get out of our head!

Practicing Dying/Training for Death

As any student of shamanism might tell you, it is a good idea to practice dying, and Archangel Azrael can help us with this sometimes-daunting task. Imagine death like a graduation: an important ritual marking a passage from school to "real" life. Though we are not generally taught to see it that way, in essence, dying is very similar: we pass from this life (where hopefully we learned many things, such as how to keep our hearts open and relax) and move back to Source, into Who We Are, Truly.

Who has never had the sense that there was "more" to this life? Who has never wished or hoped or dreamed of "more"? Once the good fight has been fought, and the Dream dreamed, the Dreamer awakens.

But often, because of the great fears we have and the limiting beliefs that run rampant about dying, people experience death not with the deep Grace that it could be but with the terror of a person who doesn't really believe that there is life afterward.

My father was like that. Even though he had gone to Mass every day, toward the end my father was deathly afraid of dying (funny phrase, that, *non*? And yet how apt!).

So many of us are "deathly afraid" of dying. Because it is misunderstood, death stands as our greatest fear and often takes our breath (and thus, our life) away, which is why practicing is a good idea!

There are many ways to "practice" dying: to train for a good death allows us the freedom of fearless life, Large Life! The exercise at the end of this chapter is just one such way, facilitated by Archangel Azrael.

But basically any "death" practice will include:

1. The intention to release our fear of death (and thus our fear of Large Life) by training for death (and thus for living Life Large!). Sons and daughters of the Creator/Creation, we create with our intention, powerful beyond our imagination.
2. Inviting Archangel Raziel to hold you and assist you in the exercise.
3. Slowing down the breath as much as possible (only possible if we can access deep relaxation, like deep sea breath-divers).
4. Imagining the last moments of this life, how it will feel, the thoughts you might have. If a strong fear arises (and it might), use your breath to calm yourself, and continue. Use your imagination to "journey" beyond this realm. Do not let your head decide that this is a ridiculous exercise.
5. Remaining in that space as long as possible, either dreaming (in true sleep, if it overtakes you) or in a day-dream state.
6. When coming back (use an alarm clock if you have limited time for the exercise or if you are worried about it), breathing and filling your body with breath. Feel your body, from your feet to the top of your head—arms, legs, torso—filled with breath and life. Feel the bed or the chair on which you are seated or lying down, the air that enters and leaves through breathing. Slowly open the eyes, and see the place where you are, this place rendered sacred as you have used it for sacred practice. Return!

When we train for death we are less fearful about our own and others' demise. Fear of living Large lessens when the fear of dying passes. Life becomes more relaxed; grateful, we can accompany others calmly along the path.

Small Deaths

These are moments when our lives take such a strong turn that the change feels almost like a death—the way life used to be has died, and we are forced into the uncomfortable position (whether we have chosen the change or not) of reconstructing ourselves and our world view.

In the last section, we used the term The Big Four (death, divorce, job loss, moving), and we looked to Uriel to help us pass through those portals of change peacefully. Azrael can also help us with such a passage, as they represent phoenix times, times of dying to one version of ourselves and rising to another, grander version. So often in our world of can't-go-fast-enough, we do not take time to properly honor such a transition, whether it be a move, a job change, a relationship ending, or a health situation that requires us to change gears.Azrael can help us to slow down and use ritual to mark such endings, recognizing them also as new beginnings, and sending our energy with our attention to the new, firing up the newest version of ourselves, the phoenix that will rise from the ashes.

One way to honor such a transition is to *express gratitude* for the lessons learned and the new opportunity before us, the wide-open space to create that is left after what is gone.

Another important way to honor a transition and live well through it is to *allow ourselves the time we need to mourn*, to allow the attachment to what "was" fall away. In being so gentle with ourselves, we can actually move more wholly and rapidly into the new because we have given due respect to what was. In honoring the transition, we can consciously (and why not with the help of Azrael?) allow what *was* to move away from us peacefully so that we are free to embrace our life as it will be.

Release the "was." Do the "is!"

CHAKRA: Seventh Chakra—Crown—Piercing the Veil

Archangel Azrael is one of the Archangels that help us bridge the divide between our earthly existence and that which is beyond this life. As such, He can greatly assist us in opening our channel of communication with the other side of the Veil, friends and family who have died, or Guides and Ascended Masters from whom we have much to learn.

Such a connection helps us in daily life. not only through the guidance it may bring but also as it gives us a different perspective with regard to the trials and tribulations of daily life. When we see the bigger picture, we are less impacted by the vagaries of our day-to-day ups and downs.

COLOR: Black

The color associated with Azrael is most often black, as we pass through the passage of darkness to our own light.

CRYSTAL/STONE: Rainbow Obsidian

Though it is not the only gemstone that can help us connect to Azrael, rainbow obsidian is recognized for its protective capacities, just as Azrael is willing to help us through the portal of death, affording us all protection. With a brilliant black sheen, the stone holds deep within a rainbow of color, in the form of an iris. It invites us to look into the depths, to see that wondrous rainbow of an eye looking back at us, daring us to look into the depths of our being to find the treasure that is there. The stone, like Azrael, helps us to look beyond what appears to be (death) to what is truly there (Life), and can be an excellent aid in practicing any death exercise.

Connecting to Archangel Azrael: A Life-Death Practice

Play with Archangel Azrael!

1. Connect with your breath, and come into a peaceful place of quiet. Set your intention to practice stretching beyond this life and cultivating your connection to Archangel Azrael.

2. Use your channel to anchor (ground) yourself, following your ribbon of light into the center of the earth, then open to the highest good with your intention, tracing your channel of light from the center of the earth through your heart and then up to the heavens to connect with the Angelic Realm. Return to your heart, setting your intention both as the human being that you are and on a soul level. (If you are undertaking this exercise, it is without a doubt the will of your soul.)

3. Sit, feet planted solidly on the ground, shoulder-width apart, shoulders pulled back so that your spinal column— the bridge you create between the earth and the heavens— is straight. Allow the arms to relax at your sides, palms facing forward in a position of energetic openness. *Breathe in* the presence of Angels and Archangels all around you.

Breathe out anything that blocks your opening to them. Allow yourself to fill with Light and peace, with a sense of the Love that is there for you; to feel and experience, perhaps, the Joy that your presence brings in this space. Take three or four deep breaths at least before continuing.

4. With your eyes closed, imagine that Archangel Azrael stands before you, and awaits your signal before he undertakes to assist you in the freeing practice to release fear of death.

5. *Breathe in* again, deeply into the diaphragm, and on the out-breath, lie on your stomach, imagining that your intestines are already recombining with the earth. Allow yourself to imagine that your body, heavy, is welcomed by the earth, offering you a resting place for these moments, as assisted by Azrael.

6. Slow down your breath as much as comfortably possible; this is only possible if we can access deep relaxation. Relax and breath more and more slowly, knowing that you are safe and accompanied by Archangel Azrael.

7. Imagine the last moments of this life, how it will feel, the thoughts you might have. If a strong fear arises (and it might), use your breath to calm yourself, and continue. Use your imagination to "journey" beyond this realm; do not let your head decide that this is a ridiculous exercise. The more we can remain present for this exercise, the more we can remain present and calm for any demise, our own or someone else's. Remaining in that space as long as possible, either dreaming in true sleep, if it overtakes us, or in a day-dream state.

8. *Breathe out* any tension you might feel as you release any vestigial weight associated with the exercise. Then, coming back (use an alarm clock if you have limited time or if you feel more comfortable with it), *breathe in* and fill your body with breath. Feel your body from your feet to the top of your head—arms, legs, torso—every cell filled with breath and life. Return!

9. Sit or stand now, and invite Archangel Azrael to place His wings around you, creating a cocoon to ease your transition back into everyday life. Allow yourself to be held and helped by your Friends in High Places. It is time! Continue until you feel satisfied that it is complete. (You cannot make a

mistake here: your intention and the request for assistance from Azrael render the exercise effective; how long you remain in that space is training your instrument over time.) Know that you are being held in Grace. Your clear intention that it be so made it so, with the help of the Divine Calm and Power of the Friend of God that is Azrael.

10. When the healing work feels satisfied and you feel relaxed and complete, thank Archangel Azrael and your Guardian Angels by bringing your hands to your chest, a gesture of gratitude for this sacred moment of opening and sounding and Joy and Power. NOTE: If you prefer, omit numbers 5, 6, and 7 in order to connect with Archangel Azrael without the death training. This connection will also boost your gusto for life and cultivate your clairvoyance and mediumistic capacities.

The Aftercare noted on p. 56 is a very good way to help yourself integrate this important work.

CHAPTER 6

Archangels Chamuel, Jeremiel, Haniel, Raguel, and Raziel

This is the third of three chapters that explore and invite a deepening of connections with the Archangels. The five discussed herein are certainly less well known than the Big Five but no less powerful. All are aspects of the Source, or God, and each serves to allow more of certain Divine qualities to find their way to expression here on Earth.

As in the previous two chapters, each section describes an Archangel. It includes a description of the energy carried by each Archangel, examples of how they can assist us in our lives, specific chakras they impact, crystals or stones that carry their frequency, as well as unique exercises to try if you should decide you would like to connect directly and more deeply with that aspect of the Divine.

The "Mysterious Five" with whom we will work in this chapter may be the least known but carry a very big impact that helps us to find the Truth of who we are, to take care of ourselves, gain peace, and align with the highest good within us; that is to say, the Archangels with whom we really need to be working to more peacefully and easily live the Life that awaits us and Large Life!

ARCHANGEL	DIVINE QUALITY
Chamuel (Samuel)	Seeking/Finding
Jeremiel	Dreaming
Haniel	Sensitivity, Natural Healing
Raguel	Social Justice, Energy
Raziel	Esoteric Wisdom

❧

ARCHANGEL CHAMUEL

QUALITY: Seeking and Finding

Archangel Chamuel, whose name can be translated as "Seeker of God" is a very helpful Friend in High Places, particularly if you, like me, tend to lose things. In this case, the friend has a sufficiently high perspective to help us find things that are lost or things we seek. A little like Saint Anthony, who in the Catholic tradition is known as the Patron Saint of Lost Causes, Chamuel can help us, in small ways and large.

Small Things

"A little help here?" How many times have I asked Chamuel for help with this query (answer: too many!), but each time I do, I am either somehow impelled (not compelled, but somehow prompted by an inner compulsion) to turn my head this way or that, or I may simply see the location of the object (keys, for example; car or house, no matter) in my mind's eye, on my inner screen.

"Really? On the toilet?!" I may mutter, as I grudgingly direct my feet the way I have been bidden, and sure enough, keys on the back of the toilet. Go figure.

As you can imagine, this sort of relationship can be delightful, and trust, confidence, even laughter grow as it is cultivated.

Often one hears talk about Angels finding parking places, or other things we need to live peacefully. This is a great way to begin to connect with Angels—a good starting point. In such games of hide and seek with the Angels, Chamuel is a great Ally!

Angels Help Us, Beginning with Small Things

As noted earlier, I am sometimes asked (at times in an almost accusatory manner), "How can you ask Angels for help with that? They have more important things to do than to find you a parking spot!"

Do they?

Remember that an Angel is around us to assist us on our path, the highest and most shining version of the life we are meant to live. Now think about how stressed you may have been (or seen someone else become) when they can't find a parking spot, especially if you are going to be late for something important. Is that a peaceful state? Are you shining Love's pure Light at that moment? Probably not!

"There is no order of importance in miracles," according to the wonderful (if arduous) channeled to me called *A Course in Miracles*.

That is true. Anything that can increase our peace (and thus the peace on the planet) is worthwhile work for the Angels around us. They know that starting with small things is a very good way to create confidence, and it increases the bond with us suspicious, doubting humans.

They may even "help" us lose our keys, just so they can connect with us to help us find them. Just sayin'. . .

Large Things

Even if you are not prone to losing your keys or you don't drive, Chamuel is still a wonderful Ally to have, as not all we seek is small, is it?

Maybe at different times of life, we might seek other kinds of "keys": a key to the highest and best work or job . . . or a harmonious relationship . . . or greater health . . . or our spiritual Self.

Whether we seek the keys to the apartment or the keys to the Kingdom, the seeker of God, Chamuel, can help.

CHAKRA: Fourth Chakra—Heart—Alignment

Archangel Chamuel brings us help with our seeking, thus bringing us ever more into alignment with our Heart chakra, where our soul has seeded the plan for this lifetime. Whether we seek our house keys or the keys for professional success, the heart chakra directs us best to what will truly serve us and the highest good.

COLOR: Yellow

The color associated with Chamuel is most often yellow, with varying degrees of white or light.

CRYSTAL/STONE: Citrine

Citrine is a stone that is recognized for its manifestation capacities, a stone that carries with it the frequency of Abundance. As such, it is a good accompaniment for the Seeker Archangel Chamuel, who responds to every knock on the door with a resounding, abundant YES!

Seeking with Archangel Chamuel

Play with Archangel Chamuel!

1. Connect with your breath, and come into a peaceful place of quiet. Set your intention to practice stretching beyond this life and cultivating your connection to Archangel Chamuel. *Decide what it is you are seeking* and how you are going to let Archangel Chamuel (who lives for such moments!) assist a child of God (you) to find what is important to you at this time.

2. Use your channel to anchor (ground) yourself, following your ribbon of light into the center of the earth, then open to the highest good with your intention, tracing your channel of light from the center of the earth through the body up to the heavens. Return to your heart to set your intention, both as a human being and on a soul level. (If you are undertaking this exercise, your soul is definitely on board!)

3. Sit, feet planted solidly on the ground, shoulder-width apart, shoulders pulled back so that your spinal column is straight. Allow the arms to relax at your sides, palms facing forward in a position of energetic openness. *Breathe in* the presence of Angels and Archangels all around you. *Breathe out* anything that blocks your opening to them. Allow yourself to fill with Light and peace, with a sense of the Love that is there for you; to feel, perhaps, the Joy that your presence brings into this space. Take three or four deep breaths at least before continuing.

4. With your eyes closed, imagine that Archangel Chamuel stands before you and awaits your accord before He undertakes to assist you in finding what it is you are seeking.

5. *Breathe in* again, deeply into the diaphragm, Imagine, or simply think about, what it is you are seeking. If it is a thing, remember what it looks like, how it feels, but most of all, *imagine how you will feel to find it.* What Joy! Peace! Excitement! How wonderful to have assistance in finding what we most need. Insofar as possible, stay in the feeling. If you are seeking something less tangible, like the right job or relationship, again, *imagine how you will feel to find it, then leave the details to Chamuel and the Angels.* Most often, we block or own highest good by imagining how success will look, with whom that

harmonious relationship should happen, the kind of job we will flourish in. When we do this, we severely limit our possibilities. So the key here, when working with Chamuel the Key Finder, the Archangel of Seekers, will be to set the intention, feel the feeling, and then *allow* the Angelic realm take over.

6. Imagine that even as you sit in that space, the Angels and Archangel Chamuel are preparing the very best for you, a surprise! What you are seeking but also much more—the pure magic of Divine intervention for the child of God, Who You Are, Truly. Remain in that Joy space as long as possible, either dreaming (in true sleep, if it overtakes us) or in a day-dream state.

7. *Breathe out* any tension you might feel as you release any vestigial weight associated with the exercise. Invite Archangel Chamuel to place His wings around you, creating a cocoon to ease your finding, like an incubator of dreams and of keys and the finding of them. It may be that in that space you "see" where your item is or you have some inspiration to take a specific action. If this is the case, *do it*! In this way, we cultivate a partnership with an Ally that is indeed one that can help us to live Life, glorious Life, Large!

8. When the work feels satisfying and you feel relaxed and complete, thank Archangel Chamuel and your Guardian Angels by bringing your hands to your chest in a gesture of gratitude for this sacred moment of opening and sounding and Joy and Power.

The Aftercare noted on p. 56 is a very good way to help yourself integrate this important work.

❧

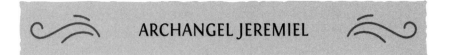

ARCHANGEL JEREMIEL

QUALITY: Life Review (No-Judgment Day) Dreaming

Archangel Jeremiel, whose name can be translated as "Mercy of God," is a very helpful Friend in High Places, particularly if you, like me, tend to dream. But mainly he is known as the Archangel to whom we are brought after we die to do a quick recap of what happened in our lifetime.

Jeremiel is known for doing our Life Reviews, which happen after we die but also, if we wish, while we are still alive here on Earth, as well as for helping us to understand the messages we receive though our clairvoyance in our dreams. As an expression of the mercy of God, Jeremiel helps us to look upon ourselves with compassion, in a nonjudgmental way, even as we stretch toward our Light, and he assists us in gaining access to such messages as may come through Divine mercy into our consciousness through the "Dreaming."

Life Review (Afterlife)

As an expression of God, Jeremiel is the Archangel that assists us when we leave this life by carrying out our Life Review, what I call the "Divine Debriefing," which some people erroneously call "Judgment Day."

Judgment Day, in fact, is what happens every single day of our lives here on Earth. We judge ourselves, we judge others, and they judge us. Judgment is not the stuff of a loving Creator, or of Angels. Judgment and punishment are entirely in the human domain. It is how we function, because we (most of us) do not yet express the unlimited Love and compassion of the Creator.

Unfortunately, the myths around a Divine Judgment Day are so powerful and terrible that it *increases* our fear of dying, especially those who imagine they will be badly judged and thus, punished. As a result, when some lost souls are being called to the light (Azrael), they refuse to go, sometimes creating such unfortunate situations as hauntings, lost souls that stay in the energetic field of the earth (another good reason to practice or train for death with Azrael, as discussed in the last chapter).

Thankfully, God is not a God of rancor but of Love, unlimited by our smallness, so the exercise with Jeremiel looks at the debriefing as simply that: what worked and what did not in the soul's plan for a given life. This information then serves as the basis for the next steps. If life went hard on us, the life review determines what sort of healing or rest might be needed to nourish the soul. If we did not manage to realize our objectives (the primary reason behind death-bed regret and why living Large is so important), the plan for our next life begins to take shape here already. If we did manage to live in alignment with our soul mission, the plan for the next life with a new objective (if there will be one) begins to take form.

That's it. No hellfire and brimstone. Unless we stay in the earth's field and punish ourselves, we are not punished by anyone. Some would say that being here on Earth is already a hard way to go, and punishment enough, despite the physical beauty that is present.

Life Review (During Life)

Jeremiel is best known for the role he plays in our lives *after* we leave this life. He is much less known for the role he can play for us as an Ally while we are still alive, but this is a positive and interesting Angelic assistance for certain periods of life, if we ask for it—a sort of Angelic "How am I doing?"

When we find ourselves at a crossroads in life, particularly, it is an excellent time to accept His invitation to experience a Life Review midstream, while we are still here. By going through this exercise, Jeremiel can help us to stop judging our past harshly, and to adjust our game plan in alignment with our soul's vision, preparing a future that focuses on our strengths and positively supports our dreams.

A Word about Judgment

God is merciful; humans judge. The Universe in its entirety understands how difficult it can be to walk the earth in human form, how the pull of darkness and light in the illusion of duality that seems so real can pull even the best-meaning souls downward from time to time. Mostly, we are applauded for even accepting to come into the earth plane!

Sadly, this is not often the tack we take with regard to ourselves. Many (if not most) of us learn from a world that is harsh in its judgments to look down on our meager efforts, as the shiny objective is always just out of reach. We learn to fix more and higher objectives, and not so much to slow down and celebrate the successes we have achieved. Sadly, the tendency is to judge ourselves on what we have not yet done, instead of patting ourselves on the back for what we have achieved. But wow! If you are reading this, look at how far you have come! Take a moment to appreciate the skills you have cultivated, how you have come through the rough patches, and maybe are still coming through them. Take a moment to appreciate that you are ever seeking to reflect the Light that is yours more and more.

Yep. You show up! You are pretty incredible. But how often do you hear it?

A Life Review (like in the exercise at the end of this section) will allot time and intention to take stock of what has been for you to see or remember how incredible you have been so far, then from there, to decide consciously what is good enough for such an amazing person to suit the Large Life you are now recognizing that you deserve!

The Dreaming

Archangel Jeremiel is also known as the Archangel who assists Dreamers. As the world is turning and the role of the Dreamers will once again come to the fore, it is helpful that He become more known at this time for this specificity.

Earlier, when we explored the idea of clairvoyant seeing, we included dreams in this category, as that clairvoyance includes all understanding arrived at due to extraordinary sight. There are always images associated with this form of clairvoyance.

Some people, those we will call Dreamers, access their clairvoyance through dreams. This time-honored gift has been recognized through the ages, and still is today in societies that are more open than the typical Western world.

In cultures close to the land or the Veil, there may be one or two leaders in the tribe or community who do the dreaming; that is, they go into the dream world and receive information for the benefit of the group: where to migrate, what to plant, how to heal a sickness, and so on. Such people are often called shamans or medicine men, although they are not always men.

As we became "civilized" (and what's so "civil" about it?), we left behind the Dreaming and the roles associated with it; however, the gift still exists, and the role of Dreamers is on the rise. My understanding is that the Dreamers will once again be holding roles of leadership—as we seek to remake the world in new ways, as time goes on, and as we find ourselves finally forced to change. Or sooner, if we wake up! If you are a

Dreamer, then Jeremiel is an excellent Ally to have. His is an alliance to cultivate, perhaps sooner rather than later, before we really need it. But how do you know if you are a Dreamer?

A Word about Dreams

Every dream is not important. Mostly, even for Dreamers, dreams are a rest period that permits the superfluous to be discharged and cleared out of our psyche. But sometimes, dreams do mean something. And it is good to know the difference, so we don't go chasing after meaning in what would be essentially a dream dumpster dive. So how do we tell the difference?

Dreams that matter move us.

We may awaken in tears, or laughter, or we may simply be impacted energetically so that we carry the energy or mood of the dream with us all day.

Dreams that carry a message stay with us.

Dreams that don't matter evaporate, often instantly, upon waking. It is of little use to write it down right away because if it is quickly leaving our consciousness, it is because we don't need it.

A loved one visits.

When a loved one who has passed away has transitioned comfortably to their new way of being, they sometimes stop by to let us know they are okay. This is most easily done (and in the least frightening way) through our dreams.

Repetitive dreams.

When we experience repetitive themes, places, and people in our dreams, our soul is trying to get a message through to us. Take time to go into the silence and ask Archangel Jeremiel what we are meant to understand from the experience.

Here's an example from my own life:

Back when I was a banker (and using drugs and alcohol to diminish my sensitivity), I had a recurring dream. In it, I was made aware of having bought a house at the seashore (my lifelong dream before it became a reality) that I had forgotten.

In various dreams, because I had forgotten the house, it either was deteriorated by the elements, taken over by the government for back taxes, had squatters living in it, or on one occasion, the Mafia had taken it over and wouldn't give it back ("Finders keepers!").

These dreams were so real that upon waking, I would rack my brain to determine if I had actually bought a house and forgotten about it! And it was such a strong dream message, I can still "visit" it and feel it.

Later, I "happened upon" a book of dreams that indicated that when we dream of houses, the house represents ourself. Yikes!

I got the message! I had forgotten myself, and following this determined to get myself back.

Dreaming can be useful for us Dreamers, both for what it can mean and what it doesn't mean. We are free to let go, because if the soul sees fit, the dream won't let go. Archangel Jeremiel can help us with such clarity.

CHAKRA: Sixth Chakra–Third Eye–Dreaming

Archangel Jeremiel is one of the Archangels known for helping us with the reopening of the sixth or third eye chakra, which helps us to see more clearly and in eternal context that which appears around us in the illusion. This impacts our daily life as well as our clairvoyant gifts, especially through the gift of dreaming, wherein we can be imbued with the understandings we require in waking moments.

COLOR: Various

There is no consensus around color for Jeremiel, as those who see and receive the Angelic realm report hues that vary from a bright orange to the deep blue of a night sky. How you perceive Jeremiel will be your unique experience.

CRYSTAL/STONE: Sodalite

Sodalite is a stone that is recognized for its ability to facilitate communication with the highest realms, including that of our Higher Self, but in a manner that is down to earth. As such, it accompanies the Dreamer well, reaching the heights of the soul's message and then bringing it into concrete earthly understanding. It works in unison with Archangel Jeremiel to aid us (with great mercy) in seeing beyond the limited perspective the world offers us.

Archangel Jeremiel and the Midlife Review

NOTE: This exercise takes time. For optimal results, allow yourself a day or two to do the work.

Play with Archangel Jeremiel!

1. Connect with your breath, and come into a peaceful place of quiet. Set your intention to see the past clearly in order to prepare well for the future of your path in this lifetime with the help of and cultivating your connection to Archangel Jeremiel.

2. Use your channel to anchor (ground) yourself, following your ribbon of light into the center of the earth, then open to the highest good with your intention, tracing your channel of light from the center of the earth through the body to the heavens. Return to your heart to set your intention, both as the human being you are and on a soul level. (If you are undertaking this exercise, it is without a doubt the will of your soul.)

3. Have a paper and pen handy. Sit, feet planted solidly on the ground, shoulder-width apart, with shoulders pulled back so that your spinal column is straight. Allow the arms to relax at your sides, palms facing forward in a position of energetic openness. *Breathe in* the presence of Angels and Archangels all around you. *Breathe out* anything that blocks your opening to them. Allow yourself to fill with Light and peace, with a sense of the Love that is there for you; to feel, perhaps, the Joy that your presence brings in this space. Take three or four deep breaths at least before continuing.

4. With your eyes closed, imagine that Archangel Jeremiel stands before you and awaits your accord before He undertakes to assist you in doing this midlife Life Review. *Breathe in* again, deeply into the diaphragm, and ask Jeremiel to help you call to mind the information that will serve your highest good as you look back to review your life.

5. *Breathe out* and begin to write. Beginning at the beginning (your childhood), write down those moments that come to mind, as those are the moments that serve the Life Review. Take the time to allow the highlights to come forward in chronological order. Don't worry about missing anything; Jeremiel will ensure that the most salient

points come to your mind. Include both the "good" and the "bad" moments/periods—whatever comes up. Do not filter anything (only you and the Angels will be privy to this information). Allow the moments to come, writing down only the key phrases that will denote the moment intended. You will use the list afterward. When your list is complete, breathe in and out and ask Archangel Jeremiel if there is anything that has been left out. If something else pops up, add it. If not, you are ready to go.

6. *Breathe in and out,* and ask Jeremiel to give you the understanding, the takeaways, for each circumstance on your list. Whether the item on your list is "good" or "bad", no matter: just note down what you learned from the experience and what can stand you in good stead for the future!

Personal Examples

Event	Takeaway
Birth of little brother	Love – so much
Staying out too late— Mom slapped me.	Compassion for (m)other, truthfulness
Put myself through Georgetown	Able to take on a hefty long-term project

7. When you have written down at least one ability, skill, or quality that was gleaned from each experience, look at the whole of it as being your credentials to do anything you want to do! For example, the qualities gleaned from the experiences above helped me to write this book!

8. When the work feels complete and you feel more relaxed and competent, confident, you can thank Archangel Jeremiel and your Guardian Angels by bringing your hands to your chest in a gesture of gratitude for this sacred moment of opening and sounding and Joy and Power.

The Aftercare noted on p. 56 is a very good way to help yourself integrate this important work.

A Word about Confidence

When we did the "With Whom Am I Relaxed?" exercise at the start of this book journey together, we learned that we can Love easily (and thus, fearlessly live Large Life) when we are confident, when we trust those around us. Children who are loved and supported grow up with this confidence and carry it with them into new situations. They are used to being loved, and that confidence is in their energetic field, attracting even more Love and support.

But that is not the case for many, if not most, of us, so the exercise above can bring us face to face with the Truth of our value. It enables us to integrate all of our experiences from the past, taking what treasure can be found there and letting go of the rest.

The exercise is truly a gift of mercy, as is God's way. It invites us to no longer judge ourselves for the past (which keeps us in the past, unable to move forward) but to take the lessons and move forward with a new-found confidence; hopefully, with a new habit of looking at our activities in this new-and-improved, no-judgment way!

ARCHANGEL HANIEL

QUALITY: Grace of God

Archangel Haniel, whose name can be translated as "Grace of God," is a wonderful Ally for those who consider themselves sensitive. She is aligned with the energy of the moon and comes to us in that form with healing presence if we so desire (and ask!).

Haniel is the Archangel most closely connected to natural healing modalities, such as crystals, essential oils, aroma or light therapies, and so forth. As such, She is a very helpful Friend in High Places for those who receive such healing sessions, and for those who offer them to others. If you are attracted to any of the many natural healing modalities (I love crystals, for obvious reasons) and wish to work with Haniel, it will suffice to be clear about our intention and to call upon her to bring her wonderful energy of grace to the healing sessions, a bit like the exercise with Haniel and crystal at the end of this section.

Sensitives—Moon Children

We are living in a time when humanity is evolving alongside the earth of which we are a part.

New humans are being born who do not fit easily into the molds and traditional roles that were the only choices in the past. For this reason, old structures are disintegrating, and new ones must arise to take their place: new institutions flexible enough to hold a humanity that is becoming more human.

What does that mean?

Socialization heretofore meant something very precise: society expected us to fit ourselves into the molds that were created for the good of society as it had been. But the children arriving now (and the youth already here, as well as some of us old folks, too) are not comfortable with the harsh energy of this earth as it is currently, so these generations will be the ones to effect change.

Until such change is effected, however, Haniel helps us to remember that our sensitivity is an important and *powerful* part of our being, to be respected and honored. The world deems extreme sensitivity a weakness; in reality, it is a sign of the presence of great strength in the person bearing it. Only old souls are sensitive. From childhood on, that sensitivity can prompt or force us to build defenses around us to keep out negative energies (my own defendedness was like a castle with a moat and crocodiles . . . lots of crocodiles!).

But those defenses, necessary when we are children, do not serve us as adults. They do not keep out very much; we remain sensitive, and being in large groups or with negative people can suck the life right out of us. On the other hand, those defenses *do* block or diminish the strength of our hidden gifts or clairvoyance, the super-powers hidden behind all sensitivity.

Haniel reminds us that we can let go of our defendedness, which does *not* help, and instead, follow the example of the moon, a strategy that *can* help.

In the next section, we will speak more directly to the idea of how to manage our energy, but one way is Haniel's: *Own your sensitivity!* This world wants us working at 200 percent, 300 percent of the time. We are constantly besieged with requests for our attention, for our time, for our energy. The world wants us at full moon power all the time.

But we can't be! No one can, not all the time!

Haniel invites us to see and appreciate our sensitivity and recognize that our bodies are like a sensitive instrument that must be allowed to be temperamental—allowed to play and shine when the time is right, but also to retreat and rest when the time is not right.

When we are at our natural "full moon" phase, we feel ready to take on the world. In that space, everything flows naturally, and the universe moves in concert with us. But such periods are followed by a waning and then a waxing. When we are not "full," it behooves us to respect our instrument and allow it to rest. The moon does not always show herself, so why should you? Tangibly this means to wait until enthusiasm rises, pushing us to action—nothing forced before its time! This will optimize both health and efficacy.

If we need help with this unlearning of the world's rhythms, Haniel helps us to learn how to play our instrument, to allow it to rest when it needs to pull back, and to "let 'er rip" when it is ready to go full tilt! By Grace, we can learn to honor ourselves instead of behaving as if it were of no importance to push ourselves beyond our limits.

But we know it *is* important, don't we? When we try to go at the rhythm of the world for too long, poor health, burnout, and depression can result. So calling on this Ally can really help us get into a shape that can hold a lot of light to live Large.

A Word about Sensitives and Autism

The term "autism" is applied widely these days, with a whole spectrum being recognized. New treatments of the condition are researched, but the Angels invite us to consider the following to put it all in context.

Autism is taking on more importance as more sensitives are arriving on the earth plane every day, to bring along the transition to a more peaceful planet that is our future (believe it or not!).

The souls whose human forms express autism are not less than the rest of us; they are more. Think on it: if only old souls are sensitive, what can we say about the hypersensitivity of people who are autistic? The world as it is currently is simply too harsh for these sensitive souls. They remind us, slowly but surely, to slow down, to do things more quietly, deliberately. And they are showing us how. Their severe reactions to disruptions are a strong metaphor for how our soul reacts to our disruptive state; the soul can't shine through when monkey mind is present, for example. As we move into a more peaceful state as a planet, these beings (and all of us) will find more and more ease (relaxation) and will be more at peace as well.

As you can imagine, Archangel Haniel is an excellent Ally for people with autism, as well as extremely sensitive people. Her healing modalities can assuage the pain of living with autism, for both the sufferer and their caregivers.

CHAKRA: Second Chakra—Sacral—Sensitivity and Sensuality

Archangel Haniel is one of the Archangels that can help us balance and strengthen the energy of our second chakra, the seat of both sensuality and sensitivity in our human experience on Earth. The Archangel of Natural Healing can help us to naturally heal our blockages around these areas, surmounting the harshness of past experience to open fully to the Life that awaits us.

COLOR: Silver

The color associated with Haniel is the silver of the moon, at once peaceful and brilliant, full of Grace.

CRYSTAL/STONE: Clear Quartz

Clear quartz is a stone that is recognized for three main qualities. First, the quality of its clarity can help us when we need to get clear about things that have us perplexed in our lives. Second, quartz is used in radios as an amplifier. In the same way, it can be used to amplify or increase the Power of our intention. The earth backs us up energetically in our intention. As such it is a great stone for manifesting intention. Third, clear quartz is a special stone because of its "white effect"—white holds all colors; clear quartz thus holds the energies of all crystals. As such, it can be programmed to resonate at the frequency of any crystal the earth holds; Grace indeed, in an age when there are weight restrictions when we fly on airplanes!

A Word about Crystals

Crystals are to the earth what Archangels are to God or Source: not separate from but part of the earth and simply carrying a particular vibrational quality of the whole. As with Archangels, which do not intervene on our behalf unless we have that intention and ask, a crystal is not magic in itself. You are! A crystal cannot do any kind of work without you, without the accompanying intentionality that sets the frequency or quality in motion.

Sometimes, a worried mother will ask me if she can put an amethyst (which helps us to free ourselves from addiction and so align more with our Higher Self) in her son's room as he is abusing drugs. The answer is sure you can, but will it help? No! A crystal cannot countermand free will; it has not the power to impact a person if they have not agreed to the healing it offers.

If this modality speaks to you, watch out for my upcoming book on crystals, which delves more deeply into the subject than we have time for, here.

Connecting to Archangel Haniel:
Healing Grace

NOTE: We will use crystal work as the example here, but you can use the same protocol for any work with Haniel: essential oils, aroma healing, herb work, light therapy, and so on.

Play with Archangel Haniel!

1. Connect with your breath, and come into a peaceful place of quiet. Set your intention to practice healing with crystals, cultivating your connection to the grace of Archangel Haniel. Decide which crystal energy you would like to work with, and keep a piece of that crystal at your side for the work. Here, we will use clear quartz, with the intention to get clarity on a particular issue.

2. Use your channel to anchor (ground) yourself, following your ribbon of light into the center of the earth, then open to the highest good with your intention, tracing your channel of light from the center of the earth through the heart and then up to the heavens. Return to your heart to set your intention, both as the human being you are and on a soul level.

3. Keep your crystal (or essential oils, herbs, or whatever) handy. Sit, feet planted solidly on the ground, shoulder-width apart, with shoulders pulled back so that your spinal column is straight—a bridge between heaven and earth. Allow the arms to relax at your sides, palms facing forward in a position of energetic openness. *Breathe in* the presence of Angels and Archangels all around you. *Breathe out* anything that blocks your opening to them. Allow yourself to fill with Light and peace, with a sense of the Love that is there for you; to feel, perhaps, the Joy that your presence brings in this space. Take three or four deep breaths at least before continuing with the next step.

4. With your eyes closed, imagine that Archangel Haniel stands before you and awaits your accord before assisting you with the (crystal) healing you have decided to undertake.

5. *Breathe in* again, deeply into the diaphragm. Take the crystal in your nondominant hand (the one you do not use for writing). Feel the crystal in your hand, and set your intention to receive more clarity through this quartz crystal work. Ask Haniel to assist you in the work, then place your dominant hand over the clear quartz, about 2 or 3 inches above it (if it is too big, you can place it on the floor or a table and place both hands above it, the nondominant hand touching it, and the dominant one hovering just above).

6. *Breathe.* Notice how the stone feels to the hand that is touching it, and also how the palm of your hand feels that is not touching it. Just notice; no judgment. There may be heat or pins and needles or even coolness, but no matter; it is your intention (and the Grace of Haniel) that will make the work effective. The "feeling" is gravy (the "gravy" will come with a regular practice if it is not there at the outset). Imagine that you are exchanging energy with the stone (which you are; strengthened by Haniel, of course). You are offering the earth holding and respect in exchange for clarity. Imagine clarity like a clear bright light flowing through to you from the stone, both down into the hand that is touching/holding it and beaming up into the hand hovering above. "See," "feel," or "know" that you are also showering this part of Mother Earth with Love and respect (perhaps—it is up to you!), a wonderful movement that will act as a counterweight for the thoughtless treatment she receives at the hands of many humans these days.

7. Breathe in and out until you feel at peace. When you feel it is complete, place your dominant hand on top of the crystal, in a completing ritual that can "seal in the goodness." When it is complete, do not fall into the trap of worrying about what had confused you before the work. Leave the details to Archangel Haniel and the Angels! Most often, we block our own clarity by worrying about things. Your intention, amplified and clarified by the clear quartz, has been received and supported by Haniel, the Grace of God. All is well!

8. Invite Archangel Haniel to place Her wings around you, creating a cocoon of peace to finish the Light clarity work and ease the transition back into the "real world." In this way, we tenderly cultivate a partnership with an Ally who can help us live Life—glorious Life!—on our terms, at our rhythm, gracefully.

9. When the "hug" feels complete, thank Archangel Haniel and your Guardian Angels by bringing your hands to your chest in a gesture of gratitude for this sacred moment of opening and sounding and Joy and Power.

The Aftercare noted on p. 56 is a very good way to help yourself integrate this important work.

ARCHANGEL RAGUEL

QUALITY: Social Justice, Energy

Archangel Raguel, whose name can be translated as "Social Justice of God," is a very helpful Friend in High Places, particularly if you work or have experience with justice, either the cerebral, governmental, law-related kind or the social justice, heart-based kind. He is also a very good friend when the weight of this world wearies us and we need rest. Yes, there *is* rest for the weary, and His name, the Justice and Repose of God, is Raguel.

Legal Aid

Archangel Raguel is an excellent Ally for those who work in the field of justice: police, lawyers, aides, judges, lawmakers, and so on. Upon request, Raguel helps these people find the balance between firm and flexible that upholds communal values enshrined in the Ten Commandments, such as "Thou shalt not steal," while recognizing that where human beings are involved, there is a need for compassion.

Raguel is also there for any of us who may find ourselves mired in the tangle of legal procedure like trials or mediation. But be careful not to ask Him to take your side; rather, when invited in, Raguel will help us cope with the situation and ensure that the result is for the highest and best good of all concerned, which may not always fall where we might think it should.

If Raguel is called, the result will always be in alignment with the soul plans for all concerned, and not always in alignment with what we think should happen. When we engage with the Angels more and more over the long term, we begin to recognize the truth of this, and we come to relax, knowing that even in this sometimes intimidating domain of law, all is well!

Social Justice

Archangel Raguel also is a strong Ally for people who work in social justice. The justice of which we speak here is not the world's justice, but God's, which calls us to aid and support those less fortunate than we are, in this lifetime.

Here's an example from my own life:

One wintry evening on my way to hold an Angel party at l'Univers d'Esther in the center of Paris, I went down into the Metro at the Mirabeau station and walked the platform to the end. As I walked, I noticed a homeless person under a blanket in a corner where the wind was blocked by a candy machine, making it the warmest spot in the station.

"Tough spot to be in," I thought, knowing that there but for the grace of God I go, and so I dropped something into the bowl by the (I assumed) sleeping form before turning as the train came into the station. I got on and sat down, my seat facing the platform. There I saw that the form had arisen from underneath the blanket, and a man was now seated, staring straight at me.

Our eyes locked and I admit that what I saw there surprised me—depth, compassion (for me), and wisdom. I knew instantly that that man was much more than met the eye, and that this moment was a gift—not for him, as I had thought, but for me. I knew it to be a moment of Grace to bolster me as I headed to the energetically intense exercise of an Angel party. I felt the Love and the support in the few moments before the door closed, and those few moments will suffice for eternity.

This is only one of a number of times that I came upon the Christ in the form of a homeless person, that intense shining in the form of one whom the world, with blind eyes, might judge harshly.

Note well, recognizing that a homeless person (or a poor person, or a person in despair, and so on) is where they are because they are on their path does *not* give us a pass from demonstrating compassion and aiding the poor! Many times, they are living their situation to be a catalyst for us to develop even more compassion. Such soul contracts allow each and all to grow and evolve to full open-hearted movement and bring us more and more into alignment with the Truth that we are all connected. Archangel Raguel can help us with such situations.

A Word about Judgment of the "Less Fortunate"

As discussed earlier, we humans identify with the roles we play here on Earth so completely that we, with very few exceptions, completely forget Who We Are, Truly, why our soul chose to come here, and what mission or objective it has. As such, it is not surprising that, just as we forget who we are, we don't have a clue who the other person is! This is why we can be so off the mark when we judge souls who we consider less fortunate around us. How can we know if this homeless man or that crippled woman is not in fact a very evolved soul who agreed to come here to elicit compassion from cold human hearts (or try to, at least . . .)?

Archangel Raguel, the Energizer Angel

Another specificity that is attributed to Archangel Raguel is one that renders him an excellent Ally for, well, all of us: *Archangel Raguel is the heavenly version of the Energizer Bunny.*

What I mean by that, with no disrespect, is that when we are tired from the enormous energy and effort that living here on Earth requires, when life has taken a toll, Raguel will fill us up with energy, if we ask. Like the Energizer Bunny in the battery commercial, his is an endless supply of energy. This is not a small ability, and one that perhaps can serve all of us. The key here is not to take my word for it, but to try it.

Here's another example from my own life:

A few years back, I walked the pilgrimage path across the North of Spain that is called the Camino to Santiago de Compostela, or the Saint James' Way. Saint James, the disciple of Jesus who would travel far and wide spreading the news about Jesus after the resurrection, is said to be buried in the Cathedral de Santiago (which means Cathedral of St. James).

The Way I had chosen to walk would take me about a month, from St. Jean Pied de Port in the South of France across the Pyrenées Mountains into Spain and then hard walking for about a month, between 12 and 20 miles a day, depending on the terrain and the desire of the pilgrim to continue. As I walked, the state of my feet deteriorated, which shook my resolve to continue. About two weeks into the daily packing of the backpack, walking, finding a place to sleep, showering, and caring for my banged-up feet, washing out clothes, eating, and sleeping, only to do it again in the morning, I was bone tired!

I wondered if I should continue and decided to take a real room in a small hotel for one night (most of the time I slept with other pilgrims in inexpensive—sometimes with reason!—albergués, often a large room with many bunk beds, like a barracks). I decided to treat myself to a room with a bath; a good soak and a good night's sleep was needed to take this decision, as my pilgrimage had been a dream dear to my heart ever since I had read Paolo Coelho's book on the walk, The Pilgrimage, some five years earlier. I'm not one to throw away a five-year plan lightly.

That night, in the comfort of a real bed, after a wonderful warm bath (the things you learn to appreciate on the Camino), I asked the Angels around me to help me gain clarity and then drifted off to sleep.

In the morning, everything was clear! When I awoke, I laughed out loud, as I was reminded (and not for the first time) that I actually teach the key that was required: I had neglected to call on Raguel! From that day forward, I called on Raguel each day on the Camino and completed the Pilgrimage, being sure to thank Him when I got to the cathedral in Santiago.

Since then, I know to watch over myself like a hawk. When I am tired, my Love and Light is diminished, so I call on Raguel right away and give myself a good time out!

A Word about Early Morning (or Late Night) Messages

As we embrace our clairvoyance, our capacity to receive messages from our Angels (or from our Higher Self, or guides) is greatly enhanced. Each night, we re-Source ourselves through sleep. Each night, while the human that we are sleeps, the soul takes over and allows for a replenishing (insofar as the state of the instrument—us!—will allow), and so the liminal space between sleeping and waking is a very open space where the Veil that separates us from the reality of the invisible becomes very thin indeed. For this reason, it is very good to begin our day (and/or to end it) with a quiet period of openness, some practice (and there will be many suggested in the chapters to come) that allows us to stay calm and receptive, ready to receive guidance with regard to what is going on around us at any given time. This is the optimal space to anchor connection to our Angels and to receive guidance that opens wondrous doors for us in alignment with the highest version of Life that awaits us.

CHAKRA: Third Chakra—Solar Plexus—Energy Boost

Archangel Raguel is a great ally for us all as the world seems to spin faster and faster and we try to keep up. In the too-fast pace of the modern world, our third chakra can become unbalanced, our power sapped. Calling on Archangel Raguel is a good idea if or when we find ourselves lagging and in need of an energy boost from above!

COLOR: Brown

Although there is no consensus, a color associated with Raguel is a deep brown, grounding and solid like the earth.

CRYSTAL/STONE: Red Jasper

Red Jasper is a stone that is recognized for its grounding capacity, bringing our human BE-ing to the fore, and allowing the recognition that we must handle our human exigencies with Divine aplomb.

Connecting to Archangel Raguel
(Power Me Up!)

Play with Archangel Raguel!

1. Connect with your breath, and come into a peaceful place of quiet. Set your intention to be filled with the power of Love, so that your very presence becomes a vehicle for God's justice (Love) here on Earth. This practice will strongly cultivate your connection to Archangel Raguel.

2. Use your channel to anchor (ground) yourself, following your ribbon of light into the center of the earth, then open to the highest good with your intention, tracing your channel of light from the center of the earth through the body to the heavens. Return to your heart to set your intention, both as the human being you are and on a soul level. (If you are undertaking this exercise, it is without a doubt the will of your soul.)

3. Sit, feet planted solidly on the ground, shoulder-width apart, shoulders pulled back so that your spinal column—the bridge you create between the earth and the heavens—is straight. Allow the arms to relax at your sides, palms facing forward in a position of energetic openness. *Breathe in* the presence of Angels and Archangels all around you. *Breathe out* anything that blocks your opening to them. Allow yourself to fill with Light and peace, with a sense of the Love that is there for you; to feel, perhaps, the Joy that your presence brings in this space. Take three or four deep breaths at least before continuing.

4. With your eyes closed, imagine that Archangel Raguel stands before you and awaits your agreement before he undertakes to ensure that you are filled and empowered, ready to bring God's justice—Love!—into the world.

5. *Breathe in*, deeply into the diaphragm, placing your hands on your solar plexus, the seat of your human power. Fill your hands with that power, then slowly raise your hands to the center of your chest and breathe out into your heart chakra, filling your heart with the power in your hands. *Breathe in* again into the diaphragm, deeply, keeping your hands on your heart center. Fill your hands with Love, then slowly lower your hands and place them on your solar plexus. Breathe out and fill your seat of power, the solar plexus, with Love. Repeat several times slowly. Invite Archangel Raguel to place His hands over yours, facilitating and deepening the filling, the power, and the realignment with God's justice, Love.

6. Finishing, *breathe out* any tension you might feel as you release any vestigial weight associated with the exercise. When the work feels satisfying and you feel relaxed and complete, thank Archangel Raguel and your Guardian Angels by bringing your hands to your chest, a gesture of gratitude for this sacred moment of opening and sounding and Joy and Power.

The Aftercare noted on p. 56 is a very good way to help yourself integrate this important work.

ARCHANGEL RAZIEL

QUALITY: Esoteric Wisdom

Archangel Raziel, whose name can be translated as "Secret of God," is a very powerful Friend, particularly if you are moving consciously into your own power and Light. He is known as a purveyor of Wisdom, as He is privy to the esoteric Truths one might imagine as God's Secrets.

Like Metatron, he can help us with wisdom and understanding, but their points of entry are different: Metatron was once human, and so with compassion, helps our human aspect to understand what is necessary for us to relax into an en-light-ened existence. Raziel, on the other hand, works with our Divine aspect to facilitate the incarnation of the soul and its inherent wisdom into the human form.

A Word about Soul Alignment

What I mean by soul alignment is the conscious recognition that we are more than the world tells us we are. We are eternal, we are Light, our true nature is Love, and when we can get out of our own way, when fear can be set aside, we are pure Light and Love.

Each one of us is a portal for the Divine. How much we let in is sometimes a function of how much we have been "tenderized" by this harsh world—softened instead of hardening as a result of the hardships we have encountered.

I love these Leonard Cohen lyrics:

"Ring the bells that still can ring; forget your perfect offering.

There is a crack in everything; that's how the light gets in."

With that in mind, perhaps we can recognize that hardship often hardens us. When we "go hard," protecting ourselves, we distance ourselves from our Heart—the sacred heart that beats within us and aligns us (and our actions) with Love.

Thus disconnected, we are very rarely in Consciousness, and fall easily out of alignment with our mission and the help (angelic and other) that is available for us. We can feel alone, lost, weakened, a victim . . . not a good place to be!

In such a case, from the soul's perspective, the incarnation—the embodiment—is in peril, and with it, the mission. Unless something happens to awaken us to the Game, as it were, the fullness of the incarnation, this lifetime, is not reachable. Although many are currently awakening, still many sleep.

A very small percentage of people are living at more than 50 percent alignment; that is, consistently conscious of their mission and their Self. Every awakening counts, though, as the "tipping point" of humanity is lower than we might think. We do not even need half of human beings to awaken as a species, as consciousness carries a stronger vibration than unconsciousness.

Raziel can help with our awakening once we get conscious enough to ask. He is particularly involved whenever a human being lives though some sort of initiation: a ritual/portal through which the soul will incarnate even more.

Initiation often opens doors to other aspects of ourselves, and renders the path even more fluid. No matter the modality to which we are attracted, it is always the path to the highest good for us. We have an inner GPS that makes things more and more clear, the more we listen; our desires are planted like Hansel and Gretel's breadcrumbs (but impervious to eating!), showing us the way—our way.

As we journey, it is good to call on Raziel, and welcome Him for the big steps that initiate us, that allow us to up-level. Raziel is the Presence at all initiating events, and all moments that bring us consciously into further alignment with Who We Are, Truly.

CHAKRA: Seventh Chakra—Crown—Soul Connection

Archangel Raziel is the Archangel who most directly works to remind us of the context of this lifetime, our incarnation. Thus, naturally, Raziel is the perfect Ally for helping us to open the channel to our soul and our purpose, and to keep it open! Remembering who we are and why we have come renders our life ever richer and more rewarding, and our service to others and to the highest good all the easier.

COLOR: Deep Purple

The color associated with Raziel is most often deep purple. It is an energy that can be linked to the Violet Flame and the raising of consciousness that allows a more ample incarnation of the Higher Self, bringing us forward naturally and easily toward the realization of our mission.

CRYSTAL/STONE: Amethyst

Amethyst is a stone that is recognized for its capacity to help us release all habits that prevent our human aspect from reaching our Light, such as any form of addiction that holds us back from that Light as it expresses in the fullness of this incarnation, the domain of Raziel. The two-fold work of amethysts is to help us release what is holding us back and to align us (naturally, as a result) with the highest Self we can be.

A Word about Addiction

The word "addiction" most often calls to mind immoderate indulgence in "bad" habits, such as drinking, smoking, drugging, having sex, eating, and so on. But the more cogent definition would be: addiction is any practice that, in excess, holds us back from our Light. Such practices are basically "hideouts": fear has us hiding in a space from which our Large Life is not accessible. Shame and other low energies can keep us locked away in there, if we are not conscious of what is going on.

Such a definition would include other immoderate behaviors that take us out of the Game, such as indulging in too much television, even exercise or meditation, can distract us from our mission, and from the healthy, balanced movement toward our Light. Sensitive people are those most likely to fall into the trap of addictions. The world is harsh, and the sensitive take it on the chin. Addictive behaviors provide respite: a time-out, if you will. But the relief can be such that, over time, we lose sight of our Selves and the Dream that is deep within us. In the energetic equivalent to sitting our Self out for an inning or two, we can accidentally sit ourselves out for the rest of our Game.

Initiation with Archangel Raziel

Play with Archangel Raziel!

1. Connect with your breath, and come into a peaceful place of quiet. Set your intention to *accept initiation* in order to allow your soul level to take the wheel more and more, with the help of your connection to Archangel Raziel.
2. Use your channel to anchor (ground) yourself, following your ribbon of light into the center of the earth, then open to the highest good with your intention, tracing

your channel of light from the center of the earth through your heart to the heavens. Return to your heart to set your intention, both as the human being you are and on a soul level. (If you are undertaking this exercise, it is without a doubt the will of your soul.)

3. Sit, feet planted solidly on the ground, shoulder-width apart, shoulders pulled back so that your spinal column—your bridge between earth and sky—is straight. Allow the arms to relax at your sides, palms facing forward in a position of energetic openness. *Breathe in* the presence of Angels and Archangels all around you. *Breathe out* anything that blocks your opening to them. Allow yourself to fill with Light and peace, with a sense of the Love that is there for you; to feel, perhaps, the Joy that your presence brings in this space. Take three or four deep breaths at least before continuing.

4. With your eyes closed, imagine that Archangel Raziel is standing in front of you, awaiting your accord before He ensures the efficacy of the initiation that will allow further awakening and incarnation, alignment with your soul and movement toward your mission. The question is asked: "Are you ready?" If the answer is *yes,* state it, and if desired, demonstrate it in a way uniquely your own, using your body to punctuate the word (this could be a thumbs up, or a fist pump, or a jump in the air, and so on). Find what feels good to you. You can't do this wrong. It is private, and what comes to you will be just perfect, the whispering of your soul.

5. *Breathe in* again, deeply into the diaphragm, and raise your arms to the sky, palms facing each other. Imagine a flow of Light (and Love and Joy) flowing down from the heavens through the channel you create with your arms, through your crown chakra at the top of your head, into your being, filling you completely. Imagine that the flow is so strong that it acts as a flushing out, so that anything that diminished your Light that is ready to be released is now let go. With the Power of God, expressed through Raziel, all is possible. You have only to agree to *receive!*

6. When you feel filled (or if your arms get tired—the cultivation of compassion for yourself is exceedingly important for Large Life!), place your hands on your heart to seal in the goodness.

Know that Raziel covers your hands with his, in a powerful gesture of solidarity and Unity.

7. *Breathe out* any tension you might feel as you release any vestigial weight associated with the exercise.

8. When the work feels satisfying and you feel relaxed and complete, thank Archangel Raziel and your Guardian Angels by bringing your hands to your chest in a gesture of gratitude for this sacred moment of opening and sounding and Joy and Power.

The Aftercare noted on p. 56 is a very good way to help yourself integrate this important work.

PART THREE

ENERGY AND ANGELIC HEALING

CHAPTER 7

The Power of the
Inner Child

Truly I tell you, unless you change and become like little
children, you will never enter the kingdom of heaven.
— MATTHEW 18:3, The Bible

The words of the Ascended Master called Jesus are at the heart of our next step into Large Life with the Angels. Although the Angels do not belong to any single religion, for all of us, Jesus' words here capture perfectly the importance of the inner child when we move into our Power with the help of the Angels.

If we can enlarge the idea of the kingdom of Heaven from some lofty cloud perch after we die to something more akin to a Joy vibration here on Earth, the message is quite evident—children have the key!

To be clear, this Master was not encouraging us to adopt Peter Pan complexes, or inviting us to be childish, but rather, encouraging us to perhaps look at and take up again a part of us that the world pushes us to lay aside altogether as we go through the process of socialization within the context of family, friends, school, and work.

That process? It kills our Joy . . . or at least tries to.

The process of which I speak takes a child—pure, sprung fresh from the Source, and capable of the spontaneous, the Joyful—and teaches them that being themself is not always correct. The world even teaches us that sometimes it is important *not* to be ourselves, *not* to speak our Truth. Anyone who has ever been a parent and wriggles in their seat as their child speaks, hoping they won't tell Grandma (again!) that she has a mustache, or tell the priest or the rabbi that Mommy and Daddy had a fight, or say that Aunt Clara smells, and so on, knows whereof I speak.

This socialization is in a certain sense important: barreling forward and dispersing truths will-nilly can hurt those around us, given the way the world is today. We want to prepare our children to live in this world, and so, most often, it is the parents who teach their children to squelch their truth.

That is, to lie.

Oh, sure, we find euphemisms for it—white lies, being nice—but basically, we learn to lie from a very young age, most often from those who are closest to us.

The example I love to use is that of my dear, departed, sainted mother (having had seven children to raise in a sixth-floor walk-up apartment in the Bronx of the Sixties, "sainted" is perhaps an understatement), who went to church religiously and taught me to lie with this gem:

"Say thank you, and tell your aunt that you love the pajamas."

But I didn't!! I did *not* love the pajamas. What kid wants pajamas for Christmas?!

I protested, "But they tell us at church not to lie!"

To which came the fated words that started the whole thing: "It's a white lie. It doesn't count as a lie because you do it to be nice to somebody. Now *tell* your aunt you like the pajamas!"

I knew better than to question further, so I did as I was told, but I hated it—and I was right.

Children tend toward honesty because the soul can only live in honesty. It is our human aspect, trying to fit in and be safe and loved, that learns to lie. Unfortunately, there is no order of magnitude of lies, and the whole "white lie" thing is, well, not a thing.

Every single time we lie, or obfuscate, or play with the truth, we distance ourselves a bit more from our soul. And sadly, it can become a habit—it is after all easier than telling the truth in many cases ("no, my friend, your butt doesn't look gi-normous in those jeans!")—and then an addiction. Remember the definition of addiction: "Any habit that does not serve, that distances us from our Light." So children are Truth-tellers; as such they are closer to our soul, which is both individuated and part of Source/God. And who else is part of Source/God? (If you said, "Everyone and everything," bravo, but that is not what I was going for.)

Angels!

As we will see in the next chapter, which is all about energy, one of the universal Laws of Energy is this: "Energy seeks equilibrium." Therefore, when we are most aligned with our Truth we are also most aligned energetically with the Angels—plugged into our Friends in High Places and ready to fly!

But how to deal with the vagaries of this world? How can we help children (or ourselves?) to get along in the world without white lies? We would probably agree that it is important that children learn to go through life *both* speaking their truth *and* not hurting everyone's feelings along the way, *non*?

For this reason, as we evolve, more and more parents will know to teach their children discretion instead of lying, that is, simply saying thank you for the pajamas, rather than lying about loving them when we don't, for example.

The ability to know when to speak our Truth and when to hold onto it—without ever betraying it!—is discernment, a quality that is absolutely necessary if we are to live our Life, Large and true, comfortably on this planet.

Coming back to what Jesus said, then, we can imagine that He was teaching us the importance of being true to Who We Are, Truly, without becoming childish and feeling like we have to give everyone around us what-for.

Mature discretion and being true to ourselves is important for tapping into another specificity of the child within us: Joy.

A Word about Joy versus Happiness

If we look around us, I imagine we can agree that, even on a good day, this world is not particularly Joyful. Oh, maybe in a particular city on a given day, if the local team wins a championship of some sort, raucous cries of happiness may ring out in the streets, but that is passing, which is why it isn't Joy.

Happiness is passing; Joy is eternal.

Happiness comes and goes with the tides of events we judge to be "positive" or "negative." Sometimes we ride high on a wave, and other times, the wave might turn into something like (pardon the expression) shit and crashes on us or spits us out onto the beach . . . hard.

In this life, about the only thing of which we can be certain is that there will always be ups and down sand those waves will sometimes feel like they are made of shit . . . which means that we won't always be happy but we can always be Joyful.

Happiness is human; Joy is Divine.

Joy is the quality that can allow us to surf when those waves come (and they always come); to remain upright, and flexible, and playful, like a child facing play-obstacles. Joy is a quality that surpasses and yet enfolds our human experience, an energetic experience of the Truth that we are more than what we see in the mirror.

To err is human; to forgive, Divine.

Both our happiness and our unhappiness at any given time are a source of suffering, as the Buddhists say. If we are happy, we anguish over how to hold onto that happiness; if we are unhappy, we struggle over coming out of that state. This is the truth of human error. In fact, if we can gain a different—higher!—perspective, we can remain more stable as the waves roll in; we can remain in the Truth that all is well, and—at the level of Who We Are, Truly—know that we are fine. If we can regain that perspective (and what is the point of hanging around with Angels if we are not looking to share in that perspective?), we can "forgive" the illusion that disappoints so, and move on to a more Divine experience of the earth plane, which facilitates Life with a capital "L"!

The more we tap into the Truth of Who We Are, Truly (and hanging out with the Angels can help us in that quite direct route to Joy), the more we realize that our true Source of Life is not in the details of ups and downs of our lives but in something *more*; something constant and loving, stable and strong. A foundation upon which we can construct something of high value, with Friends in High Places helping us out!

Anchored in that knowing, coming to understand that we are accompanied and that the Game is rigged in our favor (it is!), we can begin to relax and live the Life of our deepest heart-dreams. Joy is Divine . . . and children hold the key to it. So our Joy is in the hands of the child within us.

Children and Joy

If Joy is the transforming factor, how do we get some? Well, as it turns out, we were born with it! The highest energy, Unconditional Love, is Source energy, which expresses itself as Light or Joy—these are three facets of the same energy.

The soul you are (at the deepest level) is chock full of it, as Joy is the "stuff" of God. As such, it is our heritage, and, like anything worth having, it is worth working for. The trick is that you have to know where to find it. Here is the secret: *The child you were still holds the key to Joy, and that child still exists!*

Huh?

Don't worry, I haven't lost my mind. (Okay, some might argue otherwise, but I assure you, my feet are planted solidly on the ground.) The child who *was* you has grown into the adult who *is* you, so we know that the physical child is no longer here. But is any part of the child still with us? Yes. We know this to be true, right?

There's the part of us that can be "ouchy" when people are rude or brusque or when we don't get our way. There are the little idiosyncrasies that are carryovers from childhood ("Don't touch my plate, please. Thank you!"). They let us know that the imprint of those years is still with us. But what about the positive? What about the Joy?

Imagine yourself as a child—or any child—excited and happy, coming into this world ready to wow 'em! With a big, open heart, trusting, and playful, most children shine at the beginning unless and until the world does not respond in kind. A "Look what I can do!" answered perhaps with a "Not now" or other slights, real or imagined, and the child who shrieked joyously for attention learns that it is not always a good idea to do so.

We come into this world with our hearts wide open, loving and joyful, and the world often takes that away from us, one step at a time. Slowly, many of us learn to keep our great big Love cloaked generally, only to be released with a very select few with whom we feel safe and comfortable, or not at all.

Hence the importance of the question at the outset of our journey: With whom are you comfortable?

It's an important question, to be sure, but this one is even more important: Can we be comfortable with ourselves? Can that tender part of our heart feel safe with . . . us? Have we been good stewards of our hearts, of the child within? Or have we, too, been hard and judgmental toward ourselves, pushing against our own grain, in the way of the world, always looking for *bigger* or *more* or *better* instead of (at least once in a while) patting ourselves on the back and *celebrating ourselves* with a rousing "Good job!"

The part of the child that perhaps retreated when their sensitivity was too much for the harshness of this world is still with us—a part of ourself hidden deep in the recesses of the heart. Until that precious cargo is recognized and celebrated, we are not—can never be—completely relaxed, even with ourselves.

This is why so many people can't stand to be alone, or in silence. The distance between us and our hearts has gotten too large, the alienation too complete. We hide from it with noise and activity, all manner of addictions, which assuage our anguish but do not allow for Joy.

There is only one person on the whole planet who understands how difficult it was for the child you were to adapt to a world that was not as welcoming as we would have liked: you! Even the best of families can't provide a context of Unconditional Love 24/7, which is what we are coming from, in Source.

Further, if you are reading this, it is very likely that you are a Light-worker, a person who is filled with Light and has the potential to share it, once you accept it for yourself, which means that you are "sensitive" (like it or not).

To do that, and to live Large in the great Joy of ease and safety, with easy contact with the Angels, it is important to take time to reconnect consciously with that which had been set aside unconsciously, the inner child, so that we become comfortable in our own skin, relaxed, and ready for Joy.

Think of children you may know or have known. Think of the difference between a child who is secure with loving parents and a child whose life is more difficult. We can always tell, can't we? The first child, sure that he or she is loved, is often bolder, more confident and trusting, because the world has proven itself to be a pretty safe place. As such, the child is easier to be with, to love, and better received by the world (which is made ill at ease by those who are ill at ease.)

On the other hand, a child who is not in a comfortable or comforting context may be timid, or conversely, act out. Such a child may be evasive or try to hide, all due to a lack of security and confidence.

This is why inner child work is truly all-important for us: either to increase the Joy already present, as it will connect us even more easily with our Angels and our Highest Good, or because that child may still be in hiding, waiting for someone (*us!*) to show ourselves worthy of their presence.

Any time we push aside our needs for those of another, we put that child back into a corner, in the dark, reaffirming, as it were, that the child (us) does not merit attention. And we know better than that, don't we?

When we remember the child we were, imagining that being still within us, treating ourselves gently in accordance with that knowledge, and becoming the reliable adult who shows Unconditional Love, we become the solution and the reason confidence will grow and Joy be revealed more fully.

Without the Joy and confidence and spontaneity of the child, we are living life impaired, unable to access our audaciousness, tenderness, spontaneity, and innocence. Mind you, this is not at all to say that we should *not* be of service to others. As Lightworkers, we are called to be of service! It is simply a question of *how* we do it. Do we always put the needs of others before our own? Or do we ensure our well-being and then, ready, willing and Joyful, help others?

A Word about Self-Sacrifice

Imagine that you are a cup—not a small one, but a big one; let's say, a chalice. Let us further imagine that you, as a chalice, are pretty full, standing tall between heaven and earth. Given your soul's mission to be of service here on Earth, it is natural that you are ready to share.

Now we know energy will always tend to equilibrium, so it is easy to imagine that a chalice that is ready to give will attract those who will want to receive, right?

Right! So imagine that all around you a number of small glasses organize themselves in a circle, each one asking you to fill them up in some way. Sound familiar? This is often the lot of Lightworkers, from very early on. Normally, we are perhaps eager to help, and that is natural; it is after all in alignment to a degree with the soul's purpose to serve. It is the small detail of how we are to serve that is sometimes a bit "off" . . .

Imagine that you as a chalice bend over to share what you have with all the glasses around you. In a generous gesture, feeling the need to be fair and sure that everyone gets some, you serve all. The result is that each one gets a bit and you are left with. . . Nada. Niente. Rien. Nothing.

The next thing that happens is predictable: the glasses around you gulp down what they got and ask for more. The requests, coming when you are finding yourself already emptied out, may now meet with a different initial response within you.

Are you Joyful? Probably not. There may even be a tiny voice inside that says something like, "Well, who is going to fill me up?"

That rancor may be hard to hear, hard to admit, and perhaps we choke it back. After all, we often grow up in a world that insists that we must always put others first (and look where that has gotten us!), so it is natural that we may feel a bit guilty about that tiny but insistent voice.

So often we choke it back and render the service anyway ("Oh, I had something planned, but okay, sure, I can do that for you. Just need to cancel my appointment").

The problem with this is energetic, and it is two-fold:

The person may not know that you are not wholeheartedly enthusiastic about the service you are rendering, but you do. You know that while you may do the service (babysitting, shopping, airport pickup, and so on) with a smile, you know that the smile does not go very deep. Imagine the energy we offer when we force ourselves, feel obligated to help another. Is it Love and Joy? Probably not!

In fact, energetically, forcing ourselves to serve and dissimulating our unhappiness is actually infecting the earth plane with the rancor we think we have suppressed. So we bring fear (afraid to say no) into the earth plane, instead of its opposite, Love, which we as Lightworkers are meant to be doing.

The second energetic problem with this scenario is that such an action represents the ultimate betrayal of the child who retreated deep within our heart, waiting to break free. Instead of coming to their assistance, with such an action we confirm the attitude of a world that understood nothing, essentially showing that the needs of the child are not important, that our needs are not important! The rancor we feel belongs to the child. And they are right!

Now, I am not saying that we should not serve (we are here for that, non?), but rather, that we should do it differently.

Let's go back to the scenario at hand. Emptied, and surrounded by demands on your time and energy, the appropriate response is simply, "Not today." Not "No!" (unless, that is, you have a visceral reaction, one that indicates that you should never do it, whatever "it" is) but "Not now."

The idea is that you take the time to fill your chalice. This will seem strange to "givers" who do not have to habit of receiving, but it is necessary in order to shift things energetically and play our instrument with Joy. The idea is never again to bend over, spilling ourselves out for others, but to stay constantly aware of the importance of filling your chalice so that it overflows. In this way, all the glasses around you will be filled—and not just in small amounts, and not just now and then.

> Your "Yes" to yourself (expressed in a "No" to others) creates a movement of spontaneous abundant giving through overflow. By caring for the needs of the inner child—your needs!—you can ensure that the enthusiasm (a word that means "full of God") that connotes the presence of Joy and Light and Love will be of service to all around you. Furthermore, your very presence will be Presence (capital "P"), and will render service to all around you as well as the earth.
>
> In the end, we render more service—and render it better!—when we ensure that our inner child, inner self, inner instrument is doing well!

To this day, the words ring true:

Truly I tell you, unless you change and become like little children, you will never enter the kingdom of heaven.

In this case, the "kingdom of heaven" is not some fictitious faraway cloud place, but the state of Grace where we shine, where our Light and Love flow naturally from our Joy, and where our inner child—innocent and joyful, creative and nonjudgmental—is free to live our highest dreams, in alignment with our mission!

The good news is, No matter how ingrained the (Joy-sucking) habit of ignoring our own needs may be, we can reverse those trends any time, and the Angels can help us!

Connecting to the Inner Child with the Help of Our Angels

1. Connect with your breath, and come into a peaceful place of quiet. Set your intention to *connect with and love the child within,* accepting the help of your Angels to do so. Decide to invite your Guardian Angels to help with this. This is natural as they were present when the child was walking the earth, and witness to whatever difficulties the sensitive, perspicacious child (you) may have experienced. Also invite the female energy of the Archangel Gabrielle, as She carries the Divine Mother energy that can fill any lack of tenderness or Love that the child may have experienced at any time here on the earth plane (even when it came from yourself).

2. Use your channel to anchor (ground) yourself, following your ribbon of light into the center of the earth, then open to the highest good with your intention, tracing your channel of light from the center of the earth through your tender heart then up to the heavens. Return to your heart to set your intention, both as the human being you are and on a soul level. (If you are undertaking this exercise, it is without a doubt the will of your soul.)

3. Stand, feet planted solidly on the ground, shoulder-width apart, shoulders pulled back so that your spinal column is straight and tall, allowing the truth of your grandeur to be expressed. This standing position supports the largest version of your Self possible. Allow the arms to relax at your sides, palms facing forward in a position of energetic openness. *Breathe in* the presence of Angels and Archangels all around you. *Breathe out* anything that blocks your opening to them. Allow yourself to fill with Light and peace, with a sense of the Love that is there for you; to feel, perhaps, the Joy that your presence brings in this space. Take three or four deep breaths at least before continuing.

4. With your eyes closed, imagine the child you were stands before you—a smaller version of you, at the age that comes naturally. The child is simply standing there, perhaps wondering which "you" has come this day: the one who forgot them, the one that is sometimes harsh to them, or the one they have been waiting for all this time? Is today the long-awaited day when the child will be remembered and called on, called back into the Game, this time free to *shine*? Perhaps the child before you will be diffident. It will depend on how you have treated yourself—the most sensitive side of yourself—all these years. But no matter! If you are certain that today is the day to reconnect with the strong Light and Joy potential, and the wide-open creativity that is the domain of the child, all will be well!

5. It is time to communicate with the child. Imagine yourself explaining, perhaps, that you understand how hard it was sometimes, why they started "toughening up," or hiding out. You understand because you were there. You couldn't help then, at the time, because you were small then, too, but now you have grown up! Since you are a grown-up, you can now ensure the safety of the child, create the context where that tender and powerful part of you can relax in your own presence because no longer will you

allow the world to take precedence over the needs of your person. Assure the little one that you will take care of everything if they will only team up with you. You need the child to really live, to fulfill your destiny. Now reach down and open your arms and your heart, inviting the child to trust you, to come into your arms and your heart. If appropriate tell them you are sorry for the past but that you understand now and can ensure that the child will have every opportunity to play and to shine! Ask them, "Are you ready?" When you "feel," "see," or "know" that the answer is "yes," invite the Angels around you to create a cocoon of their wings for you and the child to bond and realign in that space of Grace.

6. When you feel it is complete, place your hands on your heart (the home of the child) to seal the pact between you both. Know that the Angels and Archangel Gabrielle cover your hands to strengthen the seal, in a powerful gesture of solidarity and Unity. Thank Archangel Gabrielle and your Guardian Angels by again bringing your hands to your chest in a gesture of gratitude for this sacred moment of opening and sounding and Joy and Power.

The Aftercare noted on p. 56 is a very good way to help yourself integrate this important work.

CHAPTER 8

Master Your Energy:
Frequency and Amplitude

We have all heard language that uses highs (or lows) to describe how we are feeling, or doing, haven't we? Expressions like "I am walking on air!" or "Flying high!" or "high energy" are used to denote when things are going well for us, while others seem to connote that we are not doing well, such as "I am feeling kind of low today" or "under the weather" or "low energy."

This scale of low to high is not only used in "spiritual" circles but in all circles: common parlance reflects common experience. We humans experience our lives on an up-or-down scale ("life's ups and downs"). Since a spiritual path will intensify ordinary experience, when we get onto such a path, it is normal that our highs may become higher, and our lows, lower. Just knowing that that is "normal" can help us to keep ourselves on a more even keel. As we progress on our journey to living the life that awaits us in alignment with our soul's mission, we often hear it said that "our frequency rises" or "we carry a higher frequency." Many spiritual practices seek that aim: to enable us to rise in frequency, even to ascension.

Anyone who has ever had a deep sacred experience can attest to the "high" of being in that ineffable Presence (and the "low" that sometimes follows, which we will discuss here). But the high is not the whole story, is it? How powerfully our "high" or "low" is anchored will decide if we are impacted by the energy of others, if they are impacted by ours, if both are impacted, or neither are.

Here are examples of those four scenarios:

SCENARIO ONE
Tangling with Mr. Jones (Being pulled down)
Imagine that you participate in a workshop, maybe my workshop Take Action with the Angels. During the workshop, we work in the presence of Angels and you learn to step into and stand in your power with the help of the Angelic Realm. Your frequency rises.

After the workshop, you feel great! Monday morning, you rise and truly Shine, heading back to work, ready for anything. You are a beam of Light, ready to shine on all, a Lightworker who has found their wings, ready to soar, until . . .

"Ms. Hudson!" (Gulp! It is Mr. Jones, the big boss man, in a dark mood, as usual.)

"How nice of you to *deign* to come in today! You were *supposed* to give me the numbers *before* you left to do I-don't-want-to-know-what on your very long weekend during our busiest season!"

Pssssssssssssssssssssssssshhhhhhhhhhhhhhhhh. That is the sound of the air leaving our balloon. Perhaps you know it?

In the wink of an eye, a Mr. Jones can deflate us, even after an intensive pumping-up like an Angelic workshop. How can we explain it?

Because it is not only frequency that matters.

Two elements comprise our power: the up-and-down of *frequency* and the width of the *amplitude*, or power, of our energy field.

If we use the metaphor of voice waves, a high-frequency sound moves faster than a low-frequency sound; the faster the movement, the higher the sound. But the amplitude of that sound will be the width (how stable the sound) indicative of the force or power of that sound.

A strong voice, like a strong "us," requires both: high frequency and power.

So in the example above, our high energy is pulled down by another person's low energy. We arrived at work at a very high frequency, and our *very high* frequency met up with Mr. Jones's very *low* frequency, and Mr. Jones's low energy won out. Why?

We know already that energy seeks equilibrium. As such, two people in contact for any length of time will impact each other's energetic fields until equilibrium is attained.

What happened there then? Why did the equilibrium swing Mr. Jones's way?

Because Mr. Jones was more rooted and more powerful—60 years of practice at being grumpy—in his low energy than we were in our new-found, just-finished-the-workshop practice of high energy. The more powerful energy field will sway the less powerful one, as energy seeks equilibrium.

So many times I hear people say, "I am too sensitive to see that person/ attend that event; the energy brings me down."

Such a person is right to assess that certain situations negatively impact our experience energetically, but this is not a life sentence! In order to be stronger in the face of the Mr. Joneses of this world, we need only go to the spiritual gym: work on both our frequency and our power!

But first, two more examples.

SCENARIO TWO
Lifting Up Another

Imagine now that it is three years later, and we have been working on our energy! Furthermore, we have just come off another workshop with the Angels (maybe my follow-on Angelic Co-creation workshop), so we are feeling *great,* shining and powerful.

Monday morning comes, and we head into the office, ready to shine all day long! We stop briefly in the restroom, only to hear a soft sobbing from one of the stalls.

"Are you okay in there?" we ask.

"Yes, I'll be alright." The answer comes as the door opens, and we see our friend Anna come out, eyes puffy and red. "My kitty Chance passed away last night. . . " she tails off, no need to go any farther.

We pass a few moments together, as Anna speaks of Chance, and we remind her that cats are often familiars and stay with us even after their departure, that the ties that bring us together with our animal family are not just of this world.

A hug before going back out to face the working world, and Anna says, "Thank you. I feel better now, ready to get back to work."

What happened there?

In Scenario Two, our high energy was sufficiently strong to buoy Anna's newly deflated energy. Her energy was very low but had not been so for very long, so we were able to lift her up. I imagine this sort of scenario has happened to you (as a Lightworker) before, with others perhaps saying something like, "I don't know why, but I always feel better when I am around you."

The trick is that we want to be sufficiently powerful in our high energy that we uplift the other without their field lowering our energy level to meet them in the middle, as with the next example.

SCENARIO THREE
We Help and Hurt Each Other

Imagine that our energy is quite high, but perhaps we are a bit under the weather. Still, we feel strongly that we need to go visit our friend John, who has been going through a particularly hard time lately. We know that our chats usually lift him up, and so we head off to see him, despite the slight fatigue we may feel.

Upon arrival, we sit at the kitchen table and chat for a long while, allowing our good friend to air all that he is feeling—that he is no longer where he is meant to be, that his marriage is no longer a space of trust and intimacy, but that he feels guilty about leaving. We can listen without commentary (most people only really need an ear and a shoulder) as he then goes on about his work and his health, all of which, if you listen to him tell it, "suck."

When it is time to go, John says, "Thanks. You don't know how much it means to me. I always feel so much better after spending time with you. It's like you're my Xanax."

As you leave and begin the journey home, you notice that you are feeling a lot worse than you did on the way over. You may attribute it to that cold that was coming on, but we know the truth, don't we?

What happened there?

You were able to lift Steve up as your high frequency was still stronger than his pessimism but *he* was also able to pull you down, as you were not at your tip-top best! Energy did indeed seek—and find!—equilibrium, as it always will. This maybe will teach us to make sure that when we do such a "good turn," we ensure that *our* state of being is pumped up enough not to suffer the experience too greatly!

This scenario describes the interaction that some refer to as the "energy vampire effect." Personally, I do not like the term (although it is very dramatic!), as the person we are calling a "vampire" in this case is not doing anything intentionally, not like a vampire would!

SCENARIO FOUR
Tangling with Mr. Jones (the Rematch)

It's a bright Monday morning, and having spent time over the weekend hiking in nature (so very high frequency and amplitude!), we arrive at work and stop in the staff common room for a moment before heading to our desk. Anna is in there, and as we stop to say hello to her, we hear someone, huffing and puffing and grumbling, come into the room. We know at once it is Mr. Jones.

Turning, our eyes meet, and (for once!) Mr. Jones simply glares and then turns his back and leaves the room.

"What was that about?" Anna asks, "That man always has something mean to say to you! I can't believe he just turned heel and left."

You smile and say, simply, "I can."

What happened there?

When we work on ourselves and muscle up spiritually, if and when we meet someone of equal power but a different frequency, neither person will be able to shift the other's energy field, so one or the other (or both) will simply leave.

This happens often with couples or friends when one starts to grow spiritually and the other does not. More and more, we are called to put our Light and our Shining first, not "playing small," so that those around us are not bothered by us.

But we were made to "bother."

As Lightworkers, we are made to Shine, made to awaken a world that very often would like to stay asleep. Most people would like nothing to change, even if it is not great "as is."

Imagine that the sleepyheads around you experience your Light like a morning alarm clock, one that shines a spotlight in their eyes. When we accept our Light and step into our Power, that is sometimes the effect of our presence on others. This can lead to people putting distance between you, and sometimes they leave treadmarks!

It can be sad, naturally, when people close to us move on, unable to accept the "new" us. But since this is the "us" that is more authentic than the roles we played before, maybe it is all the better that they move on, as it means that they liked us faking who we were and appreciate less who we are.

A Word about Playing Small

In certain circumstances (and almost always linked to wanting to be loved and accepted), we may be inclined to hide our Light. In these situations, we ensure equilibrium by faking small, which actually diminishes our energy; it's like going to the "anti-gym."

I sometimes have people come to my workshops who want to pay cash so that their spouses won't know what the workshop was really about. They shine during the three days, but at the end begin hiding that Light, even as they prepare to leave.

If you are ever tempted to make yourself small in any way, a word of warning: as we discussed earlier, energy always seeks equilibrium—not sometimes, but always. So, if you are trying to hide your Light, your energy will shift to adjust lower to simplify things. It is why sometimes living a lie (of any kind, not just spiritual) can make us physically, mentally, or emotionally sick. Something has to give.

As such, we need to be very aware of our instrument and how we are being impacted by others, or how we are impacting ourselves. Allowing our Light to shine, once it has begun, is the only path to full glowing health.

The best news I ever had on the path was a good example of the fact that once we begin on the path, no backsliding is possible. Oh, we may try to go backward, but it never works—we can't "un-know" what we know once it is known. There is no need to fear slipping backward into bad habits or limiting beliefs, especially when we are keeping good company with the Angels!

Keeping company with the Angels helps us to cultivate high frequency and amplitude as, there too, energy seeks equilibrium. Not bad, huh?

Let's explore some other ways to work with our frequency and amplitude in order to get our shine on!

Frequency

You know how to get high, right? No, I'm not talking about that! I mean, you know what floats your boat, right? What makes you happy? Peaceful? Exhilarated?

Whatever comes to mind when I ask that question is the specific route to a direct rise in your frequency.

No aspect of your being is an accident; it all serves your mission, even (above all!) your personal preferences, your likes and desires, your passion, your "bliss." This is why mythologist Joseph Campbell's famous exhortation to "follow your bliss" is the key to finding and living your soul's mission in this lifetime, but that is for another book.

The quickest (and most fun) way to fill our "cup" to overflowing, and overflow with Light all around us, is to *do what we love*. When we do what we love, we express Love and shine: our frequency is at its highest level. What we love is specifically tailored to best support our life purpose, so anything we love is an activity that can be counted as going to the spiritual gym—even going to the gym! (I am fairly certain that when I go to kick-boxing class, I am likely the only one there doing it as spiritual practice!)

Aside from *doing anything we love*, there are some other possibilities for augmenting our frequency, which I have listed below. There are two key points to remember here:

It is our *intention*, not a specific ritual, which will have the intended effect. The ritual we use simply allows our intention to be fortified, and thus, more effectively realized.

Anything we can do, we can do with the Angels, which will render the action even more effective and at the same time cultivate our connection to our Friends in High Places.

Chakra Work

The chakras are often mentioned but not always explained, so let's take a moment at the outset to do that.

Imagine that we have not just a physical body but also an energy body. This is why we can "feel" comfortable (or not) around a person we don't know, even before they speak. Just as energy seeks equilibrium, our energy bodies seek to be with people who resonate at the same or similar frequencies, barring soul contracts or situations with karmic resonance.

We know that veins in the physical body carry nourishment throughout our body, to all physical cells, don't we? Well, the energy body also has "veins," which are called *meridians*, along which the acupuncture points mapped out in Traditional Chinese Medicine are located. The free flow of energy along these pathways is recognized as important for good health by, oh, about half the people on the planet.

At each point where the meridians cross, there is a *chakra*, which means "wheel" in Sanskrit. The body holds 114 chakras, but there are seven main chakras, seen or intuited as balls spinning, places where many meridians cross and specific energy is concentrated and held. While there is largely consensus regarding the descriptions included below, some points, such as the color of the seventh and fourth chakras, are sometimes seen differently depending on the tradition. Notwithstanding such slight cultural differences, the descriptions below are largely accepted and helpful to understanding our instrument and being able to both rise in Frequency and Power.

The following descriptions of the seven chakras include the chakra number, alternate name, aspects of life they reflect, gemstone Ally, and Archangel Ally that can help with balancing that specific chakra:

THE FIRST CHAKRA, also called the **root chakra**, is **red** and is located at the juncture of the torso and legs. **It relates to the vital aspects of our human life on Earth,** including the acceptance of our Life and mission (incarnation), and all issues regarding health, home, money/ spending, job, and so on. It is the "I am" chakra: the presence and existence of our human aspect (as opposed to the seventh chakra, below). **Red jasper** is an excellent crystal Ally for bringing us into harmony with these aspects of our lives.

Archangel Ariel can help us find equilibrium with regard to our presence on Earth and our consumption habits, which impact the planet and our energetic health.

THE SECOND CHAKRA, also called the **sacral chakra**, is **orange** and is located three or four finger-width below the navel. **It relates to our creativity and its physical expressions of sensuality and sexuality** and is the "I feel" or "I accept to feel" chakra. **Carnelian** is an excellent crystal Ally for bringing us into harmony with these aspects of our lives.

Archangel Jophiel, the Archangel of Beauty, can help us balance this energy center, which intimately reflects how we feel inside the beautiful (it is!) body we inhabit.

THIRD CHAKRA, also called the **solar plexus chakra**, is **yellow** and is located in the region of the abdomen, above the navel. **It relates to our Power**—whether we stand in our Power or give it away. This chakra is the key to living Life Large. It is the "Yes, I can!" chakra. **Orange or yellow calcite** is an excellent crystal Ally for bringing us into harmony with this aspect of our lives.

Archangel Michael, the Archangel of Power, can help us balance and cultivate this energy, center, which allows us to dare to live the Life that awaits us.

THE FOURTH CHAKRA, also known as the **heart chakra**, is sometimes seen as either **green or rose colored** and is located at the center of our chest. It relates to our capacity to give or receive Love. It is the "I love" (or "I Am Love") chakra. **Rhodocrosite** (also linked to healing the inner child) is an excellent crystal Ally for bringing us into harmony with this aspect of our life.

Archangel Raphael, the Archangel of Healing, can help us balance this energy center so that we may keep our heart open in a world that tries everything to get us to shut it down.

THE FIFTH CHAKRA, also called the **throat chakra**, is **light blue** and is located at (what a surprise!) our throat. **It relates to our ability to speak our Truth**, to sing our song, and is the seat of communication, creativity, and strength. The phrase associated with this chakra is "I say" or "I sing." **Blue chalcedony** is an excellent crystal Ally for bringing us into harmony with this aspect of our lives.

Archangel Sandalphon, the Archangel of Gentleness and Music, helps us to gently balance this energy center, which reflects how free (or not) we feel to sing our part in the symphony of Life, no matter who is listening!

THE SIXTH CHAKRA, also called the **third eye**, is **midnight blue** and is located in the center of our forehead, just above the eyebrows. **It relates to how we see the world** and understand it and to our clairvoyant capacities to communicate beyond this dimension. **Amethyst** is an excellent crystal Ally for bringing us into harmony with these aspects of our lives.

Archangel Metatron, the Archangel of Wisdom, can help us balance this energy center, which is crucial to understanding and aligning with our mission.

THE SEVENTH CHAKRA, also called the **crown chakra**, is **silver** and is located at the top of the skull, the fontanelle, the soft part that is the last to close after birth, as we start off this life journey as a baby. It is the center that connects the human beings we are during this lifetime with the soul we are lifetime after lifetime. It is the opening to the Source, the Divine, and Angelic connection. **Quartz crystal** is an excellent crystal Ally for bringing us farther into alignment with Who We Are, Truly by opening and clearing this seventh chakra.

Archangel Raziel, the carrier of the Secrets of God and present for all forms of initiation, is eager to assist us in opening and clearing this energy center, which is necessary for the fullness of this and any incarnation.

⁓

In the next chapter we will look at specific ways to do chakra healing with the Angels, but what follows are three quick clearing practices to heal and balance our chakras and elevate their frequency.

Before beginning, open your channel as we have learned and practiced, inviting your Guardian Angels to support your energetic system by purifying and balancing the chakras, thus giving ourselves a boost in the different areas of our lives. (I include the eighth chakra here, which is found about arms' length above our heads. In a pinch, we can also simply place our attention at the level of the eighth chakra, as we know that "where our attention goes, so goes our energy.")

At the end, be sure to thank the Angels in your own words, from the heart.

Each of the following methods can be identified as working with one form of our clairvoyance, so we can clear the chakras and cultivate our "clairs" (hearing, sight, or feeling) at the same time.

DO-RE-MI: (this practice helps to cultivate our clairaudience, or clear hearing). Starting from the first chakra, sing the scale, supporting your energetic system as each note clears and balances the chakra in question:

First chakra	*do*
Second chakra	*re*
Third chakra	*mi*
Fourth chakra	*fa*
Fifth chakra	*so*
Sixth chakra	*la*
Seventh chakra	*ti*
(Eighth chakra)	*do*

This is a quick, fun and easy way to keep our energy system foundation, the chakras, in good form. I like to sing this "on the fly" or, when I have more time, or to sing it repetitively, like a mantra.

BALLS OF LIGHT: (this practice also helps to cultivate our clairvoyance, or clearsightedness).

Starting with the first chakra, imagine each chakra as a ball of its associated color. Next, imagine it filled with light, brightening each chakra with your strong intention and "seeing" the results as a brilliant ball of light, in perfect balance and harmony unto itself and in relationship to the others.

First chakra	red
Second chakra	orange
Third chakra	yellow
Fourth chakra	green or rose-pink—you choose!
Fifth chakra	light blue
Sixth chakra	midnight blue
Seventh chakra	silver
(Eighth chakra)	pure white

HEALING HANDS: (this practice also helps to cultivate our clairsentience, or clearfeeling).

This way of clearing our energetic field relies on the fact that energy passes very easily through the palms of our hands. It is one way in which the body, our human instrument, is played. We know this to be true, don't we? What do we do when we have a headache? Do our hands go to our forehead? And if we have a stomach ache? Do our hands naturally go to our belly? The fact that energy passes easily through our hands is illustrated by the fact that we humans instinctively place our hands on the places on our body where we are experiencing pain. Probably not an accident, right?

With that in mind, after opening the channel and inviting your Angels to assist, rub your hands together. When they are warm, drop your nondominant hand to your side facing forward, like an energetic anchor. Next, place your dominant hand (the one with which you normally write) a couple of inches in front of the first chakra, palm facing toward your body. Allow the hand to connect energetically with the chakra and to fill it with energy. When you sense or feel it is complete, do the same for all of the chakras, one after the other.

Remember that the Angels are guiding and helping you. Take your time. Notice if you feel anything at all; just notice . . . no judgment. The first time you do the exercise, it will be your baseline experience. Notice in what ways your "feeling" and overall experience shift and change and open as you continue this practice.

Move Your Body!

We know that working with our energy body can help us physically, but it is important to remember that the opposite is also true: working out physically can help us energetically. In fact, the more we take care of our instrument, the more Light we can hold and the more we get into the "flow" toward our highest and best destination: high frequency and Power, in alignment with our soul's mission.

It is a good idea to invite our Angels along in each case, as by sharing experiences with them, our connection solidifies further.

Here are some ways to take good care of your physical body. I bet you can think of others!

Walking or Running in Nature

When we breathe in fresh air in Nature, the Life within us (carried on the in-breath) is raised to a higher, purer frequency. In Nature, we relax. Nature puts no pressure on us. Unless we go to the woods putting pressure on ourselves to do or achieve while there, normally we will come out feeling higher and more powerful.

Exercise

Any form of exercise that we do for the fun of it will help us to rise in frequency. Of course, energy-based movement practices, such as yoga, tai chi and qi gong, will in the main help elevate or energize, but remember, not every practice is for everyone. The gentle nature of these practices (when we do them gently, without competition and with great attention to our bodies) makes them ideally suited for many people, however.

In my own life, I remember taking a "hot yoga" class in the center of Paris once and leaving it in an ambulance on the way to the hospital!

Both my insensitivity to my body back then and my competitive nature made me exactly the wrong kind of person for such a practice. As the heat in the room gave me a false sense of "warm-up," I pushed my body too far. Thankfully, I have changed, but I am still more of a *vinyasa* flow person (thanks, Cheryl and Juli at Momentum) than a hot yoga gal. Any kind of exercise you enjoy doing is a good thing. For me, this includes spin cycling and kickboxing, so it is not limited to gentle practice. Just make sure you listen to your body if it tells you to quit!

Singing and Dancing

These two often go hand in hand, and both can aid in the expression of Joy as well as the fluidification or relaxation of the body (release of tension) that marks higher-frequency beings.

SINGING: For singing, it is always good to call in Sandalphon, the Archangel of Music. The idea here is not necessarily to join a choir or to sing in public (karaoke, or no), but rather, to create space in your life to sing with the Angels; to sing the song that comes to mind when you set the intention to sing with the Angels around you . . . which may not be a hallelujah! You can choose whatever song tickles your fancy at a given moment:

- Songs that make us laugh help us rise in frequency.
- Songs from our childhood help us to engage with our Joy, bringing the inner child along for the fun of singing with the Angels.
- Songs that make us cry are also helpful. When we remember that every tear we ever swallowed or choked back has crystallized within us and blocks our channel to some degree, we can see the wisdom in allowing for spontaneous healing through song. I don't need to know what I am healing; I can simply allow the grace of the release.
- It can be interesting also to "open up" and ask your Guardian Angels or Sandalphon what song they would like to sing with you. Then sign whatever comes into mind, or whatever is playing on the radio, knowing that both are suggestions orchestrated by the Angels! (This is a good way to cultivate Angelic communication and confidence in what we are receiving.)

DANCING: Life on this planet can be tension-filled, and the body holds all that tension. Such tension can block our channel to the Angels and the fluidity of our energy body, and thus, our whole being. Dance can be a great solution for the release of that tension, and it also stirs up our creativity.

Which type of dance? It's up to you! Personally, I feel that, to release tension, certain forms of dance (tango comes to mind) may not be exactly the right idea for tension release as they require a certain amount of bodily tension (although tango is soooo beautiful!). Often, meditative dance practices, such as Open Floor, Five Rhythms, or Biodanza release tension and will serve to make us a better tango (or other) dancers!

Of course, we can simply ask the Angels to dance with us and put some music on, allowing our body to flow freely with the music. No one gets to watch, not even you! That is to say, leave your inner critic out of it, and if the critic sneaks in, feel encouraged when you hear any censure from them, such as "Ridiculous!" What the adult in us feels is ridiculous is absolutely the work of the child!

Eating Right/Eating Light

"We are what we eat" is a truth that is self-evident. We can rise in frequency only by deciding to be nourished by high-frequency foods—or Light! (I discuss eating Light in my first book, *The Angels Told Me So,* coming out in English shortly.) The movement toward more conscious consumption, vegetarian and vegan practices, and organic foods shows that humanity is waking up to the importance of what we eat.

The key aspects here include:

1. Listen to *your* instrument, *your* body. What works for one person may not work for another, just as you wouldn't tune a guitar the same way you would, say, a piano. Don't let any "spiritual bullies" tell you what to do (and don't tell anyone else what to do!). Let the Angels and your inner wisdom guide these choices. We are always brought along at the speed that works for our highest good.
2. Drink plenty of water, knowing that it cleanses and purifies and thus helps us to rise in frequency.
3. Whatever enters your body, bless it. Thank Nature (animals or plants, or Light), which furnished the nourishment and then

consume it with gratitude. Gratitude is of the highest importance. If or when we cannot control the quality of what we consume (at a restaurant or when we are invited to eat at someone's house, for example), offering gratitude for the meal raises the frequency of the food and makes each eating experience a high-frequency blessing we offer ourselves.

Creativity

We are sons and daughters of the Creator, and as such, we create. Flexing that muscle by expressing our creativity in any way (singing, dancing, writing, sculpting, painting, acting, and so on) ensures that we align with the Creator within us, and thus, rise in frequency. Artistic creativity also allows us to be more engaged in conscious creation every day, in making our very lives works of art.

Meditation

In cultures all over the world, meditation is considered a key to connecting with the highest good, to raising our frequency. As such, of course we cannot overlook meditation as a means of doing so, but it should be noted that it is not the *only* way to raise our frequency, despite what one may hear. As it is commonly viewed, meditation is regarded as the act of sitting in silence; this is crazy, because for many people, sitting in silence is the farthest thing from meditative they can imagine!

Huh?

If we look at meditation as "any practice that brings us into our inner selves, into that deep space of calm and peace," we know that often (at least for beginners), sitting in silent meditation is more like kicking a hornet's nest!

We have to start somewhere, but it may be the case that our meditative practice can most successfully start with activities such as walking meditation, breathing meditation, drawing, or dancing. Well, you get the idea. Doing something gives our overactive mind something to focus on, allowing the rest of "us" to get quiet, a sure-fire way to raise our frequency!

As for seated silent meditation—when the time is right, we thirst for it; we want it. But if we prematurely engage in it because we are told that it is necessary, if we are forcing ourselves to do it, little good will come of it. Anything done by obligation and not by Love is *low* frequency, not high!

Energy Work

Scientists now tell us that everything is made of energy, including us, so recognizing this, if the desire is there, doing energy work in any form will help us to rise in frequency.

Whether we use the 15 different Archangelic energy healing exercises outlined earlier; the chakra clearing work noted above, which relies on energy to balance and clear our energetic system; or any of the gazillion energy healing modalities available these days, it all comes down to this: Our intention will render all ritual effective, and the ritual (or modality) you choose to practice will render your intention even more powerful.

When we invite in the Angels to assist us, we allow our work to be strengthened enormously, so for even the loners among us (like me), it makes sense to work with the Angelic realm to densify and intensify all energy healing work.

Personally, I have chosen to work with Reiki as my primary modality of energy work (in addition to Angelic Healing, of course). I am a Reiki Master Teacher and take pleasure in teaching Reiki classes and doing treatments around the world. My choice of Reiki is the result of being guided to a Reiki lineage that suits me and is simple and effective.

I find that the word *reiki* (Japanese for "universal energy") can be off-putting for non-Japanese people, so here I will simply say "universal energy." What could be more natural than energy work, when we are all made of energy?

In a future book, I will delve further into energy work and some of the many variations of it, but here are a few keys to remember if you decide to delve (further) into energy work:

Choose the modality that makes your heart skip a beat. Listen to your body. Either in receiving energy work, or in training or giving energy work for another, make sure that you are happy with the specifics of the modality proposed.

For example, I once trained in a beautiful energetic healing modality called Frequencies of Brilliance. I was finding it a bit complicated but didn't want to drop out (due to my strident "I am not a quitter!" mindset that stomps on my happiness whenever I let it). However, when I got to the part where it was suggested to tape crystals to the person's skin, I decided it was not really for me. It's not that it doesn't work, mind you—I just find Reiki simpler, easier, and more elegant. But that is *my* guidance; each of us needs to listen to our own guidance. If we don't feel happy doing something, it is probably because our way is another way.

Choose the person you feel most at ease and comfortable with to practice either receiving or giving the work. Often we are afraid to offend someone, so we may be tempted to accept a session from or give a session to someone with whom we wouldn't drink a cup of hot chocolate (I don't do coffee).

Don't do it! If we go ahead and engage in intimate (yes this is very intimate, even more so than, say, bad sex would be) energy exchange—and that is what an energy healing session should be!—with a person we would prefer not to be around, who are we are listening to? Yes, that's right! We are not listening to *ourselves*, not listening to the inner child, and the good that could come from a session will not happen because we are not true to ourselves. Imagine being forced to kiss a relative or family friend who gives us the heebie-jeebies.

Doing energy work with someone we have reticence about is not good for anybody. This is not a question of politeness. While there is no need to be mean to the other person (avoid statements like "I don't like your energy; get away from me!"), there is no need to be mean to ourselves, either. A diplomatic "I am not 'feeling' this to be the highest and best good for me right now" will suffice. You do *not* need to explain your decision to take good care of yourself, and a good person or energy worker will understand that. If it is you who are offering a session, respect yourself and the other person will respect you, too. "This is not a good time for us to do the session" always works, and who knows, maybe you will feel it appropriate another time.

If you are receiving any kind of bodywork (massage, Reiki, and so on), make sure that you speak up if anything is uncomfortable: temperature, noise levels, the manner of touching. *You* must be your own advocate here, the best friend you can be to yourself. No professional would ever hold it against you (and most practitioners will appreciate it).

If you are the person offering a healing session, be sure to let the person know that they are encouraged to share anything with you that would render the experience more agreeable. The more comfortable and at ease both giver and receiver are, the more effective and efficient a healing session and the higher the rise in frequency for both of you. At its best, the experience brings both parties into a sacred space where there is no giver and no receiver—a rare and beautiful experience of nonduality.

Amplitude or Power

We all know them, don't we? The people who get noticed, those with charisma. They enter a room, and everyone turns to see who came in, as if their presence could be felt.

It can.

These are people whose amplitude or Power are so strong that their energy fields reach far beyond the envelope of their body, so their presence *can* be felt by those who are sensitive. Such people turn heads, and their arrival in a room, even a crowded one, does not go unnoticed.

On the other hand, just as we know that some people entering a room can cause such an energetic ripple effect, others can be in a place for hours and no one remembers they even came ("Oh, you were there? Really?").

The difference between the person who is noticed and the one who is unseen is a question of amplitude, of Power, of presence. The more we are aligned with our soul level, or Presence, the more our human presence is felt. Energy seeks equilibrium, as noted earlier, so if we cultivate relationship with the Angels, our energy field rises and strengthens; it is *so good* to have Friends in High Places!

As we saw earlier, it does us no good to cultivate a high frequency that is fleeting; we need to muscle it up, anchor into it, cultivate some Power, of presence. This section offers some helpful hints on how.

Practice, Practice, Practice

Yep. Sorry. The key to how to get to Carnegie Hall is the same as the key to cultivate presence: we need to practice. Although I imagine that some people are born that way, most of us need to work at it. So, what to practice? The answer is anything—anything that raises your frequency, any and all of the practices mentioned earlier, as well as anything else you can come up with that makes you want to practice it. Anything that connects us to our Joy, anything that serves our body, anything that floats our boat can be a spiritual practice, as long as we have the intention that it be so.

Practice Something You Enjoy

We have to want to do it, though! Sure, leaving my cozy warm bed at 6 a.m. this morning to go to the pool to swim wasn't a happy thought at first, but enthusiasm grows once we get going. Similarly, as we cultivate, for example, a sitting meditation practice we may not naturally love to sit right away; it comes over time. The trick is not to sit in meditation if we are doing it grudgingly.

If we actively don't want to sit, where is our energy going? Since "where my attention goes, so goes the energy," if my attention is on how much I *don't* want to be meditating, then we can surmise that there is no true meditation, no inner calm, and thus no Power being cultivated, right? Get up, and do something else!

I liken the "forced meditation" scenario to a grown person going to visit his parents. Imagine how sad the parents would feel if they thought that the child was there only out of obligation, and couldn't wait to leave! In the same way, we practice to "visit" with our Selves, and Joy is not what results when we force ourselves to spend time with us!

So find a practice that brings you lighthearted Joy, especially when you start out engaging with it.

Varying the Practice Can Be Very Good

We don't have to stick to just one practice; that is, unless we really *want* to! Remember, our highest frequency results from our highest desires, from "following our bliss." It depends on the person. If someone had a lot of strict rules placed on them as children, it may well be that flexibility will be more interesting than rigid discipline. The idea is to balance the firm and the flexible, the strong and the soft.

Why not ask the child within us each morning which practice sounds like the most fun for that day? Or cultivate our Angelic alliances by asking our Guardian Angels, "What would you like to do today? Sing? Dance? Both? Work with crystals? Chakra healing?" Allow whatever comes up to guide you. Let yourself be guided. Practice is unique to the individual. For example, if you know yourself to be someone who needs a firmer structure, go deep in your daily structured practice. Just practice!

The idea is to practice until each word has the power of a mantra, each thought becomes a meditation, each gesture a sacred mudra. In other words, until our human form consciously aligns with the sacred in us. Practice, practice, practice!

We are entering into a time in history when we have the possibility to contribute to the shift in values: from fear to love, from darkness to light. This is the Olympic Games of spirituality: the training is the key.

We are no longer training for some future time when we will be called to step into action. The time is now! We have been served, remember?

We are here to play, yes, but to play hard, *non*?

Yes! So let's go, Team Lightworkers! Practice, practice, practice!

Silence

Silence is another key to establishing and cultivating our power. Do you have a friend who won't—who can't—shut up? Think of the last time you spoke to them. When someone like this is speaking, do we always listen intently? Or do our eyes maybe glaze over as we think of how we can get out of there and get on with our day? (Does the person even notice you aren't listening?) Importantly, notice this: As you walk away, are you tired? If so, that is energy seeking equilibrium—Scenario Three, as we discussed above.

Perhaps you may know someone who can't stand silence, who always needs to have background noise—a TV or radio, maybe? I would be surprised if you don't, as much of Western civilization these days is really just filled with so much noise.

The noise is not an accident—not even close—though it may well be unconscious.

When we are in silence, we are faced with . . . our Selves. And if life has been such that we have strayed from Who We Are, Truly (also a common occurrence), being in that silence with no distractions, no place to hide, can be mightily uncomfortable.

So we talk, or we flip on the TV, because there is thunder in silence and comfort in sound. No one is challenging us to go deeper when the world is a noisy place . . . or at least, you can't hear it.

How comfortable we are in silence is a measure of how aligned we are with ourselves and with our Power. So to get Power, we need to get quiet, real quiet, and maybe avoid the noisy ones for a while.

For example: Think of a group dinner. Isn't there often at least one person chattering away? Imagine now that someone at the table who hasn't said a word suddenly speaks up. All heads turn to hear what they have to say. Why is that? Because each word carries energy. So if we speak a lot, energy is dispersed, not concentrated. If we speak little, the energy is concentrated. Ergo, our words carry more weight (energetically, literally) when we speak less, and people always listen more to folks who speak less.

Buddhist meditation retreats in the Vipassana tradition, also called Insight Meditation, are offered throughout the world, at meditation centers and temples, from short one-day and weekend retreats to longer retreats of 10 days and more, including more than 13 hours a day sitting in silence (which is not for everyone). When I did my 10-day retreat at a Buddhist temple, I remember that when it was time to speak again, I didn't want to. Silence, our natural state, grows on us quickly when we allow it! In the silence, we align with our inner power, and it becomes very simply our Power. Our presence becomes our Presence. The human opens to the fullness of the incarnation of the soul. And things become very, very interesting . . .

In a Pinch: Archangel Michael

While we are working on our energy levels, until such time as we feel strong and stand well in our Power, why not ask for help? Remember that Archangel Michael is here for all Lightworkers, and for all who wish to step into their Power in alignment with the highest good. So until such time as you feel strong enough to stand facing all the Mr. Joneses of the world, call on Archangel Michael with his mighty sword to pick up the slack.

In the photo on page 239 at the back of this book, that presence was there when the photographer took the photo, and only for this photo! She knew it, and I did too. Michael can bring us to Power even as we are preparing to step into it ourselves. Frequency and Amplitude: an energy mix that will stand us in strength as we walk our paths of Light!

If on your path, you find yourself in unfamiliar terrain, let Archangel Michael be your guide or sherpa. Imagine that you are crossing a forest or a jungle, a place where no one has passed before. Allow Archangel Michael to use his sword like a machete to clear the way before you.

As the "boss" of all Lightworkers, Archangel Michael is eager to help his "employees" be successful when a need arises, so be sure to let the "boss" know. Ask for help, keep on moving steadily, and watch how synchronicities appear to resolve any difficulties that may arise.

Recognizing that Lightworkers often present as hypersensitive (which some term "too sensitive"!), it is not a luxury but a necessity to be aware of how our instruments (our body on all levels: physical, mental, emotional, spiritual) work and even more importantly, to know how to help our instruments and ourselves survive and advance in a rapidly shifting and sometimes caustic environment. Realizing that we have at any time the power to stabilize and strengthen ourselves, avoiding the "weakness" of our sensitive aspect in favor of transforming it to its potential strength, power, and charisma, is life-changing for many.

Easy to remember, frequency and amplitude, both are important! Knowing what we need to elevate frequency and power levels, and using those tools with the help of Angels when we find ourselves amidst the energy traps of this world are key to not just surviving but thriving in a changing world. A world that needs more Lightworkers resilient enough to be able to mix and mingle in the corners and shine Light in the darkness therein.

◠

CHAPTER 9

Angelic Healing

Once we have a clear understanding (as gleaned from the last chapter) about how our energetic interactions with others work, life becomes simpler. Such knowledge gives us clues to ensure our well-being in a situation from this point forward.

But what about the stockpile of wounds we received in the past? How can we release the weight of those past hurts so that our own wings can open, so we can fly?

Past energetic hurts, such as those we incurred as a child and that we still carry, are the stuff of which current physical, mental, or emotional woes are made. For one who would train to step into our Power and *live the mission* our soul has chosen, it behooves us to clear away that which holds us back, whether it is rooted in the past or arising in the present.

Not a Victim

For that to happen, we need to decide very clearly that we are not a victim. These days, so many conversations (which we create with our words) focus on what is *not* going well for us, how we are victims—of sickness, or government, or big business, or other people. Victim, victim, victim!

The "woe is me" complex likely belongs to all of us to some degree (for sure, I am not completely inured to this addiction, or bad habit, if you will, though my comportment is much cleaner now than it was in the past).

Stepping into our power with the help of the Angels means deciding (with our powerful intention) to no longer point the finger at others or at our situation, but rather, to stand up and move forward to our strength (for example, with practices such as those mentioned in the previous chapter). Since the beginning of our journey, we have been engaged in a path of healing with the Angels. As we lift our attention to the Angels, their presence allows us to shift automatically, effortlessly. Have you noticed? There is more ease, more synchronicity, more fluidity along the path . . . more healing! Remember that healing, on the Angelic or higher plane, is always a realignment with Who We Are, Truly. The impact of such a realignment is, as discussed earlier, not always a "healing" such as society would expect. Our symptoms may persist, but our understanding and thus our suffering over them will be healed.

Angelic healing always allows for an energetic ritual that supports the Truth of things; that we have never left the Source, that the Truth of who we are is One; that we are playing the role of a lifetime in the theater called "Earth"; that the more we stand in our Power and Presence, the more the myth of victimhood is abolished. When we realize the truth of our Game, and see that everything that happens plays to our highest good, we can release the guilt or blame that drags us down and binds our wings, or keeps us from the experience of Joy as we walk our path of a lifetime.

Not a Savior

Not only is it necessary to release the limiting belief that we are victims here on Earth but also the equally limiting belief that we are saviors: that is, that others *need* our help to get by, or succeed. As Lightworkers, we may have already lived a life full of experiences in which we *have* been helpful to others, but being helpful to someone and saving them are two different things.

People can be eager to give over their power to someone who seems inclined to carry them, so it is important to recognize that others walk the path their souls have chosen, just as we walk the path our soul chose. And though our physical human experience may make it seem like one of us is stronger and the other weaker, it is important to remember that even those aspects are built into the instruments, into the roles that we are each playing.

In the end, each soul is "of" the Source, so while it is good to lend a hand, it is important not to get caught up in a limiting belief that places the burden of saving anyone (except the inner child within, whom you may have held captive) on your shoulders.

Moreover, the role of Savior feeds the ego, and is therefore a trap to avoid for anyone.

Finally, if we continually "save" people who give over their power to us, they may become dependent; essentially, we steal away their wings (even if they gave them to us). We are One—not a victim, not a savior, but simply Love spilling into Life through vessels that all have their own cracks.

In addition to the many healing protocols already outlined in this book, I teach three others regularly, based on protocols I learned from my early teacher, Doreen Virtue: Purification/Illumination, Relationship Harmonization, and Angel Card Readings.

Purification and Illumination

The following practice can be done either for ourselves or for someone else. It works "live and in person" or at a distance, but at the beginning it is interesting to work to gain confidence by working on ourselves or with another person who is physically present. The beauty of this Angelic Healing is that the burden of the efficacy of the healing sessions rests squarely on the shoulders of the Archangels! Which is as it should be; certainly, if we are just beginning to work with the Angels and energy.

But even if we are not new to this kind of work, it is interesting to allow the Angels to take on the burden of effectiveness. In this way, we are not attached to a particular outcome, knowing that the Archangels Michael and Raphael will always ensure the highest outcome possible for everyone concerned.

Furthermore, it allows us to avoid the pitfall of pride/ego and allows the person to realize that they are in direct communication with the Archangels and have no need of us (no savior, no victim!). This both frees us and allows the person to stand in their own Power and Love. Win-win! For this reason, the optimum physical position will be not too close to the person—just outside the person's field of energy, or about two feet, if we are not sure.

This protocol supposes that we do this healing for ourselves, but it can be adjusted to allow us to work with the Archangels for someone else as well.

Purification/Illumination with Archangels Michael and Raphael

Play with Archangels Michael and Raphael!

1. Connect with your breath, and come into a peaceful place of quiet. Use your channel to anchor (ground) yourself, following your ribbon of light into the center of the earth, then open to the highest good with your intention, tracing your channel of Light from the center of the earth through your heart up to the heavens. Return to your heart to set your intention, both as the human being you are and on a soul level. (If you are undertaking this exercise, it is without a doubt the will of your soul.) Set your intention to receive this Purification and Illumination from Archangel Michael and Raphael.

2. Sit, feet planted solidly on the ground, shoulder-width apart, shoulders pulled back so that your spinal column—the bridge you create between the earth and the heavens—is straight. Allow your arms to relax, and place your hand on your lap, palms facing upward in a position of energetic openness. *Breathe in* the presence of Angels and Archangels all around you. *Breathe out* anything that blocks your opening to them. Allow yourself to fill with Light and peace, with a sense of the Love that is there for you; to feel, perhaps, the Joy that your presence brings in this space. Take three or four deep breaths before continuing.

3. With your eyes closed, ask Archangel Michael to offer a Purification: that all that is ready to be released be released. Imagine that Archangel Michael stands before you, and at your request, folds his wings over and around you, creating a cocoon of clearing. He breathes in, and like a vacuum cleaner, sucks up anything that no longer serves you. Contact with Him allows for instant transformation of any lower energies being released. The healing continues until every level is cleared: physical, mental, emotional and spiritual/energetic. While Michael is working, *relax and breathe*. Receive this Purification, this release by Grace. You have done well, but now it is time to let the Angels intervene on your behalf. Rest in the arms of the Divine, held in the powerful embrace of Michael's wings. When you feel it is complete, thank Michael and turn to Raphael for Illumination.

4. As we move consciously toward or through our mission, it is important that we ensure that our vehicles (the body on all levels) remain full, our "cup" overflowing. This because it supports our power and our mission, as we have seen, but there is also another reason. When we have "gaps," those are possible points of entry for lower energies (such as when I get grumpy if I am tired). As we know, folks around us do not always exude good energy, and some souls do not immediately leave the earth plane for various reasons, so it is good to ensure that we do not become a stopover for any energy that does not belong within us.

For that reason, it is a good idea to immediately call upon Archangel Raphael once Archangel Michael has finished his clearing work, so that Raphael can ensure that we are illuminated, filled with His green light of healing, of renewed life, filled to overflowing, and thus in no way at risk for lower energy—ours or somebody else's, living or not.

With your eyes closed, ask Archangel Raphael to offer an Illumination: that you be filled with the green light of healing on all levels. Imagine that Archangel Raphael takes the place of Archangel Michael, standing before you. At your request, it is Raphael that now folds His wings around you, even as He places His hands over your head, creating a cocoon that allows for your filling and Illumination. His palms are over your crown chakra, facing down; from them streams bright green light—the green of new grass in spring, the green of renewal and hope, the green of the heart chakra energy.

As He works on you, allow yourself to be filled with the Light until every level is overflowing: physical, mental, emotional and spiritual/energetic. While Raphael is working, *relax and breathe*. Receive this Illumination, this renewal, this bolstering by Grace. You have done all you can under your own steam; now it is time to let the Angels intervene on your behalf. Rest in the arms of the Divine, held in the powerful embrace of Raphael's wings.

5. Continue until you feel satisfied that it is complete. (You cannot make a mistake here: it is your intention and the request for the assistance from Archangels Michael and Raphael that renders the healing session effective. How long you remain in that space is training your instrument, your sensitivity and Power, over

time.) Thank Archangels Michael and Raphael by bringing your hands to your chest in a gesture of gratitude for this sacred moment of opening and sounding and Joy and Power.

The Aftercare noted on p. 56 is a very good way to help integrate this important work.

Harmonize Relationships

During this period of great change for the earth, when we are perhaps also personally changing rapidly, we can imagine that a relationship that was fine yesterday or the day before can be out of sync today. Our energetic growth can actually have a negative impact on those around us, on those we love. Imagine we are in a canoe with pretty much everyone who is close to us (a lot of canoes!): in each case, stability exists, perhaps precariously, but if we shift energetically, imagine it is as being as though we suddenly stand up in the boat! Not particularly agreeable for our canoe partners, right?

This protocol allows us to act in a preventive manner to smooth out all passages of change for us and for our loved ones. For this reason, I use this one for myself and my loved ones probably every single day. You may find it helpful, too!

It can also be used to work effectively with aspects of ourselves! We simply invite the part of us who judges, or smokes, or gossips, whatever the habit is, to come face us, and the Archangels work the same way. At the end, we have only to reintegrate that aspect of our being by inviting that part of us to step into our arms and our heart as an Angelic soul retrieval!

The protocol can also be used to heal a relationship with someone who has passed on, a wonderful gift for both us and the loved one who has departed. We can also use this to release places (a home that won't sell, or for which we are feeling great homesickness). Be creative and listen to your intuition/inner knowing!

NOTE: This healing protocol is practiced in many forms in many different types of practices. It can be done without the help of the Angels, but why not benefit from the Help of such Friends in High Places as Archangels Michael and Raphael?

The healing is founded upon the idea that we connect energetically to those around us as our energy fields join. In our energetic field connections, there are ties or cords that can bind us to each other: when they are strong, it may be hard to feel free of the other person; if they are loose, we may feel very free in their presence.

If we imagine that these cords sometimes form around the chakras, relative to the relationship that we experience with the other person (money around the first chakra; maybe sexuality around the second, power around the third, love around the fourth, speaking our truth around the person connected to the fifth chakra, sharing how we each perceive the world and our values around the sixth chakra, and soul-level connection around the seventh chakra. You get the picture.).

Since no relationship has perfect, sustained balance around all of these levels, we can see that any relationship can benefit from a relationship harmonization. (Around the seventh chakra, we are already headed to the soul level, and no one is in our life if they have no "soul" level role to play, so that level is usually balanced already.)

Other modalities, such as shamanic practice and other energy work, suggest that we or another practitioner "cut the cords" that tie us to another person. There is even a protocol that uses wooden matches to do the work! Those practices work, of course they do. It is our intention that renders those practices effective. Our intention, as children of Creator, is powerful. But I would argue that it makes more sense to ask the Angels to take on this work, primarily for three reasons.

First, I may not want to cut all the cords with another person! What if there are levels that are flowing wonderfully? And how about our soul connection? Or the fact that we are all, truly, One? To my mind, a complete cutting is energetic overkill.

Second, sure, maybe in response to the first point, I could only cut what is in disharmony. But who's to say I see correctly? Don't we all have our filters? I may think that the other person feels comfortable speaking their Truth to me, but am I right? Asking Archangel Michael to cut any cords in disharmony precludes any such errors and lifts the burden of analysis of the relationship from my shoulders to boot!

Third, this protocol allows for healing energy to fill both parties. You can't argue with that!

Thus, though I have personally practiced this in other ways in the past, once I began doing work with Archangels Michael and Raphael, I let all other relationship harmonization practices go. Try it and see if this will be your go-to, as well.

The following protocol steps are set up to do it for yourself and a person in your life. It can be tweaked to be offered in any of the above ways, or for someone else.

Relationship Harmonization

1. Connect with your breath, and come into a peaceful place of quiet. Use your channel to anchor (ground) yourself, following your ribbon of light into the center of the earth, then open to the highest good with your intention, tracing your channel of light from the center of the earth through your body/instrument, and up to the heavens. Return to your heart to set your intention, both as the human being you are and on a soul level. (If you are undertaking this exercise, it is without a doubt the will of your soul.) Decide with whom you would like to harmonize your relationship. Set your intention to receive this Relationship Harmonization from Archangels Michael and Raphael.

2. Stand, feet planted solidly on the ground, shoulder-width apart, shoulders pulled back so that your spinal column—the bridge you create between the earth and the heavens—is straight. Allow the arms to relax at your sides, palms facing forward in a position of energetic openness. *Imagine* that the person in question is standing in front of you, facing you. This is an energetic invitation; on a soul level, the answer is always yes. Be aware that you may receive a contact on a physical level (text, email, phone call) triggered by the work afterward. Note: you don't need the permission of the other person to do this work, as you do it *for yourself.* We each have the right to harmonize our relationships. If we choose to do the work, we can be certain that on a soul level this was agreed to long ago. If you organize this healing for another person, know that always at least one of the parties in question must agree.

3. With your eyes closed, ask Archangel Michael to cut all that is in disequilibrium between the two of you. Michael will come and situate Himself between the two of you, slightly

to the side. As you have asked, his sword will raise and fall, cutting only that which is in disequilibrium, in a kind of energetic surgery. This "surgery" is very powerful. It cuts all ties or cords in disharmony thoroughly, including the history of it (disharmony is seldom just in the present moment, but most often is built on past relationship disharmony over a long time, often repetitive).

NOTE: if you live with the person, the habits of your interactions may continue, but the strength of the years that anchored these imbalances is gone. If you keep working to harmonize the relationship, each time is easier, and at some point, by the Grace of Source, expressed through Archangels Michael and Raphael, the healing will be complete.
This may not render a sick relationship well; however, it may simply heal it sufficiently so that both people feel free to leave, harmoniously.

Thank Archangel Michael, and turn to Archangel Raphael to complete the harmonization with a Healing.

4. Ask Archangel Raphael to complete the Relationship Harmonization by offering a Healing to both parties: you and the other. At your request, "see," "feel," or "know" that Archangel Raphael takes the place of Archangel Michael, standing between the two of you, slightly to the side. He extends his hands over both of you, one hand over each of your heads, just above the crown chakra. From his palms flows a strong green light of healing, which will allow for the healing of all that was cut in Archangel Michael's surgery, bringing harmony and peace and clearing all toxicity and imbalance.
    Breathe, and allow Archangel Raphael to ensure that each of you is filled and the remains of the cords that were cut by Archangel Michael dissolve easily. In this way, each one takes back their Power and releases to the other what belongs to them energetically. When Raphael is complete, each one stands in their own Power facing the other, and the only energetic connections that remain in place are harmonious.

5. Request that Archangels Michael and Raphael now enfold both of you in Their wings, for in truth you are one, even though it may not be always so easy to see it is so. Continue until you feel satisfied that it is complete. (You cannot make a mistake here: it is your intention and the request for the assistance from Archangels Michael and Raphael that render the healing session effective. How long you remain in that space is training your instrument, its sensitivity and Power, over time.)

Thank Archangels Michael and Raphael by bringing your hands to your chest in a gesture of gratitude for this sacred moment of opening and sounding and Joy and Power. If you have done the work with another person, thank them and wish them well on their energetic journey.

The Aftercare noted on p. 56 is a very good way to help yourself integrate this important work.

Oracle Card Readings

When we do an oracle card reading with the Angels, it is indeed a Healing. We prepare in the same way, and close in the same way, recognizing the sacred in the action of using a support (oracle cards) to facilitate communication with the Angels.

Cards are great: they are like bicycle training wheels for Angelic communication. In the beginning we may rely on them heavily, but eventually we will find that we are receiving the answers directly, like a child who suddenly notices that her training wheels are not touching the ground. All the better!

Remember this is just *one* way to do a card reading. Let yourself always and ever be guided by your inspiration. It is how the Angels speak to you!

This protocol is for a single card reading for yourself. It can be tweaked to do a reading for someone else, of course. Instead of one card, you may opt to do a three-card reading: past/present/future, for example, or physical/mental and emotional/spiritual aspects of the situation. A reading can be done on a particular question, or we may simply ask for the messages that are the most pertinent to us generally at this time. Let yourself *play* with it: *fun* raises our frequency!!

Angel Card Reading

1. Connect with your breath, and come into a peaceful place of quiet. Set your intention to receive a card reading with the help of your Guardian Angels.

2. Use your channel to anchor (ground) yourself, following your ribbon of light into the center of the earth, then open to the highest good with your intention, tracing your channel of light from the center of the earth to the heavens. Return to your heart to set your intention, both as the human being you are and on a soul level. (If you are undertaking this exercise, it is without a doubt the will of your soul.)

3. Sit, feet planted solidly on the ground, shoulder-width apart, shoulders pulled back so that your spinal column—the bridge you create between the earth and the heavens—is straight. Have your cards at the ready. (The cards to which you are attracted are always the best cards for you!) *Breathe in* the presence of Angels and Archangels all around you. *Breathe out* anything that blocks your opening to them. Allow yourself to fill with Light and peace, filled with a sense of the Love that is there for you; to feel, perhaps, the Joy that your presence brings in this space. Take three or four deep breaths at least before continuing.

4. Decide if you have a specific question, or if you are open to whatever message the Angels want to communicate at this time. With your eyes closed, ask your Guardian Angels to show you the card that carries the most pertinent message for you at this time. Shuffle the cards. Open your eyes and choose the card that calls to you. Choose in your own way. Some use their clairsentience to "feel" the card, some use their clairvoyance to "see" the card, others, with their clairaudience, "hear" a number and go to that card. Find *your* way, but choose quickly! The longer we linger, the more likely our head will get in the way. If this happens, shuffle and begin again.

5. Once you have the card, *breathe in* again, and on the *out-breath*, look at it. Do the words speak to you? And the image? As humans, images speak more directly to us than words, so if the words do not seem pertinent, focus on the picture. Where are your eyes drawn? Notice the thoughts that

come to you. Allow it to flow in rapid-fire rhythm without a filter; get used to allowing the flow to come. With practice, this becomes easier; eventually, we begin to receive the messages even before the cards are drawn. Have fun!

6. When you are finished, thank your Guardian Angels by bringing your hands to your chest in a gesture of gratitude for this sacred moment of opening and sounding and Joy and Power.

The Aftercare noted on p. 56 is a very good way to help yourself integrate this important work.

PART FOUR

NEXT STEPS

CHAPTER 10

Angelic Co-creation

Hopefully by now, we have explored sufficient tools for you to connect with the Angels and Archangels and empower your inner child, reinforce your energy (both Frequency and Amplitude) to make yourself ready to step more and more into your power, *non?*

Boy, I hope you said *yes!*

As we move forward, the idea is to recognize Who We Are, Truly and know that our destiny is not to cower before a God who will judge us but to stop judging ourselves long enough to see and feel and know His great Love for us. As we approach that knowing, we begin to relax, which will be the key to our Shining, to our Power, to our Large Life, in alignment with our soul's mission, in co-creation with the Angels.

What Is Angelic Co-creation?

Generally speaking, Co-creation is a collaboration, a partnership put in place for creative purposes.

Angelic Co-creation is essentially a partnering with the Angelic realm (our Guardian Angels and the Archangels) in order to live our lives to the fullest, in the service of Light, Love, and Joy.

Sounds good, right? So, how do we get there?

It takes both what we have been discussing in the book so far (Taking Action with the Angels) and a bold move toward Angelic Co-creation to work in collaboration.

Taking Action with the Angels: A Love Story

If you will, Taking Action with the Angels (the name of the first Angel Class I teach and the pre-requisite to Angelic Co-creation) is the "getting to know you" part of Angelic relationship. Like the beginning of a romance, it is the "flash and sparkle" part. We are excited to receive clear indications that we are *not* crazy: there really is a Divine presence with us, entering into communication with us in unique and individual ways that reassure us. The work we have already done together builds a nice foundation.

It is helpful to have sufficient experience with the Angels in our daily lives that allow us to go beyond the early questions like "Do they exist?" (Oh, how they chuckle at that one, since mostly, we are squeezing our metaphoric—and sometimes our physical—eyes shut to avoid "seeing" that they are there!) Hanging out more and more (by concentrating our attention on the Angels, our energy follows and connects with them) with the Angelic realm, our frequency shifts upward. But that's not all that happens!

A Word about Ups and Downs on a Spiritual Path

It is important to be adult about things and recognize that this spiritual life is not just feathers and clouds and pretty lights and colors. Just as there are higher energies (the highest including Angels), the duality of the earth also includes lower energies, acting both within us and outside of us. It is very important to note, then, this truth that is not often mentioned on the so-called "spiritual" path:

As we stretch up toward our Light, darkness will react and try to pull us back down. This may be friends or family who mock or avoid us or people who leave us. This may be injury or depression. It may take the form of things that go away (job, relationship, health, and so on). No fun (but so worth it!).

Everything intensifies on the path (just as at the beginning of a relationship!). But since the highs are so high, the "fall" afterward can seem never-ending and make us call all of it into question.

This is normal. It happens to most of us!

When, or if, this happens, do not hesitate to call on Archangel Michael for protection and healing. Use the different healing protocols in this book to reconnect with yourself and touch in with the angels. Or simply take your foot off the gas (we do tend to run forward when the path opens up for us), and slow down. Allow for some stability. Let the light settle until it is time to begin again. Even if we have ups and downs, the trend is up. You can be sure of it!

Taking action with the Angels requires a leap of faith on our path, and a stick-to-it-iveness that allows us to continue even when the world (and maybe our head!) tells us this is crazy. That is only fear—the opposite of Love—trying to slow us down!

In the beginning, we learn to *ask* the Angels for help, and we learn to *allow* them to help us! (That second part is a doozy for some; believe me, I know! If you are used to carrying it all on your shoulders, the idea of handing the reins over to someone else—even that Someone Else!—is not always simple. But boy, is it worth it!)

That is how it begins . . .

Angelic Co-creation: A Second-Half Love Story

This is how it ends. Or at least, how it grows and flourishes, and it is a lot of *fun*! There is much less drama at this level!

As we cultivate a strong relationship with the Angels, we begin to relax and *trust* that the Plan is greater than even what we have envisioned for ourselves. As in a (healthy) romantic relationship, though the flashy moments have subsided, a strong partnership is put into place, and we can deeply relax, knowing that we are safe within the relationship. We know that the Angels "have our back." We can trust it, and we know that we, too, can be trusted, that we are up for this collaboration; we are worthy partners for the long haul.

In that state of relaxation, Spirit moves, and magic happens! We enter into Co-creation, and things fall into place. The Joy is there, not in a short-lived flashy way, but in a deeply rooted, confident peaceful way. There are fewer highs and lows, more peace and stability. The Joy we experience has somehow matured, and the lessons we learn are more a fine-tuning that an overhaul in nature.

We have arrived!

If you will, the image of Taking Action with the Angels is like a human humbly asking for help. Which is often (not always, but often) how it begins, as we need to *unlearn* all the "unworthiness" crap the world has ladled onto us.

But as that is cleared away, Angelic Co-creation is the movement that sees us stand up, straight and tall, accepting our place between Earth and Sky, worthy partners to the Angels around us. When we so stand, Angelic Co-creation becomes possible; true partnership becomes possible. And *fun*! (If it's not fun, if there is no Joy, it's not Angel work! The Angelic realm vibrates at the frequency of the highest good: Joy.) Given all that, it makes sense to continue on our path with the Angels, eyeing that prize of co-creation, *non*?

Yes!

So let's look at how.

The Three Prerequisites to Good Partnership

The three prerequisites to good partnership, and therefore, to good Angelic Co-creation are:

- Equality
- Unanimity of Vision
- The Contracts

As with our fellow human beings it also helps to have some clarity with the Angels, to have a good understanding of where we stand, what we envision and how we can support each other in order to manifest this. So let's begin at the beginning . . .

EQUALITY

You know yourself to be the equal of the Angels, right? What? You don't? Well, that's no surprise, is it?

In the main, the way this world is structured tears down our confidence, rather than builds it up. Even religions often focus on our sins instead of our light, right?

Similarly, schools and tests focus on what we got "wrong" (competition, of necessity, has a loser as well as a winner). We are often judged not on our unique strengths but on how we compare with others. In short, society as it stands now is not generally made for recognizing our beauty, talent, and all-around wonderful-ness. We find the faults, we focus on them—others' or our own—and so if some Bronx chick from Paris tells us we are the equal to the Angels, well, that can be just a little hard to swallow! Maybe she's been drinking too much wine?

Not! (None at all, in fact.)

The key to any partnership lies in both parties recognizing equality—not sameness, but equality; that is, recognizing that each party brings to the partnership something valuable, probably something the other doesn't have. We may easily recognize that in the Angels, but we need to see it in ourselves as well. In the end, there are not one but two very good reasons to believe we are the equal of the Angels: (1) We are One, all part of the Source: there is no place that God is not, and (2) We have capabilities the Angels do not.

We Are One

If we recognize the Truth that there is no place that God/Source is not, we must concede that that must also include us: God is in *us* (which is already a great reason to start honoring ourselves instead of tearing ourselves down, *non?*).

Esoterically speaking, All is One: there is no separation—God/Source, the Angels, Us, the neighbor's cat. God expresses in everything and everyone. God would not be God if something outside of God were possible. So we can begin to grapple with the Truth of our energetic equality at the root level: we spring from the same Source.

But since we are hanging around on Earth these days, in the density, maybe it is easier to believe that Angels are part of God/Source than the truth that *we* are also? This is exactly why the second reason is important…

We Have Capabilities the Angels Do Not

We are equal to the Angels as we enter partnership, because we bring our own (mad) skills to the partnership. There are things we can do more easily than they can!

In a good partnership, each partner has a role to play, and we play to our strength. For example, were I to decide to form a restaurant partnership with someone, I would choose someone who is a great chef, and the way we would define our roles is clear: They would do the cooking, and I would take care of the business end (trust me!). It would make no sense at all for an artist/chef to do the books, sending a former banker/not-cook like me into the kitchen. In addition, when we do something we love, we are good at it, and we normally love what we are good at, which makes for Joy, that wonderful Angel Juice!

So, as we move toward Co-creation with the Angels, it is important to understand and know that equality exists here: each will contribute uniquely to the partnership. What, you may ask, can we bring more naturally to the partnership table than the Angels? Well, what do we have that an Angel doesn't? A physical body—with eyes and a voice, hands, feet! Our physical vessel allows us to engage with the world in a way that is simpler for us than for the Angels! For example, if I am going to teach an Angel workshop, I need to book a hall, organize the logistics, talk to people—all easier for me than it is for the Angels!

You are already partnering with the Angels. Co-creation just renders it more conscious! So often the Angels speak through us. How many times have you heard something like "You have no idea how much I needed to hear that today!"? It is important not to underestimate your role within this partnership. There are plenty of people who are not yet open enough to receive Angelic communication directly; for them, *you* are the perfect go-between!

At work, in your family, with friends, be sensitive and alert for ideas that come to you: things to say to someone or things to do for someone. When we decide to move into Co-creation, these will be divinely guided.

Have confidence. If this is coming to your attention at this time, it is Divinely orchestrated by the Angels and by . . . you. On a soul level, if you are reading this book, this is likely part of your path. You are not a young soul, but rather an old soul here to do some serious *good!* So shake off the shackles of "small" that were put on you to keep you in your place. With the Angels as our partners, the sky is the limit.

Once we understand that we are in equality, that we bring something very interesting to our Angelic partnership, it is time to get clear on what we want to create.

UNANIMITY OF VISION
(Why the Law of Attraction Doesn't Always Seem to Work)

Once we get any inferiority complex out of the way and our confidence is blooming to support Angelic Co-creation, it is time to get clear about what we will create.

The easiest way for this to go is not to set our sights on anything and let the Angels surprise us. That is not normally how we begin but rather stems from experiences where a *large* comfort level has been put in place.

Remembering our discussion in chapter 4, where we discussed working with Archangel Jophiel (who helps us recognize and refine the expression of our creativity), we know (don't we?) that *we create what we live.*

Sons and daughters of Creation, we create. It is in our DNA: we are creating machines. We create with our actions, as we all know, but not only that; we also create with our thoughts and words and draw to us what we are thinking or speaking about—the old "Where my attention goes, so goes my (creative) energy!"

We do this from the beginning of our lives, mostly unconsciously, then nobody taught us about this at school (which is changing). As such, we often consider that we are victims of life, and the world will confirm this. As noted earlier, I remember hearing the phrase "Life sucks and then you die" quite often when I was a child growing up in the Bronx. No surprise that with such a prevalent limiting belief, there wasn't a lot of magic going on back in the day. For good reason, even young, I kept my intuitions to myself. Discernment is a key ingredient to living well this life!

So remembering to watch our thoughts and words as they create our reality, let's talk about getting clear on what it is we want to create. What is our vision? And why does it have to be unanimous? And, above all . . . *unanimity with whom?*

In a partnership, it is clear that unanimity of vision is important. If we are moving in opposite directions, the push-me-pull-you effect will ensure that nothing gets done. Of course, we will want to get into clearer communication with the Angels around us so as to receive clear guidance that will facilitate things. The exercises in this book clarify our channel and help us with that, but there is another, less evident, unanimity of vision that needs to be put into place: *Unanimity of vision with ourselves!*

Did you ever try to work with the (excellent) Law of Attraction with little or no result? If so, the problem was likely a lack of unanimity of vision. Let me explain.

The Law of Attraction is really aligned with what we have been saying all along: where our attention goes, so goes our energy which creates. The energy we emit creates because it attracts! Out of all the possibilities of all eventualities, our thoughts and words call forth our experience. (As within, so without.)

Think about it. Quantum physicists tell us that everything is made of waves; nothing is truly solid. If that is true, then the limits or boundaries around us ("my body," "your body," air, water, the chair, and so on) are not as firm as we think we see. It is like we are really in kind of an "energy soup."

So what determines what emerges from the soup into my life? Or into yours? The better question would be *who* determines it?

You do! We collectively determine our common experience, and our individual experience is determined by *us*.

Staying with this idea, if there is something that is playing out in my life that I am not happy about, something that is not in line with my conscious vision (what I want), then chances are that I really don't have a unanimity of vision.

Two variables that we don't control play into what we emit energetically: our soul and our unconscious.

Soul

If the soul's mission is not going to be found on the path we have chosen (I think of me sitting on a barstool back in the day, cynical and depressed), something may occur that is out of left field that wakes us up to shake us up and onto our highest path. This is not something we can control in any way, such as my story about the Angel that visited me in the bank to hand me an amethyst crystal in order to wake me up. In addition, if our soul has some karma to unravel, this is also something we do not control in any way.

This kind of blockage is nothing to worry about. If the soul is blocking something, we can be sure it is not in our highest and best interest, and we can let it go . . . at least for now. Sometimes, it is just a question of timing, like when one part of us needs to be convinced not to work against another.

Our Unconscious/Inner Child

The second element that can impact our creation is something we can gain control over more as we learn how to play our instrument and begin to understand what motivates us deeply, often unconsciously. Sometimes, the more closely we can connect with our "inner child," the more we can come to know, understand, and love the inner workings of the unconscious and move into unanimity of *our* vision. We may believe that we are ready for a next step, whatever it is, but if we find that the energy and opportunity for it is not forthcoming (reminiscent of the discussion of procrastination we saw in the section on Metatron), if the project is not already made manifest, we can be sure that something in us is blocking it.

If consciously we know we want it, then that leaves only our unconscious to be blocking it, *non?*

When we are subconsciously blocking a next step in life, it behooves us (why not with the help of Metatron?) to get to the bottom of the fear that has us stymied. Often, as was the case in my procrastination example, the fear that blocks us unconsciously will be a limiting belief that has been imprinted on us from as far back as childhood: "Nothing ever works out for me," "It's no use; there is no getting ahead in this life," or the one that blocked my book-writing, "It is dangerous to be seen."

When we understand the root cause, we might find simply what I found in my quest around the writing: I was scared. That is, the little girl I had been—*she* was scared! When we see what the fear is, we can address it. With the help of Angels, we can reassure the part of ourselves that is putting the brakes on a project.

In the book example, once I saw the fear, with the help of the Angels I took action: I assured the little girl in me that I will always have her back; that in *no way* would that book (or any others) negatively impact her; that I can and will ensure her safety! I further assured her that, as I am grown now, no one messes with her ever again (in a world of "me, toos"—me, too). On top of that, I reassured her that we have Angels that intervene to tenderly care for her (to care for us all) and when she allows it, they always direct the highest and best good into our experience.

In short, if something is blocking our creation, it may be useful to check within to see if we are harboring some fears around the project that impede its realization, Angels or no Angels!

If you have ever seen a scared child have a tantrum, then it will not be surprising that the vehemence of the unconscious *No!* carries more power than our *Yes!* But once we have unanimity of vision, with our soul and our inner child on board, nothing can stop us!

THE CONTRACTS

When I teach the module "Angelic Co-creation," students sometimes bristle at the idea of a contract between us and the Angels, or between us and the tender part of us we call the inner child. But we know (don't we?) that a contract is a document that is meant to *help* a partnership grow and prosper (don't we?).

When two partners put things down on paper in a contract, elucidating all manner of questions, each person can breathe more easily in a safe, clear context. With a good contract, the context is clear; nothing muddy or gray will make one partner feel less comfortable or vulnerable *vis-a-vis* the other.

To be clear, the contract is for us, so that we get comfortable with the Angels for Co-creation purposes. They are already comfortable with us. Yet for humans, even among friends or family, it is good to get things clear from the outset, so emotions and judgments do not come into play . . . at least, not at the outset.

I say "not at the outset" because all partnerships evolve over time. In the example used earlier, imagine that my restaurant venture grows and my chef/partner and I look to franchise it. How will that work? Who is responsible for the cooking then? The publicity? The advertising, buying, trash, and so on? How can we ensure that no one feels like they are carrying more than their fair share? Can we ensure that the load will stay light enough to ensure Joy?

All good questions!

We can see that keeping things clear is important both at the outset of the partnership and as we go along. Since this is true for human co-creation, it is also true for Angelic Co-creation!

Again: it is not the Angels who need a contract! (Can you hear the laughing?!) It is us: the adult who we are and the child within, who may still be skittish at this much engagement with a sometimes-unpleasant world, and rightfully so, given past experience, perhaps. So that we feel relaxed and comfortable, a contract we create *must* play to our strengths. It must allow us to set the bar low enough that things stay fun for us. It must allow the child within to be playful, curious, open, and en-Joy!

To ensure and codify the Unanimity of Vision, two contracts are called for: one with our inner child, and the other with our Angels. Creating such contracts is a sacred act and should be accorded the honor that it is due. It is a good idea to use ritual and energy, inviting the Angels and Archangels to participate fully, but it is also critical that we use our heads and invite the child within (our heart) to help write the contracts, ensuring that they leave us wide open for Joy. The idea will be to commit to provide certain things, and in exchange, the Angels (or the child) will provide others. These are living documents, but it is good to write them down, as they do evolve over time.

The contract I have with my inner child evolved when I understood she was deathly afraid of being seen. I added protection and privacy to the contract to assuage that fear, and it worked! In exchange, I got her *yes!* and her enthusiasm and willingness to be seen in support of our writing and common mission. Good stuff! Remembering that each of us is different, your contracts will likely look different from mine, but here are my examples, to give you an idea, a starting point perhaps.

If you are looking for what you can offer your inner child, maybe just finish this sentence: "When I was little, I would have loved to have more_____." That is where I found my inspiration. Good luck!

Kathryn's Inner Child Contract (example)

Dear little Kathy, I love you and am so grateful that you decided to bring Joy back into my life, which had lost its shine and magic. Thank you!

In writing this, I reaffirm my commitment to you: my magic, my Love, my tender strength, my enthusiasm, as follows:

I commit to provide you (my child) with:

- Food and shelter, clothes, all material needs
- Stability
- Quiet
- Space (a large apartment with outside space in Paris, well worth it for my inner peace)
- Exercise, to include running and swimming
- Easy access to Nature, especially water
- Lots of laughter
- No pressure
- My strength and protection
- My Love.

In exchange, I ask of my inner child:

- Your light
- Joy and raucous laughter
- Your easy access to Angels and Guides
- Your nonjudgment
- Your confidence
- Your connection to the blueprint of our missions
- Your intuition and clairvoyance
- Your softness
- Your Love: your ability to keep your heart open, now that you are safe.

Dear one,
thank you for the continuing adventure, and together with you I also engage with the Angels.

Kathryn's Angelic Co-creation Contract

Before I set out the second contract below, let me note a few things. Overall, the foundation of my contract with the Angels is simply this: I'll set the table, and you feed the guests.

This allows me to respect my criteria for effective partnership: I am confident that what I bring to the table is unique and important. I am working with individual unanimity (by always respecting my inner child contract). I am committing to this and to honoring this sacred covenant or pact in the form of this contract.

Remember: What you commit to you must be able to provide, so set the bar low to avoid any pressure. Making your part of the partnership easily doable ensures success and that you remain in Joy. Do not worry about allocating anything that seems too big, anything that places the burden of fear, stress, or pressure onto the Angels traveling with you on your journey!

For example, as noted earlier, when I had almost finished my first book my former banker mind started to think about *how* to get it published. I envisioned Exergue/Trédaniel as my French publishing partner as they also work with my early teacher, Doreen Virtue, but when I started to feel into the question, I knew that I was in over my head! I knew nothing about publishing, much less in France, and I was writing in English!

So I stopped.

Remembering my contract with my inner child, I did not continue to go down that pressure-filled dark alley; instead, I relied on my contract with the Angels and *passed the burden of the publishing of the work to my Angels.* I literally positioned my arms as if I were carrying a burden, threw it upward to my Angels, and went back to work, writing, doing my part in our collaboration. I gave over to the Angels what was too big for me!

The very next day, I got a Facebook message from a student of mine living in Clermont-Ferrand, who wrote me, simply: "Kathryn, have you found a publisher yet?"

I had chills reading her message and responded, trying not to get excited, "No, why?"

I'll admit to not being very surprised when she said, "I spoke to my publisher, and she would like to talk to you about your book."

I dared the question, "Oh, and which publishing house is she with?"

When I read her answer ("Trédaniel"), I could hear the Angels chortling with Joy, very happy with themselves, and also with me, because I had finally cottoned on to how this could work . . . magically!

That was not the first time I had such an experience with the Angels. When I began my work, I was guided to do an evening conference (my first Angel Party!). The grumpy part of me (who didn't want to be seen, I later would learn) said to the Angels, "Okay, I will rent the room (not cheap in Paris!), but you guys have to put the *derriéres* in the chairs!"

The night arrived, and the place I had rented had 57 chairs in it, all told. Imagine my surprise when exactly 57 people sat down on those chairs! That was probably my first "Gulp! Sorry, guys!" moment with the Angels, but not (I am sure) my last. It is a very good thing that They have such a sense of humor!

So here is the contract as it has evolved for me. Maybe it will give you some inspiration if you decide to work on one yourself:

Dear Angels and Archangels,
First of all, thank you! You never let go of me, never forsook me, never lost faith... even when I gave you decades of "lost" behavior and cause to do so.

Good thing you guys are not like us/me! Thank you for pulling my butt out of the fire in Japan, Brazil, the Bronx, Inwood . . . Thanks to you I am still here, a little banged up but no worse for wear.

I am so glad that we walk together now and want the whole world to know how very grateful I am for it... for Your love. God. So this day, with deep gratitude I reaffirm my contract:

I commit to you:

- My openness to your word and your guidance
- My gratitude
- My willingness to let go
- My hands, my voice, my presence, my creativity
- My writing, speaking, singing, dancing
- My joy
- My brain: my capacity for logistics
- My time: teaching, speaking, sharing

- My willingness to love you as you express through other people
- My willingness to keep my heart open all of the time, no matter what. Period.
- My sense of humor
- My Love
- In short, I will set Your Table with Love!

I ask of you, my Dear One(s):

- Experiences / Proof (I am human, and need this) of your Love and accompanying Presence every single day !
- Your tender care
- Your huge sense of humor (help me to lighten up!)
- Flexibility (lend me your dancing shoes)
- Your clear guidance (so clear even an idiot could understand it, if you please)
- Your help with all I have committed to above
- Your Love
- In short, I ask you to be responsible for feeding the guests and me. Thank you.

Once you are happy with your Inner Child and Angel contracts, it is a good idea to seal them with a ritual. Here is one last protocol that may be used for that purpose. You may wish to seal the contracts with a stone. I use the amethyst the Angel gave me.

Consecrating the Inner Child and Angel Contracts

Consecrating the Inner Child Contract

1. Connect with your breath, and come into a peaceful place of quiet. Set your intention to commit to and seal the contracts with your inner child and with the Angels and with the help of Archangel Michael and all the Archangels and your Guardian Angels. Keep your contracts handy, along with a stone or crystal if you so desire.

2. Use your channel to anchor (ground) yourself, following your ribbon of light into the center of the earth, then open to the highest good with your intention, tracing your channel of light from the center of the earth through your sacred heart and up to the heavens. Return to your heart to set your intention, both as the human being (adult and child) you are and on a soul level. (If you are undertaking this exercise, it is without a doubt the will of your soul.) Keep your contracts handy.

3. Sit, feet planted solidly on the ground, shoulder-width apart, with shoulders pulled back so that your spinal column—the bridge you create between the earth and the heavens—is straight. *Breathe in* the presence of Angels and Archangels all around you, as well as the child that you were, the Light within you. *Breathe out* anything that blocks your opening to them. Allow yourself to fill with Light and peace, with a sense of the Love that is there for you; to feel, perhaps, the Joy that your presence brings in this space. Take three or four deep breaths at least before continuing.

4. Call in your inner child, and imagine them standing before you, at whatever age works for you (use a picture, if it helps). You might see or hear or feel or simply know the child is there, listening, eager to hear what you have to say, words so long awaited. *Read aloud your contract with them.* Feel the impact of the words as you read them—words that express what you would like to offer to yourself, what maybe you never had before. It is time to share these words, this commitment with this amazing being, the purest most innocent version of you, who holds the key to your Joy and creativity. When you are finished reading, take your crystal (if you have decided to use one) and hold it, saying something to the effect of "Signed with Love this _____th day of _____, witnessed by children and Angels, Archangels, and Guides, and sealed with Love in an _____ (amethyst or whatever stone you choose)."

5. Open your arms and imagine/invite the little one to come into your arms, then place your hands on your heart to carry them home. Remain like that until you feel it is time to continue.

Consecrating the Angelic
Co-creation Contract

NOTE: the consecrations can be done one after the other, or separately. If you do them on the same day, the inner child contract must be done first, for unanimity of the accord for the Angelic co-creation contract. This sequence assumes that you are sealing the contracts one after the other.

Call your Guardian Angels and Archangels and imagine them standing before you. When you are ready, *read aloud your contract.* Feel the words, what you would like to say that maybe you have never communicated to them before. If other words come, allow them, and amend your written contract to reflect it afterward. Above all, do not worry about this. You will be guided, and it will be perfect! If tears come, allow them. Insofar as possible, never block tears again, as they render the channel of communication clearer!

When you are finished reading, take your crystal (if you have so decided) and hold it, saying something to the effect of "Signed with Love this _____ day of _____ , witnessed by children and Angels, Archangels, and Guides, and sealed with Love in an _____ (amethyst, or whatever stone you choose). Take a moment, and imagine that the child you were is sitting on your lap and the soul you are is holding you both. Invite/allow the Angels and Archangels to come closer, enfolding you in Their loving arms, creating a cocoon of wings around you, the perfect space for consecrating the contracts now and for the Large Life that opens before you in Co-creation!

When you are finished, thank your Guardian Angels by bringing your hands to your chest in a gesture of gratitude for this sacred moment of opening and sounding and Joy and Power.

A Note of Thanks

Deep gratitude to my Angels and to the Archangels:
thank you so much for everything. So much.
For everything. I can always count on you,
and I know it.

The Angels

In closing, I now want to tell you the incredible story that changed my life—the day an Angel walked into the bank where I was working.

❧

The Dyckman Street subway station is a sorry place to start the day. That particular day was dark and hard after a night that had been darker and harder still, full of drink and drugs and dark corners of the city that truly never sleeps. At least for some.

Still, I had no choice, so after only a couple of hours' sleep, I forced myself up and into the shower, then down the stairs to catch the A train to work, descending into the station at Dyckman Street to make my way down to midtown Manhattan. It reeked of urine. The station itself was like a toilet-with-trains, and some of the clientèle apparently not yet toilet-trained. In that neighborhood, Inwood/Washington Heights, I stood out when I commuted to and from work, with my suit and my briefcase and the regulation strand of pearls, the necktie of female bankers.

That morning, I laughed to myself when the same people who had sat next to me in the darkness of the after-hours bars just a short while earlier did not recognize me on the subway platform, but then, I did not exactly court their attention, either, ducking my head and quickly making my way to the end of the platform so that I could board the first car.

As the train carried me unwilling-but-with-no-choice toward my punishment, I thought about how I had got into this mess. I'll preface by saying that I am Irish, and that I grew up in the Bronx of the 1970s. I was a sensitive kid, and those times were violent, both in and out of the apartment where I lived with my six siblings and parents, all nine of us in a sixth-floor walk-up, a red brick affair, covered in ivy and graffiti.

Three bedrooms meant my parents slept on the pullout couch. One bathroom meant there was always a line or a fight. Being at the tail end of the pecking order (child number six of seven) meant that life wasn't always much fun.

That was inside the home. Outside, the Bronx of the Sixties and Seventies was as turbulent a place as the apartment I called home.

A sensitive girl growing up in that situation has but one choice: to become *un*sensitive. Fast! Instinctively, I reached for what was available in terms of self-anesthesia. When I was young, it was books—I had my nose in a book the whole time, and my head thus very far from where I had no choice but to be. But as I got a bit older, the choices diversified, and I took up other forms of self-anesthesia, specifically two that were readily available and culturally acceptable where I grew up: alcohol and drugs.

As coping strategies go, these are perhaps not the best, but they stayed with me, more or less effective through my college years and into my years as a banker on Wall Street, pushing farther and farther away my dream of living and working and writing in Paris. (Paris was the reason I had decided to become a banker in the first place, coupled with a desire to climb out of poverty.)

Yes, I ruefully admitted to myself, they were perhaps not the best coping strategies. Those habits got me here: on this train, with my head pounding and my hands shaking, going to my punishment—for punishment it was.

You see, when you go out and "party like it's 1999" just about every night (even when it isn't yet 1999), sometimes you don't make it in to work the next day. And if you *do* make it into work the next day, sometimes you don't arrive on time. And sometimes you don't look so good, or *feel* so good, when you *do* arrive. And so, sometimes you don't get too much work done.

Turns out, employers don't generally like that. Who knew?

So this was my last chance. I had been given one last chance, an offer—a way out, really. I was to go work in a branch of the bank, opening up accounts and such for people coming in off the street. (My former work had me traveling domestically and abroad and working in a more analytical capacity.) If I managed to make it in on time to the job for the probationary period of three months, then maybe I would have a shot at going back to the work I was more suited to, and for which I had been trained at no small expense.

So I dragged myself out of bed that morning because I had no choice. There would be no more reprieves, so no more playing around. No calling in sick. No showing up late. This morning was less than a week into that punishment trial period. Ugh.

As the train carried me downtown, I happened on what I thought at the time to be a stroke of brilliance. While it was true I had no choice but to go in, who was to say I actually had to *work* when I got there? (I shake my head looking back, remembering that this seemed like a viable solution at the time.) My plan was to fake it all day: to play at working for the day, without really working. If a client came along who looked like they might threaten my peaceful existence by asking me to do actual work, I would simply give the appearance of being *really* engrossed in the work I had on my plate. Er, desk.

And so it came to pass that that particular morning found me slouched at my desk in the flagship branch of the bank on 42nd Street, across from Grand Central Station in the heart of Manhattan, praying no one would come to my desk.

I was feeling miserable and very hung over and worked at looking busy (actually working might have been easier, in retrospect), frowning or sighing ostentatiously, shutting a drawer here or sharpening a pencil (it was back in the day) there, a peacock showing its colors to frighten off possible predators—or customers. Which worked well . . . until it didn't.

I saw her enter the bank and bypass the tellers, coming instead directly to the back section, where I sat with two other bankers: two perfectly friendly and willing professionals who weren't hung over and who were in competition for clients and sales. This was their "real" job, and they took pride in it, which I figured would play in my favor.

As the woman approached I did not look up, but rather, looked down and around, hoping she would choose another path, another desk, a friendlier banker—a banker who looked like she wanted to help, maybe; someone more conscientious, someone actually worried about monthly sales goals, perhaps. Me, I didn't give a shit. I always hit my numbers and exceeded them; this job was so easy, too easy, boring, and I was just doing my time until I could find my way back to my "real" job.

Hung over as I was, I certainly did *not* want to see anyone today. But this woman kept coming closer; on she came, closer still, and incredibly, it looked like she was coming directly to me, ignoring the helpful calling out of my colleagues.

Yikes! She was almost to my desk now, so quickly, I got up from my desk and turned my back on her as she approached the "platform," the area where accounts are opened and closed and sales achieved gladly. Except today, except by me.

With very little gladness, I bent over (basically giving her my behind as a greeting) and feigned a thorough search through the lowest credenza drawer behind my desk for something, apparently of great importance.

Having given her my back as if I hadn't seen her (but knowing that she knew I had), I was satisfied. (*There*, I said to myself, proud of my slick maneuver, *that should do it!*) In my defense, I was pretty lost during that period of my life, and though it is not natural to me, I had developed very sharp edges. So this was the best I had that morning.

I hoped it would work, that she would respond to the calls of the other two bankers who had no clients with them, and who saw a sales opportunity in my callous disregard for the client. I was rooting for them.

No luck. She was still there. I felt her behind me, her eyes fixed on me, waiting. She persisted, waiting me out, at first simply standing at my desk quietly. In response, I began to make *harrumph*ing noises (an effort not unlike the use of noise by animals to scare off predators in the wild) to show her clearly that I was really, really busy. That should do it!

Again, no luck. When waiting quietly by my desk did not work (as my papers were really, *really* lost in that drawer!), the woman upped the ante and sat down at my desk, uninvited.

"What nerve!" my brain screamed. "What balls!"

But where I come from, standing up for yourself is to be respected, and I found myself grudgingly admiring her audacity. A ballsy move like that should pay off, and since this was after all my job (for the time being, however much I preferred my last position), and I was being paid for it (however little), hungover or not, I knew I had to do it. Before turning to her, I carefully arranged my face in a frozen smile.

Strangely, I don't remember much about her. I recollect a large, black woman with a big hat. How could I forget? But all I remember was that, upon turning, I appraised her, took in her outfit, and decided that she was not very well heeled and thus presented no significant sales opportunity. I sighed. *Damn. Why hadn't she gone to someone else's desk?*

However, my face still smiling, I said something else entirely. "Hello. Welcome to the bank. May I help you?"

Though they seemed friendly enough, with these few innocuous words but eyes that spoke volumes, I made sure that this woman knew she was trespassing on my territory and that she was in fact most certainly *not* welcome. I stretched out my hand for a handshake.

And then it happened.

The woman answered oddly, in slow motion, maybe, in one of those life-changing moments that we seldom recognize when they are upon us.

"No, I am here to help you," she replied, calmly. She did not take my hand.

"Ex*cuse* me?" I asked, eyebrows arching, a warning signal that went unheeded.

Instead, she took a rock—an amethyst crystal almost the size of my fist—and placed it firmly into my outstretched hand.

"This will help you with your addictions," she said. She also handed me a card on which she wrote, "For your happiness, Kathryn!"

What the . . . ?!

Okay, I thought, madly trying to recover, *I was wearing a name tag, and she had probably seen the name plate on my desk. But what the hell did she mean by addictions? Did I look that bad? Did I smell of alcohol?* My mind raced in confusion and then anger, as I tried to pull myself together to respond.

What the hell? She's got some nerve! Probably some freak or something, and she wants to sell me this stupid rock!

I grabbed hold of that idea and, thus girded, steeled for battle, looking up from the stone, ready to tell that woman that "One does not come into a bank, a serious place of business, to sell some stones."

But she was gone.

Gone! She had moved quickly and was already at that moment walking out of the bank onto 42nd Street, calmly, without even a glance back at the stupefied young banker she left behind, no hint of expecting payment nor of bank business to transact, for that matter.

What the hell . . . ? I slumped back into my chair, my heart pounding, then slowing, the frenzy fading as I sat there.

She was gone. I was still there. With this rock. The adrenaline drained from me, slowly. I felt oddly lost without her.

As the morning passed, I recovered a bit, but regarded the stone suspiciously. I moved it far from me at first, then put it in my drawer, resolving to ignore it—to ignore the whole weird scene, in fact, and to deal with it later. Maybe. But then (I couldn't help myself!), I would open the drawer again and take it back out to look at it. The amethyst became, over the course of the day, a bugaboo on (then in, then on again) my desk. Try as I might to ignore it, I couldn't. Its pull was stronger than I. My eyes were inexorably drawn across the desk or into the drawer to the stone each time my vigilance slipped. I noticed after a while that my hangover was gone completely. Pure coincidence, of course. Ridiculous! This thing was starting to piss me off.

Finally, I gave in, and just took the stone in my hands for a bit to examine it. I knew it to be an amethyst, my birthstone, by its purple hue, but I had never seen one in its natural, raw, crystal form. On one side, at its center, were tiny filaments of iron, creating a formation mirroring the crystal's point. Though I didn't know then that that particular type of formation in a crystal is called a phantom, I oddly felt like I had seen a ghost. The rock was a crystal point, in the shape of a cone, and the wide part was as purple as the narrow part was clear. But I didn't know anything about crystals, not back then.

I took that stone home with me that day and put it away, stowing it out of sight and mind, burying it in the chaos that was my apartment in those days (they say the environment where we live mirrors our inner state, and I can attest to the truth of that), and forgot about it.

But every time I moved from one place to another, the stone would turn up again. Always I'd lose sight of it again soon after. I forgot it as best I could for some three years. Until I remembered it for good, after moving to Paris. Now it doesn't leave my side.

Some ask if I think that woman was an Angel, and I always answer, "Yes."

Either she was my very own Guardian Angel who took on human form (à la Clarence in the film *It's a Wonderful Life*) or she really was a human being; like you and me, except that she had a "direct line" to the Angels, and she had faith. I imagine her as being so open to Divine guidance that she listened and acted upon that guidance (even though I certainly didn't make it easy for her), and changed my life in the process.

That woman gave me the amethyst circa 1998. Now, so many years later, I sit in Paris and live a life the likes of which I didn't dare to dream, not back then, and not when I was a little girl in a too-big-too-poor-too-Irish-Catholic family in the Bronx, writing and swooning over pictures of Paris in my sister's French book.

I sit here and look at that very amethyst now, that small stone that has played such a big part in my life's unwinding. Gratitude.

Blessings on your journey. Take action with the Angels. I highly recommend it!

About the Author

Photo by Sarah Robine

Born in the Bronx (a New York City girl), Kathryn Hudson teaches about Angels, crystals, energy, and life purpose all over the world, in multiple languages. The ex-banker's life changed forever when an Angel walked into a Manhattan bank with a message for her; in this book, she pays that forward. Kathryn has published several books in French and now in English.

She lives in France and the United States. For more information visit her website: **KathrynHudson.net**

FINDHORN PRESS

Life-Changing Books

Learn more about us and our books at
www.findhornpress.com

For information on the Findhorn Foundation:
www.findhorn.org